SUFFOLK

Miles Jebb lives in Suffolk and is the author of *East Anglia, an Anthology*, published in association with the National Trust. He has also written guide-books to three English long-distance walking trails, and *Walkers*, a history of walking. He believes that the best way to see the countryside is on foot, and so has explored Suffolk and its historic sites largely by means of local perambulations.

Pimlico County History Guides
(General editor: Christopher Hibbert)

Already published:

Dorset by Richard Ollard
Sussex by Desmond Seward

Forthcoming:

Bedfordshire by Simon Houfe
Norfolk by Tom Pocock
Somerset by Shirley Toulson

SUFFOLK

MILES JEBB

with a Foreword by Christopher Hibbert

A PIMLICO COUNTY HISTORY GUIDE

PIMLICO

An imprint of Random House
20 Vauxhall Bridge Road, London SW1V 2SA

Random House Australia (Pty) Ltd
20 Alfred Street, Milsons Point, Sydney
New South Wales 2061, Australia

Random House New Zealand Ltd
18 Poland Road, Glenfield
Auckland 10, New Zealand

Random House South Africa (Pty) Ltd
PO Box 337, Bergvlei, South Africa

Random House UK Ltd Reg. No. 954009

First published by Pimlico 1995

1 3 5 7 9 10 8 6 4 2

Typeset by Deltatype Ltd, Ellesmere Port, Cheshire
Printed and bound in Great Britain by
Mackays of Chatham plc, Chatham, Kent

ISBN 0-7126-5363-5

Contents

Foreword

Watching one of the labourers on his father's land rowing himself across the river Stour, from the Suffolk to the Essex bank, John Constable heard the man say, 'Farewell, old England!'

For centuries past and for generations to come, Suffolk had, indeed, seemed a land apart. It was, as Miles Jebb puts it in his illuminating and engrossing book, 'the Sleeping Beauty of South-East England, lying in profound slumber behind overgrown briars when many other counties were thriving on industry' or, like Essex, inexorably drawn towards the voracious maw of London. It had and has a strange beauty all its own: there are no dramatic landscapes here, no mountains, no moors; under the immense sky, the shallow valleys, the heathland and forest, the wide fields and uneven plains across which blow the winds from the sea, seem a far, far cry from the Chilterns, the Lakes, the Cotswolds and the Sussex Downs. Yet, as Lord Clark observed, recalling the countryside around Sudbourne where his rich parents lived in their Edwardian splendour, Suffolk offers the best kind of scenery for a landscape painter.

It certainly proved to do so for John Constable and Thomas Gainsborough, both Suffolk men. Constable was born at East Bergholt; and from the countryside around this once thriving centre of the woollen cloth industry, from Dedham Vale and the Stour Valley, scenes of childhood memory, he drew the inspiration for those evocations of the Suffolk countryside which represent the Wordsworthian aspect of the romantic worship of nature. 'These scenes made me a painter,' he wrote, 'the sound of water escaping from mill dams, willows, old rotten planks, slimy posts, and brickwork. I love such things . . . The solitude of mountains oppresses my spirit.'

Fifty years before and fifteen miles or so to the west, Gainsborough had been born at Sudbury, the son of a merchant who was engaged in the woollen manufacture of the town and was said to have introduced into it the shroud trade from Coventry. Active also in business on the Continent, he was 'not too rigid in the matter of smuggling'. His son was a 'confirmed painter' by the age of twelve and, while soon to become celebrated throughout the country as a portrait painter, he was also to be renowned as 'the father of modern landscape'.

Few counties in England have seen the birth of – or become the home of – more writers, artists, poets and composers than Suffolk. Following a tradition established by Constable and Gainsborough and by those utterly dissimilar Suffolk poets, George Crabbe of Aldeburgh, 'nature's sternest painter, yet the best', in Byron's phrase, and Edward Fitzgerald, reclusive translator of the exotic Rubáiyát of Omar Khayyám, Benjamin Britten was born in Suffolk, at Lowestoft; Elizabeth Frink came from Great Thurlow; Alfred Munnings from Mendham Mill on the Waveney, the son of the irascible miller. M. R. James, whose father was Rector of Livermere near Bury St Edmunds, made the groynes of Felixstowe the setting for the most haunting of his ghost stories, 'Oh, whistle and I'll come to you'; Arthur Ransome was so enchanted by the Orwell when exploring Suffolk waters that he came to live by its banks at Levington; Ruth Rendell has chosen to live at Polstead, strongly infusing her work with the atmosphere of the Suffolk countryside. Sir Laurens van der Post has lived at Aldeburgh, as fascinated by the Suffolk scene as was Rider Haggard by the constant changes of light that pass across the yellow gorse and green meadows of Outney Common. Sir Frederick Ashton lived at Eye, Sir Angus Wilson for many years in an isolated cottage at Bradfield St George, near the now demolished hall which was the home of the great agriculturist and travel writer, Arthur Young.

In this village, on the route of a Roman road and burial grounds, we are reminded of the Roman presence in Suffolk, a presence brought vividly to life by the discovery on the other

vii

side of Bury St Edmunds of the Mildenhall Treasure, a wonderfully rich hoard of silver probably buried during a Saxon raid in the fourth or fifth century. As remarkable as evidence of the Anglo-Saxon presence in Suffolk was the discovery near Woodbridge of the Sutton Hoo grave or cenotaph of a seventh-century king of East Anglia, a long ship fully equipped for the afterlife with over forty items of solid gold and numerous silver and bronze objects imported from the various foreign lands with which the kingdom had trading links.

Indeed, everywhere in Suffolk we are reminded of the past, as Miles Jebb tells us in this evocative and enlightening tour of the county as he follows the course of its rivers.

We see the fishermen in their yellow oilskins and immense yellow sea boots glistening with herring scales; labourers in the fields at harvest time, swishing through the corn, their scythes rising and falling in unison; smugglers struggling with their heavy sacks across the beach at Orford Ness while the excisemen lie in wait for them buried in the shingle; Felixstowe in its Edwardian heyday with the band playing and the sea sparkling and children playing cricket on the sands; William Dowsing, commissioned with the task of demolishing superstitious monuments and pictures in Suffolk churches during the Civil War, smashing images at Ufford and pushing the angels off the roof; Thomas Tusser at Braham Hall Farm settling down to give his fellow-farmers the benefit of his advice in the rhymed verses of his *Hundreth good pointes of husbandrie*; poor Maria Marten murdered in the Red Barn at Polstead by the father of her unwanted baby; the first Duke of Norfolk living in splendid luxury at Tendring Hall with sixty-five male servants; guests at Sudbourne eating oysters and steak and kidney pudding after shooting the birds driven towards them by beaters dressed in smocks with red lapels; the Green Children of Woolpit emerging from their subterranean cavities, speaking no known language, refusing to eat all food other than beans; Joseph Conrad working as a deckhand on a ketch-rigged trawler out of Lowestoft; and the nine-year-old Sue Ryder visiting the old people who lived in the ancient almshouses at Thurlow.

On our way to and from Thurlow we are taken into several of the most splendid and interesting of Suffolk's great churches, many of them built for glorification and display in the heyday of the wool and clothing trade of the late Middle Ages and used as courts of canon law and the meetings of guilds as well as for religious ceremonies. 'Originally they glowed inwardly in dim religious light,' in Miles Jebb's words, 'with many frescoes and much painted woodwork, faintly lit through stained glass windows, and by greasy candles burning perpetually in front of sacred objects. Today the sun floods in with a brightness intensified by the whitewash on the walls, illuminating an interior largely devoid of medieval clutter. What has been lost is the sense of mystery. What has been gained is greater architectural clarity.'

As a guide to these fine churches, St Edmund's, Southwold, the huge Holy Trinity at Long Melford, St Nicholas, Denston, Holy Trinity, Blythburgh and many more, we could scarcely find a more illuminating and well-informed guide than Miles Jebb. He is interesting not only on the architecture but also on the people who built the churches and on those commemorated in their monuments. He is equally so on Suffolk's great houses, on Euston and Elveden, on Melford Hall and Hengrave Hall, on the extravagant Victorian Somerleyton Hall, on Little Wenham Hall, built of brick in the thirteenth century, and on the grandiose structure just outside Bury St Edmunds at Ickworth, built for that rich, amusing and selfish hedonist and spendthrift traveller, the Earl of Bristol, Bishop of Derry. And, in Miles Jebb's company as guide, we can but be grateful for all the information he has gleaned and the opinions he has formed on his excursions from his own family home near Halesworth.

CHRISTOPHER HIBBERT

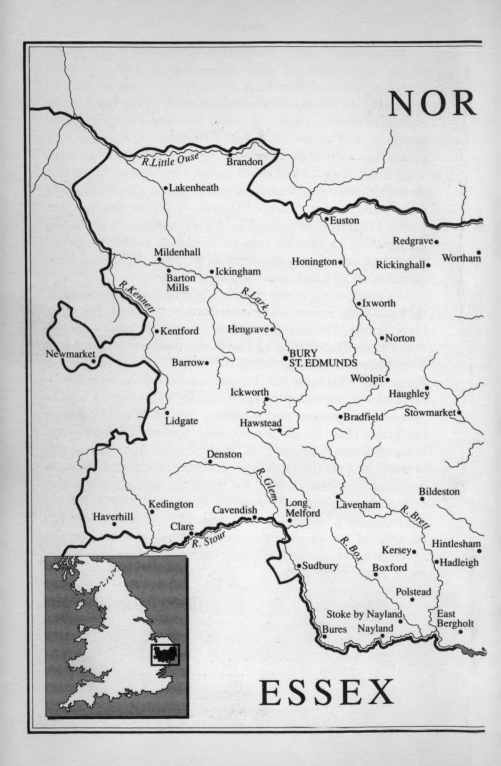

NOR

R.Little Ouse   Brandon

• Lakenheath

• Euston

Redgrave •

Honington •   Rickinghall •   Wortham •

Mildenhall •

Barton   • Ickingham
Mills   R.Lark

R.Kennett   • Ixworth

• Kentford   Hengrave •

• Norton

Newmarket •   Barrow •   BURY
ST. EDMUNDS

Woolpit •

Ickworth •   Haughley •

• Lidgate   Hawstead •   • Bradfield   Stowmarket •

Denston •

R.Glem   Bildeston •

Kedington •   Cavendish •   Long   Lavenham •   R.Brett
Melford •

Haverhill •   Clare •   R.Stour   R.Box   Kersey •   Hintlesham •
• Boxford   • Hadleigh

• Sudbury   Polstead •

Stoke by Nayland •   East
Bures •   Nayland   Bergholt

ESSEX

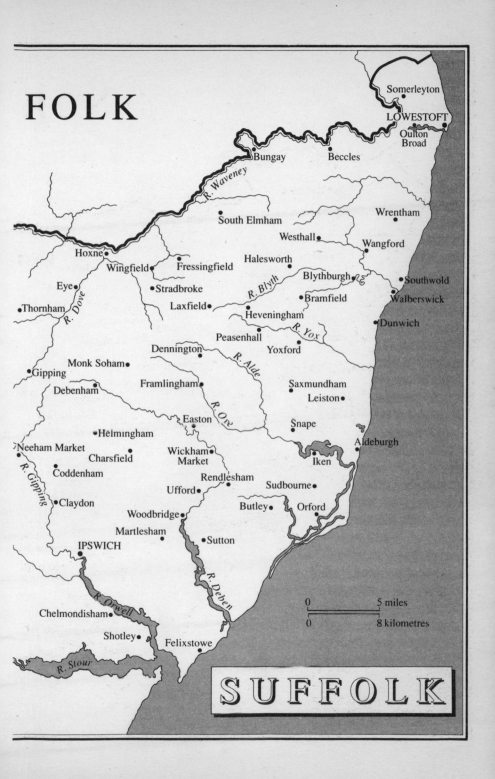

Introduction

Suffolk is a major English maritime county in which nearly two thirds of a million people live. In recent years it has become transformed from relative backwardness to the forefront of national prosperity, thanks in great measure to the realignment of Britain's trade towards the continent of Europe. Ipswich, the county capital, is, together with Cambridge and Norwich, one of the three leading commercial centres of East Anglia. Most of the population live in small towns or villages where they are surrounded by the natural beauty of the land, for the entire county has been remarkably unscathed by industrialisation. The climate is sunnier and drier than almost anywhere else in Britain. Suffolk is one of the very best corners of England for growing up in, for working in, and for living on in.

But the essence of any English county is to be found in its past rather than its present. Only by peering into the past can we sense the peculiar traditions nurtured in these time-honoured districts before they became modernised and standardised. The amazing affluence of Suffolk today, its mechanised farms and industries, its rapid communications, its well-appointed housing, its myriad leisure facilities, all these may be very wonderful – but so they are, I suppose, in Suffolk County, Massachusetts, and most of New England. The difference is that our own English Suffolk was slowly built up upon thousands of years of gradual attainment, from pastoral through to post-industrial societies, whose progressive stages are recorded legibly in a wealth of historical documents and visibly in a frail but precious display of architecture and scenery.

The Suffolk that we value is thus a complex mixture of natural and human creation, a fascinating framework for our everyday lives. The diversity of plants and animals remains a source of wonder, as it has always been. On the larger scale, however, the only purely natural aspect of the scenery is on the coast and the estuaries, for virtually all the land has been transformed through the ages by human action. In fact, it has been subjected to constant change, though never to such rapid change as at present. It took centuries for the grasslands of east and west to be out-tilled and out-grazed and to deteriorate into barren heaths; centuries for the settlers to hack down the great forests of central Suffolk; centuries for the establishment of villages and the growth of market towns; and centuries for the farmers to enclose their fields with hedges. But the metamorphosis of Suffolk into an electrified, motorised, water-tapped, chemically-controlled habitat has, during the past fifty years, been the most sudden and violent change of all, witnessed by a single generation. It follows a period during which Suffolk was the Sleeping Beauty of South East England, lying in profound slumber behind overgrown briars at a time when many other counties were thriving on industry or prospering within the orbit of London. She was bound to wake up with a shock.

One particular shock for Suffolk has been the massive increase in population. By the end of this century it is expected to be more than one and a half times its level fifty years previously. This increase has been caused not by natural fecundity but by inward migration from elsewhere in England. Together with the escalating fluidity and mobility of modern society, an ever increasing proportion of Suffolk's residents lack ancestral links with the county. Such a sudden break in inherited succession has not been seen since the Anglo-Saxon invasions. It is one reason why those of us who relish Suffolk tend to do so because of our admiration for it as a place, and not because of genealogical identification with our predecessors. Such an attitude encourages feelings of affection and respect, rather than parochial pride or fierce defensiveness. But it is surely right to increase our delight in our county by a sensitive association with those who lived here before us, usually in circumstances which we would regard as impossibly restricted and severe. All that we see around us is the result of their labours, for the most part the unremitting manual labour upon which all forms of civilisation until recently depended. And then, at the other end of the scale, the personal stories of various prominent people, whether admirable or deplorable, serve to animate the story of our adopted county.

Suffolk and Norfolk once comprised the ancient kingdom of East Anglia, and they can be thought of as sister and brother. As befits the land of the north folk, Norfolk has a stronger and more masculine identity, derived from its longer coastline and greater distance from London, an identity centred on its capital, the cathedral city of Norwich. Suffolk presents more feminine and gentle charms and, as I think, a greater beauty, and is by no means inferior to Norfolk in the richness of its character or the record of its achievement. Suffolk, for most of its long history, has been more populous and prosperous than Norfolk. When it looks at its two other neighbours, Suffolk cannot feel the same affinity. Essex is relentlessly drawn towards London, which sucks at its entrails like some voracious monster. Cambridgeshire is the land of the desiccated fens. Suffolk is thus the fresh heartland of this wider East Anglia, and displays in full variety the landscape which gives this region of England its special appeal.

One inherent aspect of this landscape is the lack of any hills worthy of the name. East Anglia is incontestably a lowland and doesn't even attempt to pretend otherwise, as do other lowland regions, by means of wolds, downs or ridges. But to say it is a lowland does not mean it is entirely flat. Almost the whole of Suffolk undulates, and shallow valleys scoop their way through uneven plains. In nature, as in art, relative scale is more important than sheer size, and the slight dips and crests of Suffolk suffice to fold the land into intimate perspectives. Complementing this calm and undramatic scenery are the universally wide skies. No great shadows ever creep over Suffolk at sunset. No clouds ever collide with the land, but float detached towards the furthest horizon for the full hemisphere of vision.

Despite its recent development, Suffolk is still essentially a rural area. Four fifths of its surface is devoted to agriculture, nearly all of which is ploughed, over half for cereals. But Suffolk can no longer be said to have a rural society. Only an insignificant proportion of the active population is engaged in agriculture. Most people go to work by car, sometimes over long distances, to positions of employment in the professions, in administration, science, engineering, trade, servicing and construction. The differences between life in a village and life in a town have in many respects evaporated. But that does not diminish the pleasure we all derive from the green mantle of the county in which we live.

None of Suffolk's three large towns – Ipswich, Bury and Lowestoft – possess any monument of national importance, Bury's great monastery being only a ruin. Instead, the true architectural marvel of Suffolk is to be found in its villages, its hundreds of flint-faced churches and thousands of timber-framed buildings, scattered all over the land and rendering every corner of the county as delightful and interesting as any other. Suffolk has five hundred medieval churches, and no other English county can claim a finer collection. They speak of a religious tradition of thirteen centuries, and their sturdy towers dominate the landscape. I like to think of them as mythological beasts, sitting watchfully and patiently in their nests of trees. For heads they have towers, for speech they have bells, for hearts they have altars, for bellies they have naves; and, to complete the analogy, for food they look for spiritual nourishment.

Around and about the grey churches are groups of brightly-coloured cottages. The contrast between the two has been likened to that between gnarled stumps of oaks and displays of wildflowers. It denotes that disparate materials were traditionally in use in stoneless Suffolk: flint-faced rubble for the churches and certain other buildings, and plaster-faced timber-framing for most of the dwellings, progressively replaced by brick. The consequent mixture of greys, reds, whites and pinks in the old village cores constitutes one of the most genial appeals of the Suffolk scene. The timber buildings comprise the organic legacy of Suffolk's woodlands, the products of hundreds of thousands of oaks. They include many examples of medieval halls, as well as carved woodwork that rivals the displays within the churches.

Suffolk was for long disregarded scenically in comparison with the wilder counties of England, especially those of the hills of the north and west. Rocky peaks and pinnacles, cascades and tumbling streams, sweeps of grassland and steep valleys, lonely farmsteads and cottages of whitewashed stone, and boulder-strewn shores, these are what excited the writers and artists of the Romantic Movement. Despite the canvasses of John Constable and the poems of George Crabbe, the hedgerows and shingles of Suffolk seemed very secondary in the minds of most people. But during the present century a great change has occurred in public perception of the countryside. Our mountains seem less remarkable now that photography has wafted us all over them, and our few remaining wildernesses are everywhere encroached and reduced. Our preoccupation has turned to the need to protect our ordinary lowland landscape from the powerful pressures that everywhere threaten it. This has led to an unprecedented appreciation of the man-made tracts of fields and lanes, for the most part hedge-lined and intricately patterned, that comprise so much of Southern England; and in no county has that appreciation been more fervently expressed than in Suffolk.

Imminent battles in the cause of conservation will undoubtedly need to be won before we can feel happy about the state in which Suffolk will enter the twenty-first century. But we cannot altogether bemoan all that has happened during the past fifty years. It was obviously necessary for new and better houses and roads to be built, and during the period of this achievement old buildings have been preserved as never before, and the open countryside closely protected from indiscriminate building. It is true that the agricultural revolution of recent years was allowed to run wild, with excessive wetland drainage and hedgerow destruction: but no one could seriously argue that we should have retained the field-patterns of the 1940s. Visitors from the Continental Low Countries will affirm that, in comparison with their own landscape, Suffolk is a veritable paradise.

By a similar process the perception of Suffolk as a cradle for artistic inspiration has been transformed. During the nineteenth century Suffolk was understandably dismissed as a land without legend or song. For whatever the reason (was it the Anglo-Saxon temperament? or the unmusical vernacular? or the taming of the landscape?), no heroes or heroines, dragons or demons, sagas or stories, had survived from ancient folklore. Even the saints to whom the churches are dedicated are trusted figures such as Mary, Peter and Andrew, as opposed to the obscure and fanciful eremites who patronise the churches of Cornwall. The rustic population seemed to indulge in a dry and cryptic humour that dampened any tentative attempts at loquacity or fantasy. But to the intellectual mind of the twentieth century this understated temperament and environment has great appeal, and has attracted and inspired the many writers, artists, poets and composers who live or have lived in Suffolk in our time.

In searching for a way to describe Suffolk, I have decided to follow the lines of the rivers. This is not only in recognition of their geographical and historical importance: it is also a protest at their present degradation. They have been starved of their natural flow by the insatiable bore-holes, which suck up the aquifer, or spongy reservoir of water in the fissured chalk beneath us, at an alarming rate. The poor rivers have largely been reduced to the status of emergency rainwater drains, and seldom rise at their official sources. All the more important, then, that we should recognise in our rivers and streams the true veins of our county, the determinant factor in the siting of our villages. None of them is a big river, and all except the Little Ouse confine their flow within or beside our county boundary. Curiously, only four have autonomous names: Waveney and Blyth, respectively Early English names meaning 'quaking-bog river' and 'gentle'; and Stour and Ouse, respectively ancient British names denoting strength and water. All the others are merely named after settlements along their banks. Each river induces some special theme in the story of Suffolk: for instance, the Stour relates particularly to the cloth trade, the Gipping to Puritanism and the Civil War, the Deben to the Anglian Kingdom, the Alde to the baronial struggle, the Little Ouse to the pre-historic settlements, and the Lark to the Roman period; together with other themes that emanate from the coast and the ancient boroughs.

Suffolk is like someone of great character who is unforthcoming but grows on acquaintance. Someone of inner serenity and authority; an elderly woman, perhaps, grown wise from an eventful life, whose personality transcends her faded beauty. I must confess it took me some time to get to know Suffolk, from when I first came to live there. I was seduced by the attractions of more dramatic counties and I loved the mountains and the moors. But recognition came in time, thanks particularly to a series of inspections of northeast Suffolk by bicycle and on foot. The bicycle rides revealed the churches, and the walks revealed the countryside. It was a challenge to find yet another walking route to some point on the coast, always avoiding roads. In the course of the eight or nine miles or so there was such astonishing variety: clay fields succeeded by sandy heaths, conifer forests, marshes and finally the beach. Unlike the primordial rocks and screes of the mountainside, here was a transiency in which the fields had once been deciduous forest, the heaths once fields, the conifer forests once sheep-walks, the marsh once a river, and the beach once dry land. And, unlike the barren moor, here were farms and villages that spoke of ordinary humanity, duly encountered in its daily round of work or play. On one such walk we arrived hot and tired at Southwold from along the line of the disused railway, and went into the former Station Hotel for tea. A simple verse was framed on the wall, and, rather than any profound poetry, it seemed to express our feelings at the time. So I shall conclude my introduction with it:

> My thoughts did dwell on Suffolk land,
> So loved by me and many,
> From rich brown earth, to endless skies,
> To seashore hours of summer days,

To autumn time of endless gold,
　So loved by me and many.
Then thought I on, of roasting beef,
Of good brown ale and fresh baked bread,
Full nets of fish from willing boats,
And lots of laughing Suffolk folk,
　So loved by me and many.

I
The Coast

From Lowestoft in the north to Felixstowe in the south, a distance of nearly forty miles, the Suffolk coast stretches along the North Sea, and for the entire length the eye is jarred only by the tall radio masts on Orford Ness and the harsh blocks of the Sizewell power station. Such a stretch of naturalistic shoreline and cliffscape is not to be found anywhere else in South-East England apart from the North Norfolk coast. In the other direction, notwithstanding brief sections of chalk cliffs along the Channel, one would have to go round as far as Dorset to find any rival of such length.

What do we mean by an unspoilt coastline? Surely the actual beach and the cliffs above it are everywhere unspoilt, except at ports and harbours. I think that by this phrase we mean that anyone looking at it, from land or sea, will be able to feel its inherent wildness, and relish the primal interplay of earth and ocean. Where there are buildings strung along the shore, or roads running closely parallel to it, or concrete embankments, or wirescapes, or even wind-farms, such a feeling is hard to catch. Where these things are absent, we are transported into a time-zone altogether more distant than anything which the man-made countryside of Suffolk can provide, to millions rather than thousands of years, as we contemplate the action of the sea through ages of ages, alternately formative and destructive.

Here, down on the beach, is the best place to consider the geology of Suffolk. The pebbles at our feet, pounded and rounded by the restless movement of tides and waves, include the flints of the great layer of chalk at the sea-bed, which stretches on beneath the entire county, hundreds of metres thick. This pure white limestone was formed during the

Cretaceous Period of 100–70 million years ago. Imperceptibly, over hundreds of thousands of years, the chalk was created from the shells of innumerable marine organisms which drifted to the sea bed, rich in calcium and other minerals. Later, within the chalk, horizontal seams of flint were formed from sponge spicules and other siliceous matter.

But Suffolk was not destined to become a chalk county like Dorset. Only in its extreme north-west corner has the chalk become exposed. For the rest, it has remained overlaid by subsequent deposits. Most of south-east Suffolk is on London Clay, a product of sands and clays at the beds of seas of the Tertiary Period, 70–40 million years ago. Eastern Suffolk is on more recent crag, an accumulation of shelly sands which augmented until about two million years ago, and which forms most of the cliffs along the shore. North of Aldeburgh we see the brown Norwich Crag, and to the south the Red Crag, with isolated patches of Coralline Crag (so called because its rough composition of mollusc shells was originally thought to have been made from coral). Today the crag is yielding to the advancing sea, the elemental force which formed it in the first place, though it is putting up a stiff resistance and providing Suffolk with at least some protection from rising sea levels.

The soil of Suffolk, superimposed on these sedimentary formations, was largely created by the Anglian glaciation of around half a million years ago. This great ice sheet or glacier, hundreds of metres thick, advanced slowly forward over many thousands of years, and as slowly retreated. At its furthest extent it covered the whole of the English Midlands and most of East Anglia, and it terminated just short of the present coast, approximately on the line of the A12. As it advanced, it ground into the rocks below, breaking them up and mixing them, and pushing a detritus of chalk across from the north-west. Later, as it retreated, it left behind a thick top soil, known as boulder clay, or till. This is the grey or brownish clay which still covers central Suffolk. Though Suffolk experienced subsequent Ice Ages, during which the soil permanently froze, it never again became covered and crushed by ice. The till plain drained and eroded, mostly to the east and south-east, by means of rivers which in time became the ones we know today. These exposed the gravels that lay in or below the till, and created loamy soils. The western and eastern extremities of the county came to be covered with sandy soils, the product of outwash gravels and river deposits. In the extreme south-east, they became covered with a yellowish-grey loam known as loess.

At the time of the last Ice Age, 24–15,000 years ago, the sea was at least sixty metres below its present level. Britain was part of the continent, and Suffolk's eastern rivers were tributaries of the Thames, which flowed into the English Channel. With the change to a warm, dry climate, the level rose rapidly to flood the southern North Sea. When Britain became an island, around 8,000 years ago, the Suffolk coast was some fifteen miles east of its present line. Since then the sea has continued to rise, but more slowly, with temporary retreats during milder climates, though the coastline has shifted quite dramatically even in historical times.

The sea is encroaching, and the crag cliffs are crumbling. The sea scours at their base and hollows it, and at their head appear the fissures which precede the inevitable landslip. The shingle beds are shifting, their movement subjected to the effects of longshore drift. Since the waves strike at them mostly from the north-east, and the backwash returns perpendicular to the coast, they tend to be pushed in a southerly direction. They are laboriously piled up in front of low-lying marshes, and sometimes block the channels of the rivers. In other places the sea comes back to breach the shingle, when in a bad mood at high tide and with a north-east wind behind it. The river mouths have been turned and twisted, some by the natural action of the sea, some by the unnatural hand of man. Although the changing sequence of woods and heath along the headlands alters the outline of the scene decade by decade, the essence of the coastal panorama is just as it was before any artificial refashioning; and nothing can exceed the thrill of walking along the beach on a windy day, beneath the looming cliffs and close beside the crashing breakers and all the foam-crested waves behind them.

The most remarkable natural feature along the coast is the nine-mile Orford Ness (ness being an Old English word for a promontory). It is Suffolk's wilderness, lonely and elemental, and the finest example in Europe of a vegetated shingle spit. Sea-peas and yellow-horned poppies grow among the shingle, and in the salt marshes are bands of grey-leaved sea purslane, the knobby stems of glasswort and the tall stalks of cord grass. Here are the sea birds, the avocets, shell-ducks, oyster catchers and sandwich-terns, the redshanks and the plovers and the geese. The River Alde, barred from the sea by the spit, flows along behind it all the way to its mouth at Shingle Street. English Nature and the National Trust between them now own the whole of Orford Ness, so it is safe from any future desecration.

The open sea is what links Suffolk to the big wide world that lies beyond East Anglia. It has always represented the greatest danger from external attack, as well as the greatest opportunity for trade. Of all the incursions made upon the coast of Suffolk, the most momentous were those that took place during the fifth and sixth centuries of our era, when a whole new population came and settled from across the North Sea. Recent historical research has obliged us to qualify any simplistic view of the Anglo-Saxon invasions. For instance, it is now recognised that the first Anglo-Saxons who actually settled in eastern Britain were tribesmen brought over to stiffen the defences of the Roman province, and granted land in exchange for military service. Also, that the early Anglo-Saxon settlement was in great measure superimposed on a pre-existing agricultural geography. All the same, there can be no dispute that the most formative event in the history of our county was the mass immigration of these Germanic tribes.

The Angles and Saxons inhabited the coastal regions of North Germany, including the Frisian Islands and Schleswig-Holstein, and perhaps also Denmark. They had developed into flourishing farming and fishing communities, whose population had expanded. But they were under pressure from the movement of other tribes who coveted their lands. They had exploited the opportunities of piracy by mastering the art of making and operating seagoing rowing boats, of clinker construction and over twenty metres long. As early as the third century they began to raid the shores of Britain. The authorities responded by a system of coastal defences based on estuarian forts, and by granting extensive power to a military commander known as the Count of the Saxon Shore. But this measure failed to stem the tide of attacks, especially when Carausius, appointed to the position in 286, used it entirely for his own ends, making deals with the raiders and sharing their booty. Though the Emperor Constantius succeeded in restoring order, the Romano-British civilisation was thereafter under constant threat and quite unable to regain its former prosperity.

In 367 the Anglo-Saxons joined the Picts and Scots to descend on the British provinces and sack them. This precipitated social disorganisation and economic decline. Theodosius attempted vainly to bolster the coastal defences, and was obliged to call in the Anglian settlers, whose numbers were increased by Vortigern. But by the early fifth century, the towns were being abandoned and the large estates broken up, as the whole province degenerated into anarchy and reverted to a tribal society which the Romans understandably thought of as barbaric. Now came the mass migration as, year by year, boatloads brought extended families and clans who settled in places allocated to them by chiefs and warlords, until the kingdom of the East Angles was established during the mid-sixth century by fresh waves of settlers who came from northern Jutland or southern Sweden. This boat-born migration was facilitated by the high sea-levels of the time, which meant that the river estuaries extended further inland than they do today.

The most obvious evidence for the total transformation of the region into East Anglia is linguistic. The Early English language entirely replaced the former urban Latin and rural Celtic. There are fewer surviving Celtic place names in East Anglia than in any other part of Southern England, even though the number traceable in Suffolk has recently been extended to fifteen by our distinguished local historian,

Norman Scarfe. For the rest, apart from a handful of Danish names, the villages and towns of Suffolk bear those given them by the Anglo-Saxon migrants. Mostly they relate to physical descriptions, and I find these so revealing that I have given rough translations throughout my text, except for those of dubious meaning. But a large minority relate to the names of the original settlement leaders, and translation would make tedious reading. Suffice to say that the county abounds with the settlements – the 'hams', 'tuns', 'wics', 'worths' and 'steads' – of people such as Amma, Assa, Cafa, Codda, Cydda, Freca, Gyppa, Hefa, Hemma, Hunta, Lafa, Leaxa, Pacca and Sibba. The place names also reveal the distinction felt by the Angles towards other tribal groups. Saxham means a settlement of Saxons; Fressingfield may imply a community of Frisians; Flempton of Flemish; and Walpole of Welsh, the name by which the former British were known.

But though the Angles undoubtedly extinguished the civilisation of the Romano-British, the actual fate of the Celtic peasants remains a mystery. We cannot tell to what extent they were driven out westwards in a process of ethnic cleansing, or died out from famine or disease, or were used as an underclass of serfs, though certainly all three fates befell them in some degree. Those that did remain must have eventually become assimilated and interbred, though the people of East Anglia undoubtedly preserved physical features which distinguished them from the large Celtic communities that survived in the west of England, and blond hair and blue eyes were by no means uncommon in what was a tribal, and hence racist, society.

The East Angles, in their turn, were destined to suffer devastation from an indefensible coast when the Scandinavian Vikings became masters of the waves. Those who ravaged and then conquered eastern England were under Danish rule, though recruited also from Norway and Sweden, and their first major incursion was in 861 when a Danish army wintered in East Anglia, commandeering anything it could lay its hands on. This was repeated in 865, only this time the army then proceeded to sweep through England on a four year campaign, ravaging Nottinghamshire, Yorkshire and Northumberland, after which it returned to winter at Thetford. Next year Edmund, King of the East Angles, decided to fight, but his forces were defeated and he himself was killed at an unidentified place called Haegelisdun. Now came the nadir in the fortunes of the little kingdom. The Danes pillaged it for several years, their chief spoils being the Christian monasteries and churches. In 878 some order was restored when, under the terms of a treaty with Alfred of Wessex, the Danish Guthram was recognised as king and Christianity was nominally tolerated among the peasantry. And in 920, Edward of Wessex ousted the Danish army and established himself as King of England. But the Danes continued to demand tribute, and the Suffolk coast was prey to their longships well into Norman times. Ipswich was their favourite target, and from there they harried wide stretches of the county and ensured that the Danegeld was paid.

The great difference between the Danish invasions into East Anglia and those of the Anglo-Saxons themselves centuries before, was that the Danes did not settle nearly so extensively. They made mainly for the north of England. Perhaps it was because of the obstinacy of the Anglian peasantry, who failed to wilt under their rule and whose population was increasing, that the conquerors forebore to oust them from their holdings. Of the small number of Danish place names in Suffolk, most are just inland from Lowestoft; and an eleventh-century list of peasantry in central Suffolk shows only one in twelve with names of Danish origin. Danish rule certainly altered and advanced Suffolk in terms of administration and trade, but the folk themselves remained mainly of Anglian descent. It was the Danes who first split East Anglia into two counties, the North Folk and the South Folk.

The Suffolk shoreline is strewn with relics of coastal defences through the ages. Of that early period of history when Roman rule was still upheld, Suffolk once possessed two important monuments, known as Walton Castle and Burgh Castle, both massive coastal fortresses. Unfortunately it has since lost both, the first to the sea and the second to Norfolk.

Walton Castle, whose Roman name is unknown, was the predecessor of the Landguard Fort in guarding the estuary of Orwell and Stour. Its site is now some two hundred metres offshore, where divers can still detect blocks of masonry, fallen from the cliff on which the fort once stood. Burgh Castle, guarding Waveney and Yare, is one of eleven recorded Roman forts between the Wash and the Solent, and was called Gariannonum. It was built within the estuary, some four miles inland. It still displays impressive fragments of its massive containing walls, whose upper courses of tiles have weathered better than the eroded flint rubble below. We may imagine the desperate efforts by those in the forts to prevent ships from entering the rivers, whether by means of slings, booms, fire, rams or sorties.

At the south-eastern extremity of the coast, on a spit of land protecting Orwell Haven, is the polygonal Landguard Fort, dating from Tudor times. Though never put severely to the test of a land siege or a naval bombardment, this fort successfully played its part in an episode in the Anglo-Dutch Wars. In 1667 the Dutch fleet under Admiral de Ruyter, after its daring attack on the shipping in the Medway, sailed up the East Anglian coast with the intention of making a similar raid on the English naval base at Harwich. But the guns of the fort covered Orwell Haven so effectively that the Dutch could not risk entry without taking it first. So they mounted a highly professional amphibious operation. Some sixteen hundred men, equipped with grenades and scaling ladders, landed beneath Felixstowe cliffs and proceeded along the dunes towards the landward side of the fort. They found it well defended, albeit only by raw militiamen, and were pinned down by small-arms fire. They were unable to penetrate the pallisades, and their fleet failed to bombard the fort from the sea. So they decided to withdraw under cover of darkness, which they did, amazingly, without the loss of a single man. This successful evacuation was made easy because the English county levies were scattered, and several had crossed to the far side of the Deben because they thought, from the positioning of the Dutch fleet, that it was about to attack Aldeburgh.

The Landguard Fort remained an important strongpoint in English coastal defences until the end of the Second World War. But recently it has found a new use as a bird observatory. Instead of scanning the horizon for Dutch or French invaders to kill, the new watchers in the fort look for geese or swallows to ring. No longer is there any garrison of bored and hungry troops or eccentric Lieutenant Governors, such as Philip Thicknesse, who directed in his will that his hand should be cut off and sent to his estranged son; or Robert Gosnold, who made six ringleaders of a mutiny in the fort draw lots as to which one should be condemned to death.

From the fulcrum of the Landguard Fort nine Martello towers line the Suffolk coast as far as Aldeburgh. These are the most northerly of a chain which extended right around the coast of South-East England, constructed by the Royal Engineers during the Napoleonic Wars when French invasion seemed to be a real possibility (as it was until the Battle of Trafalgar in 1805). Their name and design are taken from the tower on Cape Mortella, which had held up an English attack on Corsica, and they were built as circular gun-emplacements with immensely thick brick walls. Between Bawdsey and Shingle Street these abandoned forts, set in the marshes just behind the sea wall, enhance the general air of desolation. The ultimate tower at Aldeburgh is larger than the others, being in the shape of a quatrefoil for mounting four heavy guns. Its present-day function is to provide accommodation for four people in holiday lets from the admirable Landmark Trust.

Blocks of concrete, half buried in the dunes, tell of the more recent invasion scare, when Hitler, not Napoleon, was the bogeyman. But the most effective defence in 1940 was an invisible one – radar – and it was first developed here on the Suffolk coast. On the basis of Sir Robert Watson-Watt's original paper on 'The detection of aircraft by radio means', the world's first chain of radar stations was working before the outbreak of the war. Sir Robert and his team of scientists were ensconced at Bawdsey Manor, a vast mansion built for Sir Cuthbert Quilter at the end of the last century. Contemporary folklore has it that the Germans staged an unsuccessful raid on the coast just here.

But all these fortifications along the Suffolk coast were really only supportive to the first line of defence, which was on the sea itself. From the harbours and maritime towns of Suffolk came the men and ships which secured the coast, or attempted to do so. Piracy, wrecking and smuggling were practices that were never effectively stamped out, but at least it can be said that for centuries armed invasion was averted by English naval power. So the levies, militias and home guards were never put to the test. Nor was the interesting concept of the Elizabethan antiquarian, Robert Ryece, that any invading force would soon become impossibly bogged down in the miry soil and narrow lanes of Suffolk, and 'have just cause to repent of their rashness'. The Spanish Armada was harried northwards up the East Anglian coast in 1588, and the rather reluctant county levies were released in time to gather in the harvest. Suffolk has indeed been fortunate in having been spared the clash of arms, not only by invasion, but also by civil dissension, for in neither the Wars of the Roses, nor in the Civil War, did any battles take place in Suffolk. The nearest that Mars, the god of war, got to our county, was when a major naval battle was fought right up against the Suffolk coast.

In May 1672 the combined fleets of England and France intended to force the Dutch to battle. Failing to engage them, the allies, under the command of the Duke of York (the future James II) withdrew to Sole (or Southwold) Bay for provisioning. They must have made a most impressive spectacle. In all there were nearly eighty warships, and all were drawn up, in three squadrons, forming one long line of two or three miles, parallel to the shore and within half a mile of it. From faulty intelligence they believed that the Dutch had likewise withdrawn to their own coast, and so allowed the warships to remain at anchor and the crews to come ashore for the Whitsun holiday. But during the night of 27 May, the Dutch, under Admiral de Ruyter, bore down on a following wind from the north-east. At daybreak the acute predicament of the allies was suddenly apparent as the enemy ships closed in, in line abreast, each marking down for its target one of the unprepared ships along the shore.

All was confusion, as the carousing seamen in Southwold were rounded up, sails hoisted and anchors heaved, slipped or cut. The three squadrons were all pinned to the coast and lacked freedom to manoeuvre: the French went south, the English went north. The Duke commanded the central squadron – the Red – and in command of the northerly squadron – the Blue – was Edward Montagu, Earl of Sandwich. A former Parliamentarian commander and a staunch Protestant, he had come to terms with the restored monarchy but was unhappy about the sudden and unexpected alliance with France. He was dedicated to naval reform and popular with the sailors.

Sandwich's flagship was the *Royal James*, a large warship of one hundred guns and with a crew of nearly one thousand men, and she bore the full brunt of the first assault. After some hours of pounding, the ship became isolated among the Dutch. She was rammed by the *Groot Hollandia* and the two ships were locked in a bloody embrace for hours while they fired their broadsides and musket-shot in a cloud of smoke which tragically prevented the other English ships from coming to Sandwich's assistance. Eventually the *Royal James* managed to break free on an ebbing tide, but by now most of her crew were dead or wounded and unable to work the sails. At which point a fire-ship came alongside her and she was soon a mass of flame. Sandwich refused to be evacuated, probably impelled by a death-wish. Ten days later his bloated body was recovered from the sea near Harwich, recognisable by the ribbon of the Order of the Garter on his coat.

But naval power in Suffolk waters was usually that of pirates or privateers, rather than great fleets of warships. These adventurers were most active at times when royal control was weak and when royal fleets had been laid off. Several audacious acts of outright piracy are recorded in the fourteenth century, as when four ships rifled and sank all traders in the Orwell for nearly three months in 1335, or when the royal admiral's ship was boarded and looted off Lowestoft in 1344.

In Tudor times such outrages were stamped out, but were succeeded by the actions of privateers, who were really pirates who enjoyed the protection of some maritime power. The ports of the Spanish Netherlands – Dunkirk, Ostend, Sluys and Nieuport – were specially active in raiding the English coast and fond of blockading Orwell Haven. The privateers of these 'Dunkirkers', whose captains were themselves sometimes English, often had friends in Suffolk who shared in their plunder.

The regular prey of the privateers were the fishing fleets that set out from Suffolk ports for distant waters. The Suffolk fishing boats were active in the Iceland trade during the sixteenth and seventeenth centuries, and some of the smaller ports, such as Dunwich, Walberswick, Southwold, Easton and Covehithe, specialised in it. The fleet, of between one and two hundred vessels in all, would go under convoy in summer to fish for the cod off Iceland, where it had a ferocious reputation for roughing up the local inhabitants. The fact that in 1535 a Southwold ship could make £700 on a single run gives an indication of the enormous profits that could be earned. It was in expeditions such as these, as in the West Country fishing fleets off Newfoundland, that the formidable skills of the English mariners, which were to destroy the maritime power of Spain, were perfected.

It did not require such lengthy expeditions to catch the herring, which gathered in their millions off the East Anglian coast every autumn, and from early days were pickled or kippered. Coastal towns were assessed for their fisheries in terms of number of herrings as early as the eleventh century. Of all the Suffolk ports, Lowestoft came to lead the way, because it was nearer than the others to the shoals of fish, and because it was so close to Yarmouth, the centre of the herring trade. In Elizabethan times Thomas Nash eulogised the herring for bringing prosperity to the coast of Norfolk and Suffolk, where 'the patchedest Leather piltche laboratho may dine like a Spanish Duke' and where it brought work to thousands who otherwise 'would have begd and starvd with their wives and brattes, had not this Captain of the squamy cattell so stoode their good Lord and master'.

The seemingly limitless shoals of herrings also attracted
Dutch fishing boats (known as busses) to Suffolk waters, to the
detriment of local fishermen. They were seen off in the
seventeenth century. But in more recent times it was the Scots
who came south in their trawlers. At the turn of the last
century between four and five hundred Scottish fishing vessels
based themselves on Lowestoft for the herring season, an
invasion supported by troops of Scots lassies who came to gut
and clean the herrings, dextrously wielding small knives with
short, curved blades. The trade was powerfully boosted by the
railway, by which fish could be delivered to London far more
efficiently and quickly than by sea.

Perhaps the greatest havoc ever recorded on the shores of
Suffolk occurred at Lowestoft in 1770. A storm had blown for
some hours in the night, when the wind suddenly changed
direction, raging with unequalled fury. Many ships broke their
anchors and ran against each other, and by daybreak eighteen
had blown to shore, all of them broken up by the breakers
within hours. It was impossible to rescue their crews, who
clung to the masts and rigging, perishing as these broke. It was
estimated that about thirty ships were wrecked and two
hundred men drowned during this terrible hurricane. Truly,
the wild coast was very different from the placid countryside,
and the fishing communities along the shore lived in the
presence of a latent danger from the elemental forces of nature,
which sharpened their fatalistic perception of life and death, as
well as their sense of independence from the constraints of a
purely hierarchical society.

Invading armies may never have penetrated Suffolk, but
smugglers certainly did, and during the eighteenth century
their trade dominated the coast and far exceeded the fishing
industry in importance to the maritime towns and villages.
The smugglers always seemed to be a step ahead of the
customs officers, and their success was due not only to well-
planned operations but also to a control over the local
population which, at its height, was quite as strong as the
mafia in Sicily in our own time. People of all sorts connived
with them, of course, but others were simply terrorised. Juries

rarely dared to convict the gangsters who injured or killed the customs officers. The officers themselves were poorly rewarded, and not entitled to pensions if they were wounded or killed.

As examples of the smugglers' daring, in 1746 six vessels ran their cargoes together in a single night at Aldeburgh, and had three hundred men waiting to help them; and in 1786 a gang of one hundred and forty worked a cargo near Orford, with six customs officers looking on impotently. The gangs cut off the nose of an officer near Snape, and whipped and abducted an informant at Beccles. They took to flaunting the authorities in Ipswich and other towns, to the outrage of Admiral Vernon, a local worthy. As with other mafias, they justified their activities as being no worse than any other forms of tax evasion. They called it 'free trade', and reckoned they were doing the public a service.

The large-scale smuggling was organised by traders in the Flemish ports, who covered their activities with a bread-and-butter business of perfectly legal trading. For their illegal trade they specially favoured the Suffolk coast because it was relatively less well defended than Essex or Kent. Here they used their best ships, fast cutters of up to two hundred tons, and well armed. If captured, there was always a good chance that they could bribe the boarding party to spare their ship in exchange for the confiscation of its cargo. Tea and brandy, silk and lace, all subject to swingeing duties, were the staple commodities of these runs. Here are two entries for 1787 in the log book of the *Stour*, a ship used for smuggling: 'July 3rd: Desperate engagement ashore – narrow escape – two men taken – well bribed – expenses paid – kept well in prison – escaped – joined crew again . . . £0–0–0d. Oct 10th: Made good voyage – lost one man – cleared profit . . . £470–0–0d'.

These goods were swiftly dispersed by horses trotting along the byways of the county at night. But hiding places were often needed, and many are the legends attached to churches believed to offer special opportunities for temporary cover, and to pious parsons, gullible or complaisant. The rector at Lowestoft, so it is said, was persuaded to conduct a funeral for a sailor at a very early hour in the morning, on the grounds that the ship needed to sail out on the tide, quite unaware that the coffin was full of lace. But a more worldly clergyman at Leiston accepted the delivery of a cask of gin by night as follows: 'The pig's in the sty, sir.' 'An where's the sty, my man?' 'Under the old apple tree'. 'All right. Good night.'

From Richard Cobbold's novel *Margaret Catchpole* we also have a vivid account of a successful ambush made by the preventative officers against the smugglers on Orford Ness. The trap was laid by positioning fourteen men at intervals of five hundred yards along the beach, where each buried himself in the shingle with only his head visible. They lay like this for hours, fortified by rum: the password was 'King George for ever', with the response 'Hurrah!' A pole with a white flag was planted on the beach in line with two points inland – a shepherd's cottage on Havergate Island and a tall poplar near Sudbourne. This was a decoy, for the old shepherd on the island, who was known to be an accomplice and would only have raised the flag if absolutely sure the coast was clear, had been tied up in his hut. Night fell; the sea birds ceased their screaming; the full moon rose, and the wind began to blow freshly. Presently a ship could be seen anchoring, and an eight-oared boat, heavily laden and lurching through the waves, approached the shore. Out jumped the men, who beached the boat and then proceeded to carry a lot of heavy sacks to a small pit at the top of the beach. The officers by now had crept from their hiding places and moved along the landward side of the beach, out of sight from the sea, to surround the smugglers. At the sound of a whistle they opened fire. The result of the short, sharp struggle which ensued was two smugglers dead and three taken prisoner, one of them the captain of the gang: one officer was wounded.

Clamping Suffolk's shoreline at each end are the ports and resorts of Lowestoft and Felixstowe. In its capacity as a port, Lowestoft has switched from its age-old dependence on fishing to participation in all sorts of shipping activity, including servicing North Sea gas installations and transshipping freight to continental ports. Meanwhile, the old fishing days are still evoked by the thriving fish market and the old smoke-house. But the real success story is at Felixstowe. The Felixstowe Container Port is certainly the most impressive of all Suffolk's contemporary development. Taking advantage of the moribund state of some of the traditional ports, particularly the Port of London, with their intractable labour relations and antiquated procedures, a group of entrepreneurs opened Britain's first container terminal here at Felixstowe in 1967. Since then, this specialised port has become one of the largest and most efficient in Europe, handling over a million container units annually with minimal transshipment times. Its two terminals, tucked between the Landguard Point and the Trimley Marshes, exemplify the clean-cut concentration of an entirely modern port, unimpeded by old industrial clutter. Suffolk once more provides a principal link for England's trade, as it used to long ago.

In their capacity as resorts, it has to be said that both Felixstowe and Lowestoft have suffered from the lure of Mediterranean package holidays. Though they have made valiant efforts to adapt from the days of their prime a hundred years ago, they have been unable to sustain the elegance that still characterises their architecture of that period. Felixstowe was always the smarter of the two, patronised by rich families from London, and, on one occasion, by Victoria, Empress of Germany; (and a would-be queen of England, Mrs Simpson, resided at Felixstowe for six weeks in 1936 whilst obtaining her divorce). Its fine red-brick hotels and private houses up on the cliff, and its esplanade and cliff-gardens, were of a quality that could vie with some of the most exclusive resorts in Europe. On a sunny summer day, with the band playing and the sea sparkling and children playing on the sands, nothing could appear more carefree than Felixstowe beach in its Edwardian heyday. But, as an antidote to such an image, M. R. James, the scholar and writer of ghost stories, made it a scene of haunting in his most famous short story, 'Oh whistle and I'll come to you'. He was inspired to do so by the line of wooden groynes, built to protect the beach, but looking, on a gloomy day and from the beach itself, for all the world like wrecks of ancient boats. On an out-of-season day, in obscure light, a man is chased along the beach by the ectoplasm which he has had the misfortune to release through disturbing an old tomb in the abbey ruins. The man scrambles desperately over the groynes that bar his way like hurdles, but in vain: the object, 'a figure in pale, fluttering draperies, ill-defined', will not be deprived of its prey.

Lowestoft always tended to rely more on local people for its seaside trade, but had its special charm in the contrast between the old fishing town and the smart new resort. Alfred Swinbourne, a Suffolk Schools Inspector, recalled it in its late Victorian prime: 'Oh Lowestoft! Your pier bathed in an atmosphere of delicious summer dreaminess, the distant music of a band, the sunlit red-brown sails of trawlers, your harbour's sleeping water which flanks you, oh you fisherman's Venice, on one side.' The harbour, formed by cutting a channel to Lake Lothing, divided the two parts of the town.

The old town is up on the cliffs and is connected to the dunes along the shore (the Denes) by narrow passages called 'scores'. The beautiful church of St Margaret, prudently located nearly a mile inland, and the High Lighthouse up on the cliff, remain the two principal monuments of Lowestoft. Up the narrow High Street are plaques on the walls of Georgian houses, as well as on the sites of other buildings such as the first lighthouse and the Swan Inn, where Oliver Cromwell established his headquarters after his brush with the local Royalists in 1643. One of these plaques (unfortunately, in my view) marks the house of Samuel Pacey, a deplorable man who instigated the arrest of two Lowestoft women as witches in 1664. Rose Callender and Amy Drury were tried at Bury St Edmunds and sentenced to death. But the accusations were absolutely incredible and induced a wave of revulsion against such persecution. It was noticed that, as soon as the guilty verdict was announced, Pacey's two teenage daughters, the chief prosecution witnesses, conveniently recovered from the supposed ailments which had allegedly been inflicted on them by the satanic powers.

Lowestoft is the most easterly town in England and is

acutely exposed to the cold east winds as well as to bombardment from sea or air in wartime. During the last war it was
badly damaged by bombing; the insensitive reconstruction of
the town then destroyed many more of the old buildings. The
railway, opened in 1847, brought in the 'excursionists' and
expanded the market for the fish, and the new harbour became
busy with tall-masted ships and hundreds of ketch-rigged
Lowestoft trawlers, in one of which Joseph Conrad worked
for a couple of months as a deckhand. But despite the town's
longstanding dependence on fishing, there had been one early
instance of diversification in the founding of a porcelain
factory by Hewlin Luson of Gunton Hall in 1757. Lowestoft
china comprised all sorts of tableware, ranging from tea sets
(with the small handleless tea cups of the day) to punch bowls
and mugs of vigorous design, the early blue and white pieces
being copied from Dutch models. These were intended for the
lower end of the market, but have since become collectors'
items, all the more so since the company ceased production in
1799, when the seam of fine white clay became exhausted.

In between these two railway-bred resort towns is a third,
Southwold. But its development from a fishing town has been
so slight, and its scale is so small, that it has retained much of
the intimacy of those leisurely days of a century ago, and has
scorned the temptations of popularisation. Its miniature
railway line was closed well before the war, and its pier was
dismantled after its battering by the gales of 1978. Its
exclusivity is emphasised by the meadows and marshes which
surround it on the landward side. The High Street leads to the
centre of the town, where it broadens so as to provide for a tiny
triangular market place, with the dimensions of a stage set,
and with the old water pump at the centre. From here several
little lanes lead around corners to miniature greens, some of
which overlook the sea. On Gun Hill are six old cannon
(taken away during the war lest the Germans should assert
that Southwold was fortified) and on North Green is planted
the purposeful lighthouse, standing sentinel over the cluster of
small terraced houses around it. Below the cliff, on the
concrete embankment which protects Southwold from marine

erosion, are the beach huts with names such as 'Mumzut', 'Ceezruf', 'Idleours' and 'Baxrest'.

Southwold has been called variously Suwald, Suwalda, Sudholda, Southwaud, Southwood (its true meaning), and even Stowle and Sole, modifications which suggest vagaries in local pronunciation: one imagines strangers asking the way in a strong wind, and getting garbled directions from toothless mouths. At the time of the great prosperity of Dunwich, three miles down the coast, Southwold was no more than a fishing community within the bounds of the parish of the neighbouring village of Reydon. But it flourished as a result of Dunwich's decline, and the triumphal expression of its prosperity during the fifteenth century is its magnificent church, dedicated to St Edmund because the manor of Southwold had been held by the monastery at Bury.

St Edmund's serves as our introduction to Suffolk's great fifteenth-century churches. These tended to be much larger than their predecessors, not because the population had grown proportionately, but because they were built for display. Or rather, since there was no thought of people coming from afar to visit them, and the display was for the community of people who regularly attended the services, it is perhaps more accurate to say that they were intended for glorification. Besides all the religious ceremonies – the masses, baptisms weddings, funerals, and prayers for the dead – they were also sometimes used for courts of canon law and meetings of the guilds. They were built hardly a century before the Reformation transformed the services for which they had been designed. Originally, Suffolk churches glowed inwardly in dim religious light, with many frescoes and much painted woodwork, faintly lit through stained glass windows and by greasy candles burning perpetually in front of sacred objects. Today the sun floods in with a brightness intensified by the whitewash on the walls, illuminating an interior largely devoid of medieval clutter. What has been lost is the sense of mystery. What has been gained is greater architectural clarity. It is as if the Catholic and Protestant traditions have been welded together in stone, and it is a combination which is dignified by history and possesses its own nobility.

It is astonishing that a mere fishing village could have afforded to erect such a wonderful monument, and it is clear, from the many bequests that were given towards its building and furnishing, that a whole community was actively involved. But royal patronage may well have been crucial, since the King held the lordship of the manor of Southwold at the time, and the little town received its charter as a borough in 1489. During the seventeenth century the church became neglected, and might easily have suffered the fate of Walberswick and Covehithe churches in being reduced to a single aisle. When Daniel Defoe visited Southwold he found only twenty-seven people in the Sunday congregation, whereas the Dissenting Chapel was full to overflowing. The church windows were bricked up to half their height to conserve heat, the box pews blocked and obscured the base of the screen, and an unsightly wooden gallery encroached from the west end. Thanks to an inspired reconstruction earlier this century, by a young church architect, F. E. Howard, the interior of St Edmund's today looks exceptionally graceful: he re-elevated the altar, repainted the pulpit, and provided a magnificent font-cover, adornments which admirably complement the original screen and roof.

St Edmund's also draws our attention to the flint which clothes the walls of nearly all Suffolk's medieval churches. This flint cladding produces visual effects of great variety. The flints can be large and stony, or small and pebbly. Those on the coastal churches have mostly been picked from the beaches, those further inland from chalk beds or gravel deposits. The gravel deposits are generally brown in colour, the chalk beds black and white. The flints can be rough or they can be knapped. However they are treated, they are virtually imperishable, being stronger than many limestones. They form an incrustation of tiny broken surfaces, catching the light or holding the shadow, darkening in rain or brightening when dry, adding body and depth to the wall, and generally giving an impression of great ingenuity as well as durability. Humble though they may be in comparison to great blocks of masonry, the tiny flints are what give me the greatest pleasure when approaching a Suffolk church. The admixture of flint and stone in decorative patterns on the exterior of buildings is known as flushwork, which is much in evidence on the tower of St Edmund's, whilst on the west front and the south porch are large panels of chequer patterning.

Thomas Gardner, the eighteenth-century local historian of Southwold (whose tombstone has been redeposited in the church) has recorded the devastation of a terrible fire in 1659, which 'consumed the Town-Hall, Market House, Prison, Granaries, Shops, Ware-Houses, and two hundred thirty-eight Dwelling Houses, with Fish-Houses, Malt-Houses, Tackle-Houses, Brew-Houses, and other Out-Houses'. It was this which caused Southwold to be almost entirely rebuilt. The Dutch seamen brought ashore as prisoners doubtless provided much of the labour force, and may have influenced the architecture also, to judge from the Dutch gables and brick-coursing which are everywhere apparent. At least the cellars of the old Swan Hotel escaped this fire. These became incorporated into the Sole Bay Brewery, which still flourishes under the name of Adnams.

Adnams proudly proclaim 'From Suffolk's Oldest Brewery to Britain's Finest Beer'. At a time when all other local Suffolk breweries got swallowed up by conglomerates such as Cobbolds, Adnams have succeeded in preserving their independence and the quality of their real ales, and they are now renowned throughout East Anglia. Their muscular grey Percheron horses, plodding the streets of Southwold, affirm the laudable success of the policy of maintaining the highest quality in the production of beer at a time when pressurised beers seemed to have swept the market. One of their directors, Simon Loftus, has achieved fame as a wine merchant, proving that Southwold's peripheral location is no impediment to commercial success if the product is right. He seems to be in the tradition of the famous sixteenth-century wine merchant of Ipswich, Henry Tooley, who maintained a depot in Bordeaux and in a single year (1521) shipped 212 tuns of wine to Ipswich for sale to the Dukes of Norfolk and Suffolk and the leading merchants and gentry. Henry Tooley would have been surprised to learn how widely wine is consumed in Suffolk today, and even more surprised that viniculture, after centuries of complete abandonment in England, has recently been re-established in Suffolk.

Across the mouth of the Blyth from Southwold lies Walberswick, which stretches back inland for nearly a mile to its church, St Andrew's. This is in ruins except for the former south aisle, and for its great tower, which owes its preservation to being a landmark from the sea. Originally Walberswick was surrounded by water on three sides, with the Blyth sweeping around it to meet the sea further south. During the last century it was one of the first Suffolk villages to be 'discovered' for its qualities as a village, as opposed to a seaside resort, although obviously this discovery was helped by its proximity to the sea and, in the days of the regular ferry, to Southwold. In the summer of 1884 the young artist Philip Wilson Steer came to Walberswick, fresh from his training in Paris, and began to paint canvasses in the Impressionistic style which was still very much disapproved of in the Royal Academy. In the ensuing years he returned annually to Walberswick and produced a series of seascapes and landscapes which brought fame to both the artist and the place, and Walberswick became established as a sort of artists' colony.

Down by the water-front everything seems perfectly arranged for artists, with walkways over the mudflats, and shacks on stilts, and fishermens' sheds for kippering herrings, and skeletons of old wooden boats – a picture awaiting its painter. The heart of Walberswick, around the Green, is protected from inundation by a grass-covered embankment, put up after the floods of 1953. These caused severe damage to low-lying houses all along the coast, and in Suffolk forty-six people lost their lives: though the publican of the Harbour Inn (just across the Blyth from Walberswick) at least had a jolly tale to tell afterwards, being marooned in an upper room for a night and a day together with his wife, five customers, three dogs, two cats and a budgerigar, plus a bottle of whisky and a rabbit pie.

Besides these towns and villages which stand on Suffolk's shoreline, there are also several lonely hamlets perilously perched on cliffs or beaches, as if offered sacrificially to the raging of the sea. At the northern end is Corton, whose church tower still provides a landmark near where the Romans once had a signal station. A visitor to the coast of North-East Suffolk a century ago found that, after an absence of twenty years, 'the ancient manor-house, the old inn, the beachmen's shelter, and a dozen or more fishermen's cottages had all gone "down-cliff" '. Then come the former fishing villages of Covehithe and Easton Bavents. Covehithe at least still has its ruined church (St Andrew's), and its tower has also been preserved as a landmark. But the church of St Nicholas at Easton Bavents, just north of Southwold, was undermined three hundred years ago; and before that the whole of another village, Easton Stone, had disappeared, this being the most eroded part of the entire Suffolk coast in historical times. Thomas Gardner records that in 1748 a special service was held in a barn, once a chapel in the parish of Easton Bavents, itself by now down-cliff.

Finally (forgetting for a moment Dunwich and Aldeburgh) the settlements along the coast are completed by two of more recent origin, and never villages in the proper sense. Shingle Street is associated with the building of a Martello Tower and a coastguard station. It is correctly named, since the houses are linked by an access road, or street, to landward, but are actually on the edge of the beach, which towers up in front of them, so that from some of the ground-floor windows you cannot see the sea. And the shingle is very much on the move just here, busily forming a new bank just offshore. The inhabitants of Shingle Street brave it out in the short term, but it must give a curious, if salutory, feeling of impermanence to live there, like modern Cnuts demonstrating the inexorability of the forces of nature.

Thorpeness, just north of Aldeburgh, is an entirely artificial creation of the 1920s and '30s, developed by an enthusiast, Glencairn Stuart Ogilvie. It was built as a mock village for summer holiday-makers, and was much favoured by colonial civil servants in the days of the Empire. It displays all sorts of architectural fancies – imitation timber-and-lathe houses, a water-tower looking like a cottage suspended in the sky, and cottages looking like a medieval gatehouse. Amongst its sports amenities, Thorpeness has its own artificial mere, with islands and inlets associated with events in *Peter Pan*. Thorpe (the fishing hamlet that preceded Thorpeness here) is a Danish place-name, common in Northern England but rare in the South. So it is coincidental that the Liberals' lost leader, Jeremy Thorpe, should have lived in a house near here, to be seen on occasions rowing on the juvenile Meare, incongruously wearing his trilby hat.

II
Dunwich and Aldeburgh

Dunwich and Aldeburgh are the two marvels of Suffolk's shoreline, two ancient boroughs which have for centuries rolled on the beach in a twice-daily embrace with the sea. Though impoverished by their battle with the elements, both have been enriched by history, and have provided a setting for religious and artistic inspiration and attainment. Together they are the twin shrines for all who seek to find spiritual refreshment in the strange story, both natural and human, of Suffolk's coast.

Everyone who visits Dunwich knows about the town that drowned, even if only from old legends about church bells ringing beneath the water or ghoulish accounts of human bones protruding from the cliffs. It is a great place for observing the erosion along Suffolk's shifting shoreline. But it wasn't the incursion of the sea that did for Dunwich. If that had been all, the town could quite well have been rebuilt higher up the cliff and a little inland. The real killer was the blocking of the harbour.

Looking northwards from the Dunwich cliff one can see the marshes through which the tiny Dunwich River drains away into sluices at Walberswick. In the great days of Dunwich the scene was utterly different. Where the marshes are was then a salt-water estuary, with its mouth just where the car park is. Into this estuary flowed the Dunwich River, and also the Blyth River, which was prevented by a shingle spit from reaching the sea at Walberswick. This spit, known as the King's Holme, enclosed the natural harbour to the north, just as Dunwich itself did to the south, and was to be the instrument of destruction of the sea-port. Through the centuries it altered its shape, sometimes broader, sometimes narrower, but always shifting south in accordance with the prevailing coastal pattern. Unfortunately the cliffs of Dunwich stood directly in its way, and ultimately King's Holme came up against them and totally blocked the natural harbour that it had itself originally created. What we see now from Dunwich cliff is a face without a mouth.

The great days of Dunwich were during the twelfth and thirteenth centuries. The Norman Conquest brought prosperity to Dunwich in contrast to Ipswich. The number of burgesses recorded in Domesday had doubled in twenty years, and its total population of around three thousand included a small Norman community. At the time of the conquest Dunwich had been awarded to Robert Malet's Honour of Eye, but when this was forfeited the town was retained by the Crown, which worked to its great advantage. The culminating recognition came in 1199, when it was granted the charter of a free borough. Among the various privileges awarded to the burgesses was one which stated that they might 'marry their daughters wheresoever they may', the first instance in England of this particular freedom being explicitly stated; and it was a freedom for the daughters themselves, who were not to be married except 'with their own free will'.

Dunwich became a major shipbuilding port, thanks in part to the ready supply of timber from the Suffolk woodlands, and the ships usually remained in the possession of the Dunwich owners. In 1173, twenty ships were sent to Sandwich for royal use; in 1229, forty ships to Portsmouth for Henry III's passage to France. By 1279 the town possessed eighty large ships. Dunwich provided eleven ships, armed and manned, for Edward I's expedition to Gascony in 1294, which remained there through the winter without pay. Together with this went ship repair, and an entry in the Royal Exchequer refers to the purchase of 'masts, booms, yards, straps, sprits, hair-cloth, pikes and ropes for the royal galleys' to be contracted with Nicholas Fitzrobert of Dunwich for £41–4s–1d. Besides this there was more business to be had in entrepot trade, with goods transferred from the warehouses to ships following the coast or plying across to France or Flanders. And, as always, the fishing boats were constantly at work in gathering the harvest of the sea.

But already Dunwich was on the defensive. Even in the eleventh century the sea had carried away a carucate (approximately fifty hectares) of land. In 1225 it was necessary to protect the town by a sea wall, and in 1250 King's Holme had got so close that a new cut had to be made to the harbour. At the same time, the sea had made its breach through the shingle spit further to the north, and this had to be blocked so as to encourage the water through the new cut. But in a great storm in 1286 this northern breach re-opened even wider, and it required a tremendous effort, probably over two or three years, to close it again. Even then, another breach broke open in 1300.

It might be assumed that the burghers of Dunwich would not have been too concerned about the exact spot at which the tide would ebb and flow between the sea and the natural harbour behind the shingle bar. But in fact this alternative harbour mouth spelt ruin. This is because the ownership of the shingle of King's Holme was disputed with the village of Walberswick at the far end. Whoever controlled the entrance to the harbour could command a toll on all shipping entering.

There had always been friction between Dunwich and the manorial lords of Blythburgh, Walberswick and Westleton. In particular, the Lady of the Manor of the first of these, Margery de Cressy, had initiated legal action in respect of King's Holme, which was ultimately successful. But the opportunity for the local enemies of Dunwich to put the screws on came after the terrible storm of 14 January 1328. This shifted the shingle so much that it was clearly impossible to reopen the Dunwich cut. Sir John de Clavering of Walberswick took the initiative in destroying the Dunwich guard house on King's Holme. In return for this, a group of Dunwich men boarded and sank a Walberswick ship, killing sixteen men. The feud continued in the days of Sir Robert Swillington, lord of the manor of Blythburgh. He seized King's Holme in 1381. In 1400 the sheriff ordered him to release it, but a few years later his son, Sir Roger, managed to produce the old writ of

Margery de Cressy which proved his case, and a royal enquiry found in his favour. In a conciliatory gesture which cost him nothing, he then released the southern, and useless, part of King's Holme to Dunwich for the derisory rent of one root of ginger.

Meanwhile the storms had worn down and destroyed much of the lower part of the town. The timber-framed buildings could not withstand the combined onslaught of wind and waves. Thomas Gardner of Southwold has set out twenty successive disasters through the centuries. He tells of over four hundred houses, together with two churches and shops and windmills, going down in the fourteenth century. In 1570 the town suffered incredible damage, and in 1677 the sea reached the Market Place. Finally, there were the terrible devastations of 1740. After each of these, fresh ruins lay exposed in the water, to be pounded down through the years. The brick linings of former wells, standing up in the sea like round towers, were specially prominent and lugubrious reminders of these devastations. There were probably six parishes in the town at the time of its prosperity, and all their churches went under: St Leonard's, St Martin's, St Nicholas', St Peter's, All Saints, and the largest, St John's. There were also several religious houses, and that of the Grey Friars – the Franciscans – was the last great building of Dunwich to fall, being situated high on the cliff, and its impressive curtain walls may still be seen. Meanwhile, in ironic contrast, the landward rampart of Dunwich, the Pales Dyke, which had defied the Earl of Leicester's forces in the twelfth century and is still discernible, remained unscathed.

Long after Dunwich had been reduced to a mere fishing village it retained several of its ancient privileges, of which the most important was the right to return two members of Parliament until the Reform Bill. By then the electorate comprised only seventeen freemen residing in the town, and Dunwich was one of the most notorious of the 'rotten boroughs'. But at least the town died in this way with a certain dignity, and although we may deplore the bribery of these electors, and laugh at the thought of their electoral functions being conducted in a boat anchored in calm weather over the site of the former town hall, it was perhaps small compensation for all they and their families had lost.

The strange story of Dunwich has proved very satisfying for moralists. It shows the folly of building houses on sand. Daniel Defoe sees it as an example of the ultimate destruction of all human endeavour: 'we see that towns, kings, countries, families and persons have all their elevation, their medium, their declination and even their destruction in the womb of time and the course of nature'. Swinburne, in a long poem, dwells on the pathetic belief of the people of Dunwich that they would be spared from the iron inevitability of the rule of the sea; he has some macabre lines about the corpses exposed by the erosion. And Henry James, who bicycled around Dunwich, expounds on the latent menace of the sea, 'which moves for ever, like a ruminating beast, an insatiable, indefatigable lip'.

Dunwich's origins stretch back to Roman times, but its first historical reference is in the establishment by St Felix of his episcopal see at Domnoc, which is generally supposed to have been Dunwich. It was from here that the priests of the new religion spread out by foot along the rough tracks of Suffolk, and from where their bishops kept in touch with Canterbury and the Continent by boat. Dunwich was thus the ignition point of Catholicism, and the Church of England still recognises this by retaining a suffragan (or assistant) Bishop of Dunwich.

Felix, the apostle of East Anglia, found a ready response to his ministry from the moment he first arrived in 630, on the authority of Archbishop Honorius of Canterbury. Doubtless this success was largely due to his own diplomatic skills, acquired at the Burgundian court, and to the wholehearted support and patronage of the saintly king, Sigebert. But it must also have been that the time was ripe for the conversion of the people as a whole, for in other Anglo-Saxon kingdoms several missionaries met with great hostility.

It is pleasant also to learn that Felix was assisted in his historic task by an Irish holy man called Fursey, and that no apparent conflict existed between them, despite the different traditions that they represented. Felix, once established at Dunwich, busied himself in an orderly way in persuading the king and the notables to provide him with the means to build his church and set up a school, efficiently deploying his missionary priests with their portable altars throughout the land, where they quietly preached the new morality. Fursey led a more unworldly existence in his religious community at Cnobbesburgh (among the ruins of Burgh Castle). His missionary methods were more oratorical and emotional, perhaps employing an Irish loquacity that left the bovine Anglian tribesfolk gaping, for he told wonderful stories of how his soul had left his body for several days and been among the angels. After taking a sabbatical in one of the monastery's hermitages, Fursey left Cnobbesburgh and went to the court of the Frankish king, Clovis, who awarded him another monastery at Lagny, where he died.

The missionary efforts of Felix and Fursey had only just had time to permeate East Anglia when the kingdom succumbed to Penda and his Mercian horde, and the pagan gods re-emerged. The swift recovery of Christianity was helped by its firm hold over the ladies of the royal family of Wuffinga, whoses names seem appropriate for such forceful characters. Etheldreda, daughter of King Anna, founded the monastery at Ely, endowing it with royal lands in East Suffolk. She was joined at Ely by her sister Sexburga, who had married the King of Kent; and another sister, Ethelburga, became abbess of Brie in France. A generation later the daughters of King Aldwulf – Eadburgha, Ethelburga and Hwetburga – all became abbesses of monasteries in the north of England. These influential ladies must all have been concerned that the faith should be secure locally in East Anglia. Among the priests evangelising under their royal protection was St Botolph. Botolph was a learned man of noble birth, and it was said that he could foretell the future 'as if it was already past'. He founded a monastery at Iken, and he may have been a bishop. Another figure who gave inspiration to the faith in these early Saxon times was

Ethelbert, an East Anglian king who was said to have been assassinated at the Mercian court in 794.

In 673 the Dunwich diocese was divided and a new bishopric established at Elmham, as part of a policy effected throughout England by Archbishop Theodore. It has been generally supposed that this was North Elmham in the middle of Norfolk, and that the dividing line was along the Waveney. Some historians support the claim of South Elmham near Bungay. Certainly this was church property from an early date: but it would have been very odd to establish the two sees, whose authority covered the whole of East Anglia, within fourteen miles of each other. Besides, when Christianity was later re-established after the Danish interregnum, the single diocese for the whole area was based at North Elmham, and Dunwich ceased to be an ecclesiastical centre.

For ten years the Danes forcibly attempted to stamp out Christianity, and for many decades thereafter, although it was tolerated as the religion of the people, successive waves of pagan Northmen prevented it from becoming re-established. There were no known bishops during this period, nor any monasteries, and all the previous church and monastic property had been plundered: when their chalices and ornaments had been seized, they were put to the fire, together with their holy books. But, as we have seen in Eastern Europe in our own day, so long as it is impossible to stamp out a religion completely, it tends to thrive under persecution. In the case of the East Anglians it was associated with their resentment at subordination to Danish soldiers and settlers, and with their sense of identity in race and language. So when, during the tenth century, East Anglia came once again under English rule, it was with exceptional religious fervour and popular enthusiasm that monasteries were founded, and parish churches established under the authority of the bishop at Elmham.

Place-name evidence suggests that many churches had been established right across the Suffolk landscape before the Danish invasions of the ninth and tenth centuries. But under Danish rule such churches were neglected. Being constructed

39

of wood, they would have fallen into disrepair, and their sites used for pagan ritual. Indeed, several churches were themselves on the sites of earlier pagan temples, whilst others were set up on the ruins of ancient earthworks or the sites of cemeteries. But it was during the revival of Christianity in the later Saxon period that the pattern of Suffolk's parishes, as we see it today, was largely completed. In Domesday Book, the Norman audit, 417 Suffolk churches are recorded, and the best estimate of the total population of the time is 70,000. This gives an average parish of only around 170 people. In no other county was there such intensity, and Norfolk (which, after all, was part of the same diocese) had about a hundred fewer churches, despite a larger area and population. Such exceptional activity cannot merely have been imposed upon a reluctant population, and communal and popular participation in the construction of Suffolk's Saxon churches is implicit throughout. The influence of the two great monasteries of St Edmund's and Ely can also be detected, as they acted to augment the parish coverage within their extensive Liberties.

During the Middle Ages the monasteries and other religious houses dominated much of Suffolk. At the peak there were as many as seventy-six religious establishments of all kinds. First and foremost were the monasteries. The Benedictine Abbey of Bury was by far the largest monastery, with some eighty monks and over a hundred servants living within the precincts. Because Bury did not welcome other monasteries within the bounds of its extensive Liberty, the others tended to be in the east of the county. There were Benedictine dependencies at Eye, Hoxne, Rumburgh, Snape and Stoke; and Cluniac Monks at Wangford and Mendham: the Cistercians were at Sibton. The Augustinian Canons, whose main function was to provide priests for parishes, had houses in every part of Suffolk, and the Premonstratensians (from the Abbey of Premontre, near Laon) were at Leiston. At one time there were preceptories of the Templars at East Bergholt, Dunwich and Gislingham. There were also nunneries, such as Benedictine nuns at Redlingfield and Bungay, and Augustinian nuns at Campsey Ash. Throughout the county there were also colleges for the training of priests and, in all, thirty-five hospitals funded by the religious houses. The religious houses held immense estates, and at the time of the Dissolution they together owned some two hundred manors. In addition to all this property, the influence of the monasteries in Suffolk was augmented by the practice of impropriation. This meant that they acquired control of the original church endowment and appointed a vicar who was often himself a monk, whilst the running of the church was left to a stipendiary priest on a substantially reduced income.

Besides the monasteries there were the friaries. The friars differed from the monks in many ways, of which the most important economically was that they owned no land, and, socially, that they went out and about among the people and did not live secluded lives behind monastic walls. They appeared first in the thirteenth century, under a bewildering variety of orders. There were the Augustinian Friars, the Carmelite (or White) Friars, the Crutched Friars, the Dominican (or Black) Friars, and the Franciscan (or Grey) Friars. They were more numerous than the monks, as well as more in evidence, and their houses were always in the towns. The two largest establishments – the Black Friars at Ipswich and the Grey Friars at Babwell near Bury – had forty friars each.

During the early fifteenth century the Church itself was challenged on matters of practice and doctrine by the followers of John Wyclif, known as the Lollards. They held heretical views on the mass, on confession, baptism, and marriage, as well as secular opinions relating to the unlawfulness of church property and the payment of tithes. They were especially active in Beccles and Bungay. Although several in Suffolk were condemned to periods of imprisonment and public whippings, none was put to death except for an ex-priest, William White, who was burned at the stake in 1428. White had been in trouble in Kent, and obliged to make a solemn abjuration of his heresies. He was permitted to remain a priest on condition that he never preached again. But before long he was doing so actively in Suffolk, based on Bergholt, where he foresook the priestly gown and tonsure for ordinary clothes, and took a wife.

Other signs of cracks now appeared in the monolithic structure of Catholicism. The wealth of the monasteries began to be questioned, and gestures of irreverence occurred during ceremonials. In 1431, Nicholas Conon of Eye was charged with mocking the Easter Day procession around the church by walking around anticlockwise, and standing with his back to the altar while the priest was celebrating mass on All Hallows Day. In 1515, on the Friday after Corpus Christi Day, Richard Warton and Thomas Woodcock and several others broke and threw down several of the pageants which were being paraded through Bungay. Yet this was the period of the construction of Suffolk's magnificent churches of the Perpendicular style, which took place with great public support. Certainly, such churches were initiated and funded in the main by leading landowners and merchants. But from the evidence of bequests it is clear that donations flowed in from much smaller property owners, whilst the pennies of the poor were gleaned from popular local gatherings known as church ales. People spoke of 'Selig (holy) Suffolk', since corrupted to 'Silly Suffolk'.

The centrality of the Catholic liturgy in the lives of the entire population before the Reformation can hardly be exaggerated. It provided an all-embracing spectacle whose influence over the illiterate may, I suppose, be compared to television today. After all, it was elaborate and colourful, and was received rather than participated in. It proceeded through a complicated weekly and annual cycle. The principal protagonists were readily recognisable from their various images, and seemed to be as real as one's own family and acquaintances. And there was plenty of time to contemplate familiar scenes – with the difference that, instead of sitting comfortably at home being harangued by a strident young woman, one was standing uncomfortably in the church while, from beyond the rood screen, the priest was mumbling imprecations.

But this superficial comparison ignores the utterly different attitudes of people five hundred years ago. They lived in a closed society bounded with certainties, and their lives concluded with an unequivocal translation into heaven or hell. When in church they were partaking in time-honoured rituals which explained the whole meaning of life in a deeply satisfactory way. In the decades before the Reformers broke the spell, it seems in retrospect as if the Church was doing its best to ward off any deviant thoughts by increasing the splendour of its ceremonies and art; and nowhere were these displayed to better effect than in the villages of Suffolk. Whatever our attitude towards institutionalised religion, we cannot but applaud the building of Suffolk's medieval churches, for they are also temples of art and architecture. But we cannot properly appreciate them without some sympathy for the poetry and symbolism which inspired them. It is necessary to hear the words of the psalms when looking at the outstretched wings of the angels up in the roof, to be touched by the stories of the saints who appear on the base of the rood screen, and to sense the spirituality that pervades their silent spaces.

Unlike all the other coastal towns and villages of Suffolk, the heart of Aldeburgh lies right down on the beach and below the cliffs, extending for almost half a mile along the shore. A more intimate relationship to the sea could not be imagined; and, of course, it is a deathly one, because the sea has already rolled away half the old town. This destruction, which took place gradually over a couple of centuries, is most clearly evident from the sight of the venerable sixteenth-century Moot Hall, once at the epicentre of Aldeburgh, but now right up against the beach. But massive concrete sea walls now offer reasonable protection, and the long High Street, with its Georgian frontages, looks reassuringly permanent.

Aldeburgh (meaning old-fort) was a fishing village which benefited from the decline of Dunwich, and became a chartered borough in the mid-sixteenth century. But it never aspired to the importance of medieval Dunwich, and remained no more than a fishing port, with some boat building activity thrown in. Life was hard, and the people of Aldeburgh were constantly in fear of attack from the sea – first pirates, then the Spaniards, the Dunkirkers, the Dutch, and then the Royal

Navy press-gangs. The town's Hearth Tax return in 1674 shows that nearly half the houses were empty. But Aldeburgh has managed to survive in a way that Dunwich did not, despite the incursions of the sea and the adverse changes to its harbour mouth, now some ten miles south of the town's jetty on the Alde, Slaughden Quay.

Slaughden Quay, at the point where the Alde fails to gain the sea and turns abruptly south, is the harbour of Aldeburgh and where the elemental forces are felt, not in the incursions of the sea, but in the accumulations of shingle that have smothered the old harbour buildings.

The clutch of little fishing boats drawn up on the shore at Aldeburgh still bears witness to the nautical tradition, to the fishermen in their yellow oilskin smocks and huge leather sea boots glistening with herring scales. So do the two watch towers of the former 'beach companies', which specialised in salvage, ready to launch their long and graceful yawls, which bore a strong resemblance to Viking ships. The beach companies certainly saved lives, but they also acted ruthlessly in matters of shipwreck, charging exorbitantly for salvage. The great hero of Aldeburgh was James Cable, the intrepid coxwain of the Aldeburgh Lifeboat a century ago. He achieved international renown because, among the ships whose crews he managed to save from drowning, were those of the German steamer *Sirius* and the Norwegian barques *Winifred* and *Prudentia* as well as several others, including the Welsh schooner *Rambler*: 'a Cable that in storm ne'er broke!'

Aldeburgh had also earned its status as a borough by supplying the *Marygold* to the English fleet against the Armada; and also the *Susan*, the *Pelican*, and the *Greyhound*, to Francis Drake's punitive expedition in the following year. The town's seal, couched in heraldic terms, is most appealing: 'Azure on Water in Case an ancient ship of three masts in full sail a Ladder affixed to the side amidships proper the mainsail charged with a Lion rampant the fore and aft sails and the pennons charged with a Cross Gules'.

In the last decades before the use of steam power, the sailing ships which plied the coastal waters of Suffolk must have

44

looked truly magnificent. James Ford, in 1815, described the scene off Aldeburgh on a sunny day. There were thirty or forty fishing-boats to be seen within a mile of the shore. A little further out, but still close enough for their crews to be detected, great fleets of merchantmen and colliers, sometimes as many as three hundred at a time, passed by on their voyages up and down the English coast, or to and from the Baltic. The sight, he says, was 'sublime', and 'congenial to every thing that a Briton esteems and values'. At this time Aldeburgh enjoyed a brief head start over the other coastal villages of Suffolk as a place for a select few to come and take to the water. In 1804 it was 'quite a new place', with a promenade, bathing machines, circulating library and so on, attracting visitors such as the Earl of Bristol and Dr Charles Burney.

Nowadays there are said to be more knights than fishermen living in Aldeburgh, and the inhabitants are very different from the closed community that persecuted Peter Grimes. The old borough, with its stern moralities, has become transformed into an altogether gentler place, whose congenial lifestyle is focused in an August carnival, culminating in a candle-lit procession along the High Street to the Moot Hall. But the spirit of the old days pervades the scene, not only by means of the architecture, but also through the poetry of George Crabbe and the music of Benjamin Britten.

The poetry of George Crabbe expresses the essence of Aldeburgh and the Suffolk coast with such exactitude that it is as if the subject and the style had been made for each other. Crabbe is to Suffolk what his contemporary Wordsworth is to the Lake District, and it is hard to imagine what would have been the result if Crabbe had been born and raised at Cockermouth and Wordsworth at Aldeburgh, each out of his element. Crabbe is never melodramatic, he is never enthusiastic, he never lets go. He is short in imagination and long in realism. He avoids metrical experiments. But in his own understated way he can also be classified as a romantic, and the deep suggestiveness of his poetry, and the implications of what he left unsaid, are aspects which distinguish him from being just a poor man's latter-day Alexander Pope.

To the imaginative mind, the sombre marshes, the black mud flats, the grey horizons, the perpetual sighing of the sea on the shifting sands and shingles – all these induce feelings of depression rather than elation. The scene even lacks the grandeur of a rocky coast of precipices and promontories, where waves strike at fantastic boulders and scatter cascades of spray. It induces an awareness of the blind and cruel force of nature, especially if an entire community is battling against the elements, as were the fisher-folk of Aldeburgh. The fishermen had learnt to dominate the winds and the waves by generations of careful observation and testing, and so it was appropriate that the poet should likewise study nature with a verbal precision and a scientific eye. The marble bust in Aldeburgh church proclaims him as the 'Poet of Nature and Truth': if truth is accuracy and not – as Keats thought – beauty, Crabbe excels. His accurate descriptions of nature call to mind the great Dutch school of painters, with every detail anatomically depicted. But even here he directs his eye, with a precise attention, towards the meaner aspects of the scene – the humble mosses, litchens and herbs, the thistles and the weeds, rather than the more obviously beautiful flowers. He revels in the slimy banks of the Alde and the desolate stretches of swamp and shingle. 'Nature's sternest painter, yet the best' is Byron's well-known verdict on Crabbe; though, as a salutory antidote, we should also recall that Byron's contemporary, William Hazlitt, criticised Crabbe's poetry as being 'done so to the life, that it seems almost like some sea-monster, crawled out of the neighbouring slime, and harbouring a breed of strange vermin, with a strong local scent of tar and bilge-water'.

Above all, it was the sea that attracted him, in all its moods – heaving in tranquillity, wrapped in densest fog, or furious in a winter storm. He forbears to soliloquise about the elemental force of the ocean, and its impersonal indifference to humanity, as Byron did in 'Childe Harold' and as is implied throughout Coleridge's 'Ancient Mariner'. Instead, he delights in describing exactly how the waves break on the shore, curling, striking and grating:

But nearer land you may the billows trace,
As if contending in their watery chase;
May watch the mightiest till the shoal they reach,
Then break and hurry to their utmost stretch;
Curl'd as they come, they strike with furious force,
And then re-flowing, take their grating course,
Raking the rounded flints, which ages past
Roll'd by their rage, and shall to ages last.

Aldeburgh was the setting for the depressing early life of George Crabbe. His intelligent and energetic father lived there precariously, in reduced circumstances, as a customs official. This forceful man also took part in local affairs, had a share in a fishing boat, and in the evenings studied mathematics and read Milton. But sadly these qualities became submerged by his increasing violence and intemperance, which brought chronic misery to his downtrodden wife and six children. At least he recognised the mental strength of his eldest son, George, who went briefly to schools in Bungay and Stowmarket, and then was sent away, aged thirteen, to be apprentice to an apothecary. After a menial year near Bury, George Crabbe was transferred to Woodbridge, where he was left largely to his own devices in the dispensary rather than being taught medical or surgical skills. He spent his spare time writing poetry, and found happiness with other young people.

His seven years' apprenticeship over, Crabbe returned to Aldeburgh at the age of twenty-one to a pretty hopeless situation. He had no money and his medical education was deficient. He was reduced to working for some months as a common labourer on Slaughden Quay, rolling barrels of salt, piling casks of butter, and sweating and shouting on the shingle with the rough-necks, a demeaning experience in a class-bound society. Fortunately George Crabbe was able to acquire a small apothecary's practice in Aldeburgh. He now became absorbed in botany and anatomy, both subjects appealing to his gifts of minute observation. But 'Dr Crabbe' failed to inspire confidence in his patients, and his ministrations were all too frequently inefficacious. His practice diminished and he was reduced to little more than looking after the poor-house, for which he was paid a pittance by the borough. After three years he gave it up and went to London in the slight hope of finding a patron for his poems. This he secured, only in the nick of time, in the person of Edmund Burke, the great parliamentary polemicist. Besides advancing money to Crabbe, Burke also arranged for him to be ordained as a clergyman, and it was in this capacity that he returned once again to Aldeburgh. The new curate had triumphed over poverty and obscurity, but he found no welcome among the townsfolk of Aldeburgh. They did not by any means approve of this transformation, and his sermons were preached to rows of sullen, angry faces. But he got his own back on them in his poem, 'The Borough'.

In his treatment of the human scene, Crabbe appears as the poet of disillusion. He selects for subjects the maimed, the unbalanced, the depraved, the outcasts, and gains for them our pity. But then he proceeds to treat them with a certain reproof, and even contempt. In the Aldeburgh he portrays, the doctors are quacks, the clergymen are misfits, the lawyers are rapacious, the teachers are bitter and thwarted, the tradesmen are timid and corrupt. Down at the bottom of the social scale are the drunkards, the spendthrifts, the profligate, and those who are possessed by the devil. Here are Jachin, the parish clerk, who pockets the church collection money; Blaney, who runs through three fortunes; Clelia, whose marital misadventure ends her up in the almshouse; Ellen Orford, seduced by a man above her station; and Peter Grimes, the sadistic loner. What a cold and frightening place it is, inhabited by these incorrigible people, 'a wild amphibious race, with sullen wo displayed on every face'!

We may suspect that Crabbe is being excessively gloomy, and that life in Aldeburgh cannot have been altogether so miserable as he suggests. Indeed, his character sketches are intended as shock treatment, as doses of moral medicine, to shake his contemporaries from their complacency. In describing rural life, for instance, he was determined to demolish the seductive but unreal charms of Arcadia, that enchanted land so beloved of the pastoral poets, where shepherds and shepherdesses loll around on grassy banks in an eternal spring, singing songs of love. Instead he described the poor-house, where the outcasts of society did indeed dwell in squalor, as in the drawings of Hogarth:

Theirs is yon House that holds the parish poor,
Whose walls of mud scarce bear the broken door;
There where the putrid vapours, flagging, play,
And the dull wheel hums doleful through the day;
There children dwell who know no parents' care;
Parents, who know no children's love, dwell there;
Heart-broken matrons on their joyless bed,
Foresaken wives, and mothers never wed;
Dejected widows with unheeded tears,
And crippled age with more than childhood fears;
The lame, the blind, and far the happiest they!
The moping idiot, and the madman gay.

Crabbe was soon able to make his escape from Aldeburgh by means of clerical appointments elsewhere, and to repair his damaged psyche thanks to a happy marriage. But Aldeburgh is where we shall always find him, illuminating our perception of that old salt-sprayed beach-borough.

Aldeburgh was also the home of Benjamin Britten, who has added lustre to Suffolk in our time. Suffolk shaped him and inspired him, and his musical genius was affected by what he saw and learnt and felt about the county. He was born in Lowestoft on St Cecilia's Day in 1913. His mother was a soprano and organiser of the local choral society, and his exceptional musicality was recognised at an early date, so that he was sent to the Royal College of Music at the age of sixteen. His home at Lowestoft faced the sea, and he must have heard it all the time that he or his mother were not actually making music, for no gramophone or wireless polluted the Brittens' house. He got to know the countryside during holidays spent in a farmhouse near Butley, where he walked along the river dyke listening to the swishing of the reeds and rushes and the calls of the curlews. Benjamin Britten was a pacifist, and he and Peter Pears, the tenor who so powerfully inspired his work, were in America when War broke out and did not hasten back. But his deep feelings about Suffolk were pregnantly reawakened by an article in the *Listener* by

E. M. Forster on the poetry of Crabbe. Britten returned in 1942 and set to work on *Peter Grimes*. A few years later he and Pears came to live at Aldeburgh in a house right on the beach beside the Moot Hall, later moving to the Red House just outside the town.

Laurens van der Post, for long another eminent Aldeburgh resident, and one who has wandered the world, has written that Britten brought into his music 'an elemental idiom of nature', and one which is peculiar to East Anglia, particularly to the coast, where the harmony and rhythm of the natural forces are so powerful. Though Britten never kept to any particular musical idiom, but made use of any devices suitable to the work in hand, it is not too fanciful to suppose that his musical compositions were influenced by the sight and sound of the sea, especially as he went for long regular walks along the shore. It is this empathy with the natural scene, rather than the local settings of *Peter Grimes* and *Albert Herring*, that render the association of Britten and Suffolk so close, and which we can particularly detect in the Sea Interludes of *Peter Grimes* and the *Spring Symphony*. But it would be naive to suggest that Britten's music was shaped primarily by the sight and sound of the Suffolk shore. The roots of his genius are more likely to be found in his own introverted personality, his deeply repressed sensuality, and perhaps (as some think) the contradictions of his homosexuality.

Britten also bears an affinity to Crabbe in his hard orderly habit of composition, in his innate sense of anger at injustice to the underdog, and in his restrained romanticism. Fused to Crabbe by *Peter Grimes*, Britten and Aldeburgh became even more bound together through the annual Aldeburgh Festival, mounted for the first time in 1948, and still going strong. Old timers remember nostalgically the operas mounted in the little Jubilee Hall, which saw the first performances of *Albert Herring*, *The Rape of Lucretia*, *The Turn of the Screw*, and *A Midsummer Night's Dream*; and the lighthearted initiatives of the small group of enthusiasts who managed to cultivate the arts in this improbable place, which was dominated at the time by the likes of Lady Billows and the committee of the Golf

Club. They have succeeded in endowing the prosperous Aldeburgh of today with a sensitive recognition of its humble origins, expressed and understood through words and music that transcend the trivialities of ordinary daily life.

III
Lower Stour

The Stour (traditionally pronounced like dour, not flour) is
Suffolk's southern border. This makes it historically much
more significant than the northern boundary along the Ouse
and Waveney, because it was also the border of the primeval
kingdom of East Anglia. Although the Stour valley is shared
with Essex, Suffolk has the larger catchment and superior
architecture since, apart from Manningtree, all the towns
along the Stour are on the Suffolk bank. There seems to be no
single reason for this locational imbalance, so we can accept it
as a happy coincidence that so much lies along the Suffolk side
of this delightful river, from its source just across the
Cambridgeshire border to its mouth between Harwich
harbour and Shotley Point, where it is joined by the Orwell,
the estuary of the Gipping.

The Stour has the largest estuary of all the Suffolk rivers,
and by far the most extensive mudflats – some sixteen hundred
hectares of them at low tide. These rich sedimentary deposits
are host to great flocks of waders and wildfowl, particularly
Brent geese, shelduck, grey plover, black-tailed godwit and
redshank. But they are under threat – from pollution, from
lugworm diggers, and most of all from the channels dredged
for large shipping whereby the action of the tide is so much
stronger than formerly. The mudflats merge with marshes,
bright in summer with the tints of thrift, sea aster and sea
lavender. Along the edge of this inter-tidal world run the
grass-covered sea-walls or the crumbling cliffs. Where these
cliffs have eroded into woods and copses, the trunks of trees
which they have uprooted line the shore, presenting an
appearance as wild as any desert inland. Walking along the
shoreline of the estuary, all the way from Cattawade Bridge to

the Bristol Arms at Shotley Gate, is one of the most rewarding experiences for those who admire the natural scenery of Suffolk, and is best done on a bright winter day, with the low sun shimmering on the water, and the birds in winter plumage. However, this muddy, marshy scenery was not always so appreciated, and Thomas Fuller in the seventeenth century wrote that the Suffolk air is 'sweet' except for 'a small parcel of land nigh the seaside not so excellent, which may seem left there by nature, on purpose to advance the purity of the rest'.

The churches of the villages along the Suffolk bank of the estuary are mostly built with septaria from local quarries or the foreshore. Erwarton and Stutton also have Tudor halls, both much altered, but with pretty red-brick gatehouses, the one at Erwarton, with its round buttresses and round pinnacles looking like a giant octopus. At the head of the estuary the railway crosses the Stour at Cattawade Bridge and enters Suffolk at Brantham. The chemical plant beside the railway was first established here in 1887 by British Xylonite for the manufacture of celluloid, the first form of plastic. Close to it is Braham Hall Farm. Here, in the mid-sixteenth century, Thomas Tusser combined practical farming with writing his popular treatise on the subject, the *Hundreth Good Pointes of Husbandrie*, which went into several editions. It is written in the form of simple proverbs and admonitions in rhymed verses, describing the tasks of the prudent husbandman in each month of the year. January begins:

> When Christmas is ended, bid feasting adieu,
> Go play the good husband, thy stock to renew,
> Be mindful of rearing, in hope of a gain,
> Dame profit shall give the reward for thy pain.

The practical precepts of this homely Virgil were destined to help others rather than himself. Though he pioneered the cultivation of barley, 'dame profit' failed to reward him, and he twice had to sell up. Doubtless he would have had reason to remember his own philosophic lines:

The year I compare, as I find for a truth,
The Spring unto Childhood, the Summer to Youth.
The Harvest to Manhood, the Winter to Age,
All quickly forgot, as a play on a stage.

East Bergholt (hill-copse) overlooks the valley where the Stour flows past the Essex village of Dedham. There is little in Bergholt to show from the time when it was one of the leading centres of the woollen cloth industry. It is best known as the birthplace of John Constable, and today it is scrutinised as closely for its association with him, as it was on canvas by the artist during his lifetime. We can visit the site of his father's house, the cottage he bought for a studio, the tombs of his family and friends; and down the hill is the emerald swathe of Dedham Vale.

Nowhere has the essential beauty of the ancient countryside of England been more movingly interpreted than in the art of John Constable. With painstaking accuracy he depicted the details of the landscape of two centuries ago, but in such a way that he succeeded in translating the rustic scene on to a spiritual plane in its own right. It is this combination of realism and romanticism that has elevated Constable to supreme heights on the Parnassus of English art and, through him, rendered Dedham Vale a cynosure of the English countryside, representative of all we imagine to be best in our lowland scenery. The gentle valley slopes, the fields and copses, the grazing cattle, the placid little river, and the church towers half hidden between groups of oaks and poplars – all these comprise a sort of wildlife picture gallery, where his inspirational scenes may still be evoked in all their natural purity, and imbued with a glow of recognition from familiarity with his luminous, cloud-dappled compositions.

I suppose that the water meadows of Salisbury or the heath at Hampstead or the sea-shore at Brighton might each have a claim to have inspired John Constable, for several of his finest works depicted them. But he held a special affection for the Stour valley around East Bergholt and Dedham which could not be translated elsewhere; for this was the scene of his childhood, and this filial man felt for it with special intensity.

Here were his father's red-brick house and his happy family life. Here were his friends, not merely confined to people of the same class as his father, but including humble lock-keepers. Here was the love awakened in him by Maria Bicknell, for long frustrated but eventually consummated. But the over-riding sentiment that impelled Constable towards an artist's life was love of place. Love of place, however it may be analysed, can be equally overwhelming as other forms of love, and it is often most strongly imprinted on the mind when associated with the earliest forms of recognition when young. Constable, like his contemporary Wordsworth, identified himself indissolubly with his childhood surroundings.

Certainly these two men were exceptionally fortunate in the quality of the scenery around their homes, waiting to cast its spell on their infant minds. But it would be wrong to suggest that their worship of nature blinded them to the harsh realities of their times. Wordsworth when young was a revolutionary, and his poems are full of descriptions of social misfits. Constable admittedly was no political activist, nor did he depict scenes of suffering, but his paintings were of themselves revolutionary. He ignored the convention that important landscape pictures should express some form of classical or religious symbolism, and he introduced a rustic common-sense, seeing the countryside, as it were, through the eyes of a peasant. He was already middle-aged before the Royal Academicians reluctantly recognised his genius. What is so extraordinary is that his works failed to influence English landscape artists who, for most of the nineteenth century, adopted a sickly realism that smacked of sentimentality. Only in France did Constable spark off an idea which flourished, by means of the works of Corot and Delacroix, into what became the school of the Impressionists, who themselves were constantly battling with the disapproval of conservative tastes.

What makes Constable so much more the wonder of Suffolk is that he was largely self-taught. Though Gainsborough and Ruysdael influenced him, it was his own close observation of nature as seen in Suffolk, rather than any formal training in the academies of London, that directed him towards the development of his art. To produce the effect he wanted, he developed his method of painting on-the-spot oil sketches, thus creating for himself an even closer relationship with the green leaves that fill his canvasses, by prolonging the time actually spent in examination of them.

Popular appreciation of Constable only developed a century after his death. Fortunately, this was in time to preserve the idyllic quality of Dedham Vale, despite all pressures for change, pressures all too clearly evident from the A12 and the railway which confine it at either end. One can pleasurably wander along the footpaths and stand at various other points precisely where Constable painted, though attempts to see exactly what it was he saw are seldom successful. The treescapes are all different and, besides, he never sought a merely literal accuracy, as would be achieved in photography. Especially in the wider prospects, he bent and transposed the individual objects that comprised his subject, as all good artists do. Dedham church tower, in particular, was not a fixed point of reference so much as a movable marker. And then there were the clouds, which figure so prominently in his paintings, especially the cumulo-nimbus with its lowering streaks of incipient rain, broken by clear patches where the sunshine breaks through.

Wandering along the river bank we note the subtle alterations which the passage of two centuries have brought to the scenes of some of Constable's major canvasses. At Flatford Mill *The Hay Wain* is entirely encumbered with thick bushes, though *Flatford Mill* retains its unobstructed river bank, and Willy Lott's House still looks as it did when occupied by that remarkable octogenarian, who spent only four nights of his life away from it. The site of *The Leaping Horse* has lost its sluice. The mill house in *Dedham Mill* has been altogether rebuilt and its adjoining lock blocked up. Perhaps the most unchanged river scene is *Stratford Mill* (also known as *The Young Waltonians*) where the treescape seems strangely congruous and where young fishers still have their lines out, though they sit on concrete, not wooden, embankments.

The tower of Stratford St Mary, though rebuilt since

Constable's day, still faces that of Dedham across the meadows, but the village is separated from its church by the A12. Stratford means a ford on a 'straet', the Early English word for a former Roman road. This one was the strategic route from the capital at Camoludunum (Colchester) to Venta Icenorum (just south of Norwich), built during the first century. Stratford St Mary has been identified as a staging post mentioned in the Antonine Itinerary as *ad ansam* or 'the curve', descriptive of the former sharp turn at the bottom of Gun Hill. During the eighteenth century it was noted that hundreds of droves of turkeys, with up to a thousand birds each, were driven seasonally across the bridge at Stratford on their way to the London market.

A mile upstream from Stratford St Mary the Stour receives the Brett, flowing through a little valley in which the first memorable building we find is Giffords Hall. Set in a secluded bowl of woods and pastures, here is perhaps the most appealing piece of early fifteenth-century domestic architecture in the county. Sensitively restored, it has all the characteristics of a great house without being too large or too uniform, being a mixture of brickwork and timber-framing. At the front is the gatehouse, with angle-turrets, and often with a heraldic flag flying from it. At the centre is a small flagged courtyard, in which one feels far removed from the surrounding countryside and reassuringly protected. Along one side is a miniature great hall, with its gallery, oriel window, and double-hammerbeam roof with richly decorated spandrils. Facing the house are the ruins of a thirteenth-century chapel, and in the garden is a dovecote.

Hadleigh (heather-clearing), the town next upstream on the Brett, has twice experienced great economic depression – during the seventeenth century, with the decline of the cloth trade, and early this century during the agricultural slump. The present development of Hadleigh has been sufficiently recent for the old centre, lying along the left bank of the little river, to remain remarkably unblemished. The entire High Street, together with the Market Place and Church Street, is a monument to previous prosperity: in 1568 Hadleigh was third only to Ipswich and Bury as the wealthiest town in the county. The most outstanding building is the Guildhall, dating from 1430 and the days of the cloth merchants. It is three stories high, and each upper storey projects over the one below, so giving an impressive display of posts, beams and brackets. Of even earlier date is the Toppesfield Bridge over the Brett, a triple-piered stone structure widened in brick during the sixteenth century. From the days when Suffolk was England's bread-basket, are the flamboyant Italianate Town Hall (1851) and the diminutive neo-Classical Corn Exchange (1813).

Hadleigh had its very own railway branch line, coming from the mainline at Capel St Mary. It was opened in 1847, and closed for passenger services in 1932. In his delightful reminiscences, *A Suffolk Childhood*, Simon Dewes (John Muriel) describes the excitement of travelling on this line as a boy. At the outbreak of war in 1914, Simon's father, the general practitioner at Hadleigh, correctly predicted that the Germans would bomb the town from zeppelins and decided that his wife and son should be evacuated. As a great treat, Simon was permitted to ride in the driver's cab. Just as Mr Hurd, the station master, and Mr Thorpe, the guard, frock-coated and brass-buttoned, were about to supervise with due ceremony the departure of the almost empty train, the booking clerk rushed on to the platform with a 'Hold on! Hold on! There's a passenger coming up the hill'. After a slow start, and the pauses while the fireman opened the gates of the level crossing and the guard shut them, the train got up 'a bit of speed' between Raydon Great Wood and Capel, with Simon blowing the whistle for all he was worth.

The Danish King Guthram was buried at Hadleigh, which had been a Royal Vill from the Middle Anglo-Saxon period. Late in the tenth century the Manor of Hadleigh (together with the neighbouring Manor of Monks Eleigh) was given to the Archbishopric of Canterbury. In consequence, Hadleigh was excluded from the jurisdiction of the bishops of East Anglia and, in the language of the church, it became a 'peculiar' of Canterbury. The incumbent of Hadleigh enjoyed status and wealth, and in 1495 Archdeacon Pykenham, the then Rector, built a great residence beside the river, whose beautiful turetted gatehouse still stands. In this tower in 1833 Hugh Rose, a later Rector of Hadleigh, convened a meeting of like-minded clergymen who resolved to issue a series of 'Tracts for the Times', thus founding the Anglo-Catholic Oxford Movement.

It was the patronage of an archbishop that brought its most famous figure to Hadleigh. Rowland Taylor had been chaplain to Thomas Cranmer, the first Protestant Archbishop of Canterbury. He was an inspiring preacher and a loveable man of secular outlook and generous proportions, who had married and had several children. When Roman Catholicism was restored under Mary Tudor he refused to conform, and courted arrest when he ousted a priest who was attempting to say Mass in his church. Imprisoned in London by the Catholic authorities, he steadfastly refused to recant his religious beliefs and was condemned to death. Amid touching scenes he was taken back to Hadleigh and burnt at a spot a mile outside the town, recorded by a monument. Even as recently as the middle of this century, Protestants in Hadleigh were particularly vigilant in opposing High-Church practices of the sort advocated by Hugh Rose, and held unauthorised services in the nave and walked to Taylor's place of martyrdom. Meanwhile, the lead-covered wooden spire and the bell of St Mary's have presided unaltered for six hundred years over all these complicated changes in liturgical practices.

A couple of miles outside Hadleigh is Kersey, perhaps the most picturesque of all Suffolk villages (if I may use that now discredited adjective). It is by no means the only village to have been spared development, or to have a street lined with timber-framed houses, once the dwellings and shops of busy tradesmen. What makes it so special is that it lies right across a miniature valley, and suffers no through traffic. From the church at one end the street plunges down to a stream, where cars slow to walking pace to cross the ford while pedestrians use the footbridge. From here it climbs steeply up to the far side of the valley towards the ruins of an Augustinian priory. Thus the old houses of Kersey can be seen from various vertical, as well as horizontal, angles. Several exquisite features add further charm to the scene, such as the stallion's tail hanging from an eave (the old sign of a vet), or the Elizabethan brick porch of River House, or the wonderful wooden roof of the south porch of the church (St Mary's), with its sixteen panels of heavily moulded timbers. It is not hard to imagine the cloth trade in full swing at Kersey – for it was, after all, a cottage industry – or the busy Monday market. Until recently, it was supposed that Kersey and the neighbouring Lindsey had given their names to cloths, but this is now thought improbable.

Cosford, just upstream of Hadleigh on the Brett, is the site of the Anglo-Saxon meeting-place from which the Hundred of Cosford takes its name, and which we entered after leaving that of Samford. These hundreds were formed in the tenth century or earlier and represented, in theory, a hundred family holdings. For centuries they were the basis of all local administration, presided over by the king's bailiff or by the steward of the lord. Each was named after its meeting-place, some of which must have pre-dated even the formation of the hundred. Here we may imagine the Anglo-Saxon tribesmen meeting for communal justice in a primitive form of decision-making which antedated the establishment of feudal authority or legal practices. In Old English this was called a 'moot', in Danish a 'thing'.

Further up, the next riparian village is Chelsworth, where the dispersed houses, most of them thatched, face the water-meadows. One of the great attractions of the Suffolk country-side is the multitude of thatched cottages, most of them conserved as such by legislation. Their owners pay higher fire insurance premiums, but lower electricity bills, thanks to the excellent insulation; and once the thatch is in good order, the cost of maintaining it is probably no more than for a tiled and guttered roof. At least, that is the view of John Stiff, who, with his son Russell (of the seventh generation of Stiff thatchers), I found working on a Chelsworth cottage, re-surfacing the age-old reed. Above Chelsworth, and below Lavenham (described in the next chapter), the Brett flows past Brent Eleigh and

Monks Eleigh, where we come into the large hundred of Babergh, whose name implies that the original meeting-place was on a mound. At Monks Eleigh the little village green is still furnished with a water-pump and is dominated by the large tower of St Peter's church. At Brent Eleigh, so called because it got badly burnt, or 'brent', early in the thirteenth century, there is a delightful hall and a church, St Mary's, which contains a dramatic Baroque monument to Edward Colman, owner of the hall but sadly the last of his line, whose erudite father had adorned the church and provided it with a well-stocked library.

Up another stream we find Bildeston, a former market town with a fine group of timber-framed houses with oversailing upper stories. As with so many other Suffolk villages, the complex doesn't look much changed from a hundred and fifty years ago, but is utterly transformed in sociological terms. Whereas the old village then comprised a self-centred community of largely agricultural labourers and domestic servants run by tenant farmers and small shopkeepers, it is now occupied mainly by professional or retired people disconnected from any purely local economic structure. Whereas the cottages were crammed with people (whole families sometimes sharing one room), each house now normally contains at most a nuclear family group. And whereas in those days each man's status was proclaimed by his clothes, it is now impossible to tell – especially at weekends – which is the retired meritocrat or which the old farm hand.

Hitcham (hedge-home) and Whatfield (wheat-field) have had remarkable rectors. John Henslow was Professor of Botany at Cambridge. He became Rector of the fat living of Hitcham (immediately north of Bildeston) in 1837, and from then, until his death twenty-four years later, was able to get the best of both worlds by residing in his fine rectory whilst still retaining his professorship. He was altogether a most beneficent figure in Hitcham and the surrounding area. He encouraged the teaching of botany, as well as the use of a phosphate manure, derived from Suffolk Crag, in farming. He also organised parochial events such as cricket matches. Mr

Lane, Rector of Whatfield (adjacent to Hadleigh) early this century, was an enthusiast on a less exalted level. It was certainly admirable that during the First World War he should have housed Belgian children in his rectory, and have had these young Catholics, together with the Lutheran German prisoners of war who worked in the fields, bellowing out Anglican hymns and canticles at his services. But the domestic arrangements got out of hand, what with a communal bath installed in the front hall, and the attic given over to an aviary where he bred canaries; and fate struck when the house was gutted by fire, thought to have been caused by one of his cigarettes.

The next Suffolk tributary of the Stour is the Box, which rises in the parish of Little Waldingfield, just south of Brent Eleigh, and enters the father river only a mile upstream of the Brett. Boxford, the principal village on the Box, means a ford where box grew, and the stream merely got its name from the village. Like Hadleigh, Boxford prospered on the cloth trade; and like Hadleigh it lies in a small valley and has preserved its character, with many timber-framed buildings, some facing the church and some in the upward-curving Swan Street. The church, St Mary's, is flanked by two contrasting porches. On the north side is the oldest timber porch in the county, and it comes as a delightful surprise to see the moulded ribs and traceried windows of the early-fourteenth century Decorated style worked in wood, albeit decayed, rather than stone. On the south side is a grand fifteenth-century Perpendicular porch in gleaming white limestone. Inside the church is a memorial to a woman who died in 1745 in her 113th year, having been four times a widow; one wonders how old she was at her fourth marriage.

Adjoining Boxford are the parishes of Edwardstone and Groton. John Winthrop, whose father was Lord of the Manor of Groton, was born at Edwardstone Hall in 1587. He followed his father into legal practice in London, and seemed set to enjoy a comfortable life, having property both in Suffolk and in Essex. But he decided to abandon his career and emigrate to North America. He had been greatly influenced by

Puritan teaching after surviving a severe illness when a boy, and his wife, Margaret Tyndal, strongly upheld his moral principles. In 1629 the newly incorporated Company of the Massachusetts Bay broke with precedent and resolved to transfer its legal entity to America, thus creating a *de facto* colony. John Winthrop was chosen as its first Governor, and next year set sail in the *Arbella* at the head of a convoy of fifteen ships carrying nearly a thousand emigrants, together with their livestock. He was a brilliant and resourceful Governor, and was re-elected to the post several times until his death in 1649. He exercised a conservative policy in the face of pressures from those who wanted a more narrow and theocratic rule; for he was himself no Old Testament prophet, but a refined, sensitive and affectionate man, the founder of one of the leading families of New England. The first three new counties to be formed in the State were Norfolk, Suffolk and Essex.

Suffolk's contribution to the Puritan colonisation of New England was certainly significant. The *Mayflower* was registered in Harwich, on the Essex bank of the Stour, and is assumed to have been built there. It had been in use for years in the wine trade, based at King's Lynn. When it sailed from Plymouth on its historic voyage in 1620, more than half the 102 pilgrims came from East Anglia. During the 1630s, many more emigrated to North America, often going first to Holland and assembling there. Besides John Winthrop, Suffolk's other notable colonists included Bartholomew Gosnold of Grundisburgh, who helped to found Virginia; and Moses Cleveland, a carpenter from Ipswich, whose descendants included Grover Cleveland, 22nd (and 24th) President of the United States. Thomas Payne, a prosperous weaver from Wrentham, fitted out one of the pilgrims' ships, the *Mary Anne*.

This early seventeenth-century emigration abroad is important because of the impetus it gave to the formation of the North American colonies. But there was no overwhelming flight (such as occurred in France when the Protestants fled after the Revocation of the Edict of Nantes in 1685), and the main drift of enterprising people at the time was no further than London. As the economy of Suffolk relapsed, London always attracted the talented, the educated and the ambitious. Indeed, it continued to do so until recent times, when the flow has in some respects actually been reversed. A far larger overseas emigration took place in the late nineteenth and early twentieth centuries, at the time of the agricultural depression. During this period, millions emigrated from England (in 1912 alone, half a million), mostly to Canada, and preponderantly from amongst unskilled labourers in rural areas where unemployment was highest. In common with the earlier Puritan asylum seekers, these economic migrants were keen to get away from what had become an impossible situation. Great efforts were made to try to scrape together the money for the passage and to make for the brave new world, and they often left their villages without regret.

The restricted little valley where the Box flows down between Polstead and Stoke-by-Nayland epitomises the prettiness of this corner of Suffolk, where everything is small-scale. Polstead, traditionally known for its black cherries, means a place of pools, and a pool remains its central feature. On one side the street ascends to the green past thatched cottages, and on the other are the church and the hall set among park trees. A venerable oak which fell in 1953 was called the Gospel Oak because it was devoutly believed that St Cedd preached under it in the seventh century. The church (St Mary's) possesses the only medieval stone spire in Suffolk, and the Norman nave has brick arches in aisles and clerestory. This is quite exceptional, since the use of brick was generally unknown to Norman masons, and these are certainly not Roman bricks re-used. In fact it is thought that they are the earliest surviving English bricks anywhere, providing proof of English participation in the early revival of brickwork in Northern Europe. They appear all the more remarkable now that they are exposed and not, as originally, whitewashed.

A century later the use of bricks had advanced to the extent that whole houses could be made of them, and Little Wenham Hall, some six miles east of Polstead, is Suffolk's notable example. Built with white bricks during the late thirteenth century, it is less defensive than the usual baronial keeps of the day, having large outward windows. Above the brick-vaulted basement are the hall and the chapel, itself vaulted and with a solar above it. I like the names of the original owners, Sir John de Vallibus and his successor, Petronilla of Nerford, and feel that they would still feel very much at home there, because Little Wenham Hall is hidden among secluded farm buildings, and approachable only by long earth tracks, seemingly deep in a medieval time warp.

Polstead is still renowned among older people for the Murder in the Red Barn. No other murder in England has had such a run. At a time when Gothic horror novels captured the imagination, a real murder with Gothic implications was just what the clever scribblers in London were waiting for. They told the story with various degrees of accuracy, and it then took off with a stage version which was always a sure box office winner.

The victim, Maria Marten, was a girl of easy morals who had already given birth to two babies, one by the local squire's son. The father of her third was William Corder, son of a Polstead farmer. Their baby died within a few weeks of birth, and was buried secretly by them. Corder had always asserted a readiness to marry Maria, but was increasingly desperate to be rid of her. He pretended that he would marry her in Ipswich, away from scandal at Polstead. He told her to meet him at the Red Barn and change into boy's clothes for the elopement. She was never seen again, but letters from him to her family suggested that they were living happily on the Isle of Wight. That might have been the end of the matter had not Maria's step-mother led searchers to the Red Barn, alleging that she had dreamt that Maria's body was there, as indeed it was. Corder was discovered living at Brentwood with a wife who he had acquired by matrimonial advertisement (and the many eager responses to his advertisement provided splendid light relief to the horror-story). The sensational trial at Bury St Edmunds was followed by his public hanging in 1848, witnessed by 10,000 spectators. He was such an obvious villain that no one questioned the findings of the very cursory inquest, nor the precise role of the step-mother in the affair.

The mighty tower of St Mary, Stoke-by-Nayland, standing on a ridge above the Box and Stour, is perhaps the most prominent of all Suffolk's great Perpendicular towers, visible all the way down to the estuary. From whatever direction of approach, it is revealed in successive and ever closer sightings, of which the most impressive is on foot from the west. Here it is initially seen in its entirety, then it slowly sets behind the clean-cut grass margin of the hill, and finally it makes its reappearance, starting with the topmost pinnacles, in the manner of a tall sailing ship out at sea. The visual effect of any great work of architecture is always enhanced if it is in sympathy with its immediate surroundings, and this famous tower is as exceptionally favoured close at hand as it is from far off. Just in front of it are two sixteenth-century timber-framed buildings, the Guildhall and the Maltings, with nothing to spoil the illusion of the past; and the whole of the church, with its southward-facing terrace, is surrounded by plastered cottages and houses grouped together at the corners of lanes which radiate down the hill.

Stoke's tower is ornately decorated. Its western door and windows are deeply recessed and of grand proportions, and its polygonal buttresses, with canopied niches, lead the eye up to the elaborate stone battlements and pinnacles. But it is also remarkable for the texture of its materials. Its lower stages are mainly flint, but this yields progressively to brick, a lovely, gentle, peach-coloured brick, which blends most harmoniously with the stone dressings. John Constable swept a rainbow above it on his canvas, but no such artificial aid is really needed to marvel at the colouration of Stoke-by-Nayland's tower. Although it lacks the brilliance of the flushwork displayed on the finest of Suffolk's Perpendicular towers, it has a majesty all of its own, standing on its hill like a hoary monarch.

The tower also manages to dominate the interior of the church, due to the great arch which is carved out of it. Looking along the length of the nave from the chancel, this slender and lofty arch is seen to best effect when the sun shines through the open south door, lighting up the octagonal stone font, standing on its raised base like a chalice on a table. Beyond this grail-like object is the dark interior of the tower, with the coloured glass of the west window shining from within it. The south door itself is another marvel of this church. It is unvarnished and its panels are carved with all sorts of figures, such as birds and insects, and with tracery representing the genealogical Tree of Jesse.

The great house at Stoke-by-Nayland, Tendring Hall, has been demolished, and is commemorated only by a formal lake and elegant fishing lodge at the bottom of the hill, designed by Humphrey Repton. In the church is a brass monument to Sir William Tendring, who fought at Agincourt, depicted with the face of an old man but – in the fashion of the day – with the shapely body of a youth. His beautiful daughter and heiress, Alicia, married John Howard, founder of the Howard dynasty, in 1398; the church is decorated, within and without, with the arms of these two families.

We get a fascinating glimpse of the domestic economy of the original Tendring Hall in the times of the Howards from *The Household Book of the Duke of Norfolk*. John Howard, 1st Duke of Norfolk, lived at Tendring for several years before his death in 1485. The entries show that he paid wages to sixty-five men servants, and entertained in style, bringing in minstrels and actors; the private chapel was provided with an organ and a choir of three men and six boys, under the care of a priest. The price of food is carefully recorded: for instance, 23 herrings cost 4d, 100 eggs 11d; and pound weights of sugar 6d, pepper 1s 1d, mace 3s, and cloves 2s 6d. Of infinitely greater expense were the presents John Howard gave his patron, Richard III, such as a gold cup and cover; and, as Richard's Constable of the Tower of London at the time of the murder of the Princes, it does look rather suspicious that an entry for new beds for the Tower should be immediately followed by one for two sacks of lime.

The 3rd Duke also resided at Tendring for eleven years before his accession in 1524. He was often away, but when at Tendring his household consumed enormous quantities of meat at breakfast, dinner (at 10 a.m.) and supper (at 5 p.m.). But Fridays were fish only, and church fasts were observed. Meals were served in the great hall, except that when the family was away they were taken to 'Lord Henry's room', Lord Henry being the young son of the house, the ill-fated and poetic Earl of Surrey. I like to think that the doric charms of Tendring and its surroundings were inspirational to his poetry.

Nayland (an island) and Bures (a bower) are two former market towns upstream on the Stour. Both have stately churches, and Nayland abounds in timber-framed houses, most notably Alston Court, one of the most magnificent of the town houses of the cloth merchants, with oriel windows lighting the first-floor parlour where the original owner assumedly fixed hard bargains with his customers. Smallbridge Hall at Bures was the seat of the Waldegrave family, who were linked to several of the leading Suffolk families, and who twice entertained Elizabeth I here. Hidden in the delightful stretch of countryside that separates Nayland and Bures are two little gems.

The first is St Mary's, the church of a former parish variously called Wiston or Wissington. Though very much restored in Victorian times, this church gives the best impression in the county of what a Norman church was like, with arches dividing the nave, chancel and apse, a tympanum over the doorway, and a wonderful display of wall-paintings in the nave. These transport us to a time when illiterate villagers stood and gazed on them and beheld the stern lessons of morality, while in the candle-lit chancel the priest chanted in Latin and the deacon swung the censer. Among the scenes depicted in this gallery of thirteenth-century art is St Francis preaching to the birds, one of the earliest representations of that saint in England.

The second is the thatched Chapel of St Stephen outside Bures, consecrated by Stephen Langton, Archbishop of Canterbury, in 1218, on the supposition that St Edmund had been crowned at Bures. Looming large within the small chapel are three tombs of the Earls of Oxford. Ever since William the

Conqueror granted to the first de Vere extensive estates in East Anglia, this family was of great importance in Suffolk. Their ancestral seat was Castle Hedingham just south of the Stour in Essex, and their burial-place was the nearby priory at Earls Colne. After the Reformation the empty tombs remained in the ruins of the priory, from which they were brought to this lonely chapel in the 1930s, providing an important addition to Suffolk's medieval sculpture. The most remarkable thing about the de Veres is that they continued in the male line through twenty holders of the title over a span of six centuries, holding the post of hereditary Great Chamberlain. The 7th Earl was a paladin of Edward III and fought at Crécy with a following of twenty-seven knights. The one who is best remembered nowadays is the 17th Earl, Edward de Vere, a colourful figure at the court of Queen Elizabeth, believed by his devotees to have been the author of Shakespeare's plays. Here at St Stephen's Chapel are the effigies of the 5th, 8th and 11th Earls, lying on tomb chests. The 11th Earl shares his alabaster tomb with his wife; she is wearing a horn head-dress, and pet dogs play at her feet.

The Stour was made navigable up to Sudbury in the early eighteenth century, and the canal remained in use until the First World War. It was twenty-four miles in length and flowed through fifteen locks and under sixteen bridges. The locks were nearly all placed beside a mill, and strict rules pertained so as to minimise the loss of water. It was possible for barges to make the journey in a long day, but most did it in two days. They were towed by horses along the haling path, usually two horses upstream and one downstream, moving at around three miles to the hour. But the path changed banks no less than thirty-three times either at locks or bridges. This cumbersome procedure was speeded up by teaching the horses to jump on and off the barges, and also to jump stiles which obstructed the haling path, as we can see in Constable's *Leaping Horse*. When the railway came to Sudbury in 1849, the canal began to decline, relying increasingly on the carriage of coal.

The old mill-houses that still stand beside the Suffolk rivers, particularly the Stour and Waveney, provide a very special adornment to the landscape, particularly as they are usually situated in the most lush and lovely parts of the riverine scenery. Their white weatherboarded granaries, brick wheel-houses and rusting machinery remind us how essentially self-sufficient the rural economy was till the advent of rapid transport, at the time when horse-drawn wagons, painted in traditional blue and heavily laden with grain, converged on them from the surrounding villages after harvest. Domesday Book records 178 water-mills (there were as yet no wind-mills) in Suffolk. The millers were a hard-nosed lot, taking full advantage of their local monopoly in acquiring the grain at the lowest prices, and in manipulating the flow of the river to their advantage. But there was always something essentially romantic in the thought of all the flowing water and the greenery, whether expressed in Constable's canvasses or in Schubert's song cycle; and it is no wonder that the surviving mill-houses are so treasured and cherished as dwellings.

Sudbury is, and always has been, the chief town on the Stour. Historically, this had much to do with its geographical position, especially its secure situation on a piece of high ground at the centre of a semi-circular loop of the river: it was the 'south fort' of the East Angles. Its population has recently been doubled, but this expansion has been to the north, and the old core of Sudbury still looks across to a largely rural scene around the river, where the water-meadows have resumed their pastoral appearance now that the old railway line has become a walkway and the river itself de-commercialised.

Sudbury was a very early centre of Christianity and St Gregory's church may even have been founded by St Felix. From the twelfth century it became the seat of an Archdeanery which provided the ecclesiastical administration for the whole of West Suffolk. Sudbury had a market from the late ninth century and its own government from medieval times. From 1558 it returned two Members of Parliament and continued to do so even after the Reform Act of 1832. But in 1844 it was disenfranchised because of spectacularly corrupt practices, and we get a flavour of the political life of the town from the pages of Dickens, who had been sent as a journalist to cover the General Election of 1835 at Sudbury, and provided an imaginative account of it in *Pickwick Papers*. Straight bribery secured the votes for the Honourable Samuel Slumkey, but there was plenty to be done by the dirty tricks brigade. The Buffs locked thirty-three drunken electors into the White Hart to prevent the Blues getting at them, and the Blues got the band to play when Horatio Fizkin gave his address; and there were dark tales of lacing the brandy with laudanum to put the electors well and truly to sleep, and staging a coach accident to prevent them arriving.

One group of Sudbury residents who were definitely not involved in these political gerrymanderings, were the poor people unfortunate enough to be confined in the House of Industry. This was one of twenty such Houses set up in Suffolk following the Poor Law of 1834 to replace the inefficient parochial Workhouses. The Workhouses were bad enough, with insufficient food, clothing or warmth provided for the debilitated inmates. But the Houses of Industry were positively inhuman. For instance, the sexes were divided, so that husbands and wives only saw each other in the chapel on Sundays. One of the first to express revulsion against such cruelty, which was eventually mitigated, was G.W. Fulcher, a one-time mayor of Sudbury. His poem, 'The Village Paupers', describes pathetic moments, as when 'the ruined trader', 'the hopeless deaf', 'the blind mother', and the 'halt and maimed', enter the chapel for Sunday service.

Sudbury is the birthplace of Thomas Gainsborough, whose statue is on Market Hill, palette in hand. His father, John, was a cloth manufacturer who went bankrupt, though not before he had built a fine new Georgian facade onto the old house he had bought. John Gainsborough was also a prominent Dissenter, while his wife was the sister of one of the Anglican establishment, Humphrey Burroughs, Vicar of St Gregory's and Master of the Grammar School.

Thomas married Margaret Burr, the beautiful daughter of one of his father's partners. He began to paint in Sudbury before moving to Ipswich for seven years and then to Bath. He said that there was not a single tree of any beauty around Sudbury which he had not studied closely. Like many other portraitists, Gainsborough employed personal charm to gain his commissions, in addition to his remarkable ability to achieve true and accurate likenesses. But the faces which gaze at us from his canvasses are surrounded by natural scenery which is not dependent on topographical accuracy, but reveals a wistful splendour, a world of dreams, inspired by the quality of light first observed by Gainsborough in the Stour valley. In the words of John Constable: 'The stillness of noon, the depths of twilight, and the dews and pearls of the morning, are all to be found on the canvases of this most benevolent and kind-hearted man. On looking at them, we find tears in our eyes, and know not what brings them'.

Sudbury's other famous man was Simon of Sudbury, one of Suffolk's home-grown Archbishops of Canterbury. He shares with Thomas à Becket the distinction of being murdered when in office, but he can hardly be considered as a religious martyr. At the time of the Peasant's Revolt of 1381, he was in effect the ruler of England, acting as Chancellor as well as Archbishop to the boy-king Richard II. He it was who imposed the infamous poll tax and excommunicated John Ball, the heretical priest and popular preacher. When Wat Tyler and his mob overran London, they seized Simon from the Tower and executed him. He had earlier rebuilt St Gregory's in Sudbury and founded a college there, so it is appropriate that his skull is retained as a precious relic in the church.

As well as these famous men, it is refreshing to record that Sudbury has a reputation for pretty girls. Robert Arbib, a sergeant in the US Army Engineers stationed in Suffolk during the Second World War, was quite amazed at what he saw. There was Peggy in the tea-shop, 'a pert, blue-eyed blonde of eighteen'; Millie, a 'shy, dark-haired, large-eyed girl with a soft low voice'; Thelma, 'tall, winnowy, pale-skinned, chestnut-haired'; Fay, 'red-haired, sparkling with laughter'; Olive, with a 'heart-shaped face and the cascade of black hair'; Daisy, 'snub-nosed, red-haired, pixie-eyed, and saucy'; Joan, 'graceful, slender, blue-eyed'; the tiny Pat, the graceful Kay, the beautiful Molly and Audrey, and Daphne. Trying to solve the enigma of why Sudbury bred such talent, he suggested that perhaps all the ugly girls were taken out into the woods at three years of age and exterminated; but this was indignantly denied by the locals.

IV
Upper Stour

In 1599 William Kemp, a comic actor and a dancer, decided to morris-dance all the way from London to Norwich for a heavy bet. It took him nine days to cover the course. On the morning he left Sudbury towards Melford, a girl in the crowd offered to dance with him, as he records:

> A Country Lasse, browne as a berry,
> Blith of blee, in heart as merry,
> Cheekes well fed, and sides well larded,
> Every bone with fat flesh guarded,
> Meeting merry Kemp by chaunce,
> Was Marrian in his Morrice daunce.
> Her stump legs with bels were garnisht,
> Her browne browes with sweating varnisht;
> Her browne hips, when she was lag
> To win her ground, went swig a swag;
> Which to see all that came after
> Were repleate with mirthful laughter.
> Yet she thumpt it on her way
> With a sportly hey de gay:
> At a mile her daunce she ended,
> Kindly paid and well commended.

In the steps of William Kemp we come into Long Melford, whose street is longer than any in Sudbury and is lined with the houses and warehouses of centuries of cloth-makers, together with the inns and shops and chapels that serviced them, and whose prosperity was revived in the nineteenth century by the railway. The street broadens as we pass the timber-framed Bull Inn and Brooke House and then, by the bridge over the original mill-ford, we come to the green, which widens as it extends uphill to its far end a quarter of a mile away. To our left are the houses and cottages behind their garden walls and hedges.

Ahead is the red-brick Trinity Hospital, almshouses dating from Elizabethan times but largely rebuilt. To our right is the long wall beyond which can be seen the chimney-stacks and pepper-top turrets of Melford Hall. And towards the centre is the brick conduit that once supplied the villagers with water. The green at Long Melford is justly considered one of the grandest in Suffolk. And yet, to me, it is badly spoilt by the road that cuts across the middle, and the traffic that still besets it despite the bypass around the village. I wish I could have seen it before the motor age, its tranquillity disrupted only by the colourful horse fair, when it was covered with a patchwork of wagons and tents and booths, loud with the shouts of dealers and traders.

Melford Hall has its back to the Green and its front to the open country. Although its gatehouse range has been removed, and sash windows inserted, its external appearance is substantially unchanged from when it was built in the 1560s. Its six towers and its stone porch, as also its gateway and octagonal garden house, provide an Italianate flamboyance to what is otherwise an understated and common-sensical structure. With the mellow red-brick of its walls, and the rich greens of the topiary of box and yew in its garden, and the avenues of oak in its park, Melford Hall satisfies our best expectations of what a great Elizabethan house should look like.

It was built for Sir William Cordell, a lawyer who made a fortune under Tudor rule, rising to be Speaker of the House of Commons and Master of the Rolls, and cleverly steering his way through the violent changes in religious practice under four successive sovereigns. There being no rules against insider trading in those days, leading men in the service of the Crown picked up huge windfalls, notably from the Dissolution of the Monasteries; and Cordell acquired an interest in the rich manor of Melford, which had been the property of the Abbot of Bury. In 1578 he entertained Queen Elizabeth at Melford with exceptional splendour, setting a standard which her other hosts in the county found hard to follow. The household at Melford was commendably well run by his niece in Jacobean times, to judge from an account by James Howell, employed as a tutor. He tells us that the family were civil and polite, the children well brought up, the servants orderly and punctual, and the house kept clean and free of dogs. As to the garden, 'Here you have your Bon Christian pears and Bergamot in perfection; your Muscatel grapes in such plenty that there are some bottles of wine sent every year to the king . . .'. But this delightful regime did not continue for long, and the house was sacked during the Civil War because its then owner, Countess Rivers, was a prominent Royalist.

In 1786 Melford Hall was sold to Sir Harry Parker, whose successors still live there as tenants of the National Trust. This family came to fame as naval commanders, and the father, brother, and nephew of Sir Harry were all admirals: they also all bore the given name of Hyde. A splendid portrait of Admiral Sir Hyde Parker by Romney hangs over the staircase. As Admiral of the Red, he it was who ordered Nelson to withdraw rather than move in to engage the Danish fleet at Copenhagen in 1801, but whose signal was memorably ignored. It is interesting to contrast this portrait with the Gainsborough of Admiral Hervey, later 3rd Earl of Bristol, which hangs in the National Trust's other great Suffolk house, Ickworth. Together they emphasise the important links between this county and the Senior Service.

William Cordell had married Mary Clopton, whose cousin was William Clopton of Kentwell Hall, also in the parish of Melford. The two Williams were engaged on the expansion of their houses at about the same time, and it is quite possible that they employed the same surveyors and masons; certainly the octagonal towers look similar. Kentwell Hall was sold several times, and its least responsible owner was Richard Moore, who came into the property in 1782. He seems to have been a compulsive gambler who was bankrupted despite mortgaging the estate and died in a debtors' prison. He actually sold off the famous lime avenue (to the composer Clementi for making piano keys), but fortunately it was saved by his mother at great cost. While he was at the gaming tables in London, his wife was consoling herself with the steward at Kentwell, and Richard got a divorce by Act of Parliament, on the grounds of their 'unlawful familiarity, criminal intercourse and adulterous conversation'. The house suffered badly from a fire in 1826 and its contents were dispersed by successive owners.

The present owner of Kentwell Hall has devoted himself and his family to a brave battle to restore and improve this great house without any Government grants. This is done by raising income by means of all sorts of imaginative attractions. These include Elizabethan events – with a lot of thee- and thou-ing and mead-quaffing and spit-roasting – and the conservation of rare breeds of farm animals such as the Norfolk Horned Sheep, the Tamworth Pig and the British White Cow, and also, of course, the Suffolk Punch.

Kentwell Hall is linked to the village of Long Melford by the lime avenue, three quarters of a mile long and planted in 1678. From it the church can be seen to best effect across the fields. This is appropriate, because Holy Trinity, Long Melford, to many the grandest Perpendicular church in Suffolk, was built largely on the wealth of John Clopton, the great-grandfather of the William who rebuilt the Hall. The eight great windows of the aisle and eighteen windows of the clerestory prepare us for what is within – a veritable glass-house, remarkable both for the proportion of glass to stone, and the rare display of medieval stained glass along the north aisle, commemorating the patrons and connections of the Cloptons. The width of the interior, together with the shafts and panels which decorate the walls, and also the rich sculpture within the exquisite Clopton chantry, are more what one would expect to find in a royal chapel than in a remote village church. But the symmetry of the architecture is curiously flawed by the graph-like gables of the Lady Chapel as seen through the plain-glass east window, and the purity is broken by the Victorian simulation of the original west tower.

A walk up the former railway line from Melford will bring us to Lavenham. Here is the most remarkable group of timber-framed and jettied buildings in Suffolk, twisted by the years into crooked or bulging shapes, and together providing as fine an impression of a late-medieval town as anywhere in England. Time seems to have stood still at Lavenham, even though the precise semblance to early Tudor times is uncertain. For instance, no one can quite tell to what extent the timber-framing was originally covered with plaster, rather than displaying its naked wood. So the old houses do look a little like skeletons, and lack their original cosiness. What is more, many of the uncovered posts and beams still bear traces of lime rendering, which gives them a strange dream-like appearance. Much has been restored, and the Swan Inn is said to have as many Elizabeth II as Elizabeth I beams. Still, the illusion is astonishing as we wander around the streets, picturing the intense activity of the past, with houses crammed with people working the various processes in the manufacture of clothing, and deals being struck by the merchants whose names are commemorated in the streets – the Springs, Shillings, and Boltons, and by the members of the Guild of Corpus Christi in secret session in their guildhall in the triangular Market Place. There is nowhere better in Suffolk to reflect upon the astonishing prosperity of the cloth trade.

Until the mid-fourteenth century the production of woollen cloth in England had been insignificant. The wealth of the country depended on the export of raw wool, which was converted into cloth in towns all over Europe, but principally in Flanders, where the skills of clothmaking were progressively advanced. The higher the quality of the cloth, the more it required the best wool, and English wool was unsurpassed. It came from well-tended flocks of sheep all over the country, and particularly from the great monastic estates which owned many of the most verdant pastures on which the sheep were bred and fed. But this profitable trade in a most important commodity was destined to fade in the face of protectionist measures introduced at a time of political and economic instability, and the continental merchants were obliged to find other sources for their wool, particularly in Spain. In England there was a growing need for home-made cloth, and this was supplied by the enterprising merchants and artisans of East Anglia, especially Suffolk. So successful were they that cloth soon replaced wool as England's greatest export.

The rapid expansion of this manufacture was greatly helped

by Flemish craftsmen with specialist skills, who established their own communities in several Suffolk towns during the fourteenth century, though there is no evidence that they were themselves the entrepreneurs of the new trade. What they brought with them was the knowledge of how to produce woollens rather than the traditional worsteds. One important difference between these two cloths was that the woollens required fulling, a process involving water flow, thus encouraging the construction of fulling mills at places along the banks of adequate rivers. Indeed, the whole sequence of processing wool into cloth lent itself to cottage industry, since there were at least six separate procedures to be worked, and the material could easily be transported from one to the other by pack-horse.

The first stage was that of sorting, washing and scouring the wool, and soaking it in oil. From here it was taken to the carders in their cottages, who mixed the short wool together on spiked boards. From the carders it went to the spinners, who twisted it for cohesion and made it up into packs of yarn. Now it was ready for the weavers, the highly skilled craftsmen who passed the yarn through a heddle, with weft thread across warp thread. The woven cloth was then passed to the fullers, who soaked it in clean water, then beat it, scrubbed it with fuller's earth (aluminium oxide), and bleached it. After being stretched and dried, it was next submitted to the dyers, and finally to the finishers.

Dyeing was delicate and expensive, and often sub-contracted. Great quantities of dye were needed, often twice the weight of the cloth that was to be dyed. The cheaper colours were derived from local vegetables. There were greens and yellows from onions, nettles, cow-parsley and oak-barks; blues and purples from woad and elderberries, damsons and sloes; reds from sorrel and ladies-bedstraw; blacks and greys from alder-barks and yellow iris; magenta from dandelion, and saffron from saffron. But some of the brighter colours, such as vermilion and the scarlet grayn, had to be acquired from abroad. All these dyes were mixed with mordent, a metallic salt, and teased through the cloth.

The names of the cloths thus produced are bewildering because they altered in time and differed in place, just as marketing trade-names are today. The earlier worsteds had been strictly designed for the social classes permitted to wear them: camlets for the nobility and gentry, 'monks' and 'canons' for the ecclesiastics, and fustians and bombagines for the commoners. The principal Suffolk woollens were known by their colours – blues, azures and plunkets – and by their quality, the cheapest being kersies and straits, and the most expensive the broadcloths.

The clothing trade had been dominated by craft guilds. These were trade unions of master craftsmen which secured maintenance of standards and regulation of trade, and also protection from competition. With the increasing demand for cloth, and the immigration of the Flemish weavers, many local craftsmen decided to move away from the towns into the countryside to find more freedom. This trend was brilliantly exploited by wool brokers known as clothiers, who came to dominate the industry, and in time to employ huge forces of labour directly. The sorters, carders and spinners were the first to succumb, and then the weavers gradually lost their status, though the dyers were usually successful in maintaining their independence.

The cloth trade throve on the general prosperity of Suffolk during the fifteenth and sixteenth centuries, a prosperity derived from a rising population, profitable agriculture, fisheries and ship-building. But the actual manufacture of woollens was largely confined to the southern and western part of the county. Ipswich, Bury St Edmunds and Needham Market were the principal clothmaking towns. But what was most remarkable was the diffusion of clothmaking processes in the small towns and large villages of the Stour valley, particularly East Bergholt, Hadleigh, Glemsford and Lavenham. At that time the Stour valley was the scene of what was the most intensive and efficient industrial activity in England.

By the seventeenth century, however, the dominance of Suffolk woollens had yielded to the 'new draperies', produced in Holland and then Yorkshire. Though these fabrics made use of greater quantities of wool, they were lighter and stronger, and so commanded higher prices. The ability of the Suffolk clothiers to compete in these new materials was impeded by the growing influence of the London merchants in the finishing and marketing of their products, and also by the hostility of their workforces to changes in methods. As a result, their best craftsmen tended to migrate away from the region, and only in a few places, such as Sudbury, Long Melford and Lavenham, were the new draperies manufactured profitably. Still less was Suffolk able to participate in the cotton industry and the factory system of Lancashire, having no fast-running water or coal. Thus it came about that our county was mercifully spared the dirty coal mines and grim mill-towns that defaced so much of Northern England. Lavenham and other former cloth towns were reduced to running secondary industries such as horse-hair weaving and coconut matting.

The Wool Hall at Lavenham, next door to the Swan, was the subject of one of the earliest victories in the cause of the conservation of ancient buildings in England. In 1912 it was sold to an American and builders began to take it to bits for re-erection across the Atlantic, as in the old film, 'The Ghost Goes West'. But Henry Taylor and a few others were not prepared to witness this desecration passively. Faced with a conspiracy of silence from the owners and their lawyers and agents, and with utter indifference from the local authorities, he resorted to the desperate device of following the lorry that was taking the frame away, and succeeded in identifying those involved and securing a patron (Princess Louise) who paid for the restoration of the Wool Hall to its original position. This victory paved the way for a new industry for Lavenham – tourism – which has become more profitable than the sugar factory and flour mill which kept the place going during the first part of this century.

The church of St Peter and St Paul at Lavenham is in many ways complementary to Holy Trinity, Long Melford, which, indeed, it was intended to emulate. It is perhaps less of a Perpendicular showpiece because the chancel of the earlier

81

church has been retained, as has the spirelet that contained the sanctus bell, and it is without any of its original glass. But besides its stonework, which is as rich as at Long Melford, it is provided with two princely chapels which clasp the chancel on either side, and it contains some truly magnificent wooden carving in screens and stalls. And then there is its tower, tremendously powerful on its green-field site, even if disproportionately large for the delicate nave attached to it. In fact, if the pinnacles had ever been built, the tower would have been as tall as the church is long, and even as it is, the shape of the church is that of an enormous L – an L for Lavenham. Up in the tower is the tenor bell, over a tonne in weight, cast by the famous bell-founder Miles Gray of Colchester, and one of the finest toned bells in the world.

This church was built as a result of co-operation between the Lord of the Manor at Lavenham, John de Vere, 13th Earl of Oxford, and the leading clothiers of the town, particularly the 2nd Thomas Spring. Their arms appear constantly in the stonework. The south porch was paid for by the Earl, and is decorated with boars (*verres* in Latin, and so a pun on Vere) and stars (the de Vere Star recalled that Albericke de Vere had led a force of Crusaders by starlight on a successful attack on the Saracens). Around the parapet of the tower, the Spring arms are repeated thirty-two times.

There are also Tudor roses, denoting that both donors were strong supporters of the Tudor Henry VII. John de Vere's father had been a leading Lancastrian who, together with his eldest son, was executed on Tower Hill by order of the Yorkist Edward IV in 1462. John de Vere himself had been incarcerated and deprived of his possessions. His wife had to depend on charity and earn money by sewing. But eventually he managed to escape and joined the future Henry VII in exile in France. At the victorious Battle of Bosworth he was Henry's Captain-General. Meanwhile, 'The Rich Clothier', as the 3rd Thomas Spring was known, did extremely well out of the Tudor settlement, and by the time of his death in 1523 had acquired manors or tenements in some one hundred and thirty places in East Anglia. In view of their inspired co-operation at

Lavenham, it is pleasant to record that Thomas Spring's niece married a son of the 15th Earl, and that when Elizabeth I visited Lavenham in 1578, she was entertained by William Spring.

When Julian Tennyson walked up the Stour Valley over the Whitsun Bank Holiday of 1938, he made use of the lanes and encountered practically no one. Today, when even the narrowest lane bears its quota of rushing cars, and the wider lanes have been upgraded into fast roads, his route would no longer be a pleasure to walk. But, fortunately, the footpaths are always there, and I recently walked down the entire Stour Valley – all the way from Great Bradley to Shotley Point – in four days, hardly touching any surfaced roads and hardly seeing anyone other than my purposeful fellow-walkers. One beneficial result of mechanised agriculture is that when the machines are not in operation the countryside is more deserted than it ever would have been in the past. It was July, a specially good month for Suffolk, because all the corn is tall and ripe and waiting for harvest. The emeralds and golds of the fields of wheat and barley were brilliantly offset by the blues of occasional fields of flax and borage. One of the very best sections was between Long Melford and Glemsford, where we made use of some wooden planks to cross the Glem, which comes next on the list of the Stour's humble tributaries.

Up this little stream are Boxted and Denston, both with halls and churches of interest. Holy Trinity, Boxted (box-tree place), overlooks the grounds of the Hall below it in the valley, a sixteenth-century timber-framed house very much restored. It is still occupied by a member of the family of Poley (pronounced 'Pooley'). This is just as well, because the church is crammed with Poley monuments. There is even a line of descent, showing their succession through five hundred years with only one name missing. In the aisle is the screened Poley pew. In the chancel, the floor is crammed with Poley floor-slabs and the walls with Poley hatchments, and beside the altar lie a Poley and his wife, sculpted in oak. Around the corner, in the Poley chapel, we come face to face with Sir John Poley and his wife Dame Abigail standing in niches, sculpted in alabaster. Sir John stands in armour with one hand on his hip and the other lifting his robe to show his shapely leg. With his mustachio and neat chin-beard, he looks very much the swashbuckler who had fought for Queen Elizabeth and King Christian of Denmark. From his ear-ring there hangs a frog, which has led people to suppose that he is the inspiration for the nursery rhyme 'A frog he would a-wooing go', because the refrain of the song goes on 'With a rowley, powley, gammon and spinach . . .'. This has been interpreted as alluding to four landed families in these parts: the Rowleys, Poleys, Bacons and Greenes. But this is fallacious, because the song can be traced back to before Sir John's time, whilst the refrain is not heard of until the nineteenth century. More probably, a 'rowley powley' means a plump chicken (poulet), suitable for garnishing with gammon and spinach.

Denston Hall is an early eighteenth-century mansion and behind it is a long Tudor range, part of the original moated house, which also had a tall gatehouse. During the fifteenth century the manor of Denston was owned by a family of the same name. When John Denston died in 1474 he made provision for a college of chantry priests to be incorporated with the church. Ostensibly this was for the chanting of daily masses for his soul, but really its purpose was not altogether self-interested. The parish of Denston had been impropriated by the abbey of Bury, which failed to provide a parish priest in permanent residence. Hence the chantry priests could minister generally to the parish; and, what is more, the bequest involved the rebuilding of the entire church.

Though a much smaller church, St Nicholas, Denston, bears a similarity to Holy Trinity, Long Melford, and was probably built by the same masons, the Denstons having intermarried with the Cloptons. Like Melford, it runs from west to east without a break, displaying well-developed windows in aisles and clerestory. The roofs, and the chancel stalls and nave benches, with their wonderful animal carvings, are all original; and the only subsequent accretions are the holy table and rails, the pulpit, and the box-pews in the aisles, all of the seventeenth century. Besides this woodwork, the church has an octagonal font carved with panels of the Seven Sacraments and the Crucifixion, all with rayed backgrounds. No wonder Denston is famed as one of the finest small churches in Suffolk, looking all the more appealing since its sensitive restoration of 1988.

Denston is a good place to consider the astonishing variety of woodwork in Suffolk's late-medieval churches. The roof was either of a simple single frame, made by local carpenters; or else it was double-framed, in which case it was probably the work of carpenters who were specially brought in. The most elaborate of these double-frames were the hammer-beam roofs, whereby the roof was supported by posts which rested on hammer-beams protruding from the walls. Some churches were provided with font-covers, suspended from the roof, and often magnificently carved in simulation of a Gothic spire.

After the roof, the woodworkers' art was next displayed in the benches. These were made with shouldered ends terminating in 'poppyheads', or fleur-de-lys. These poppyheads are characteristic of East Anglia, since benches in the rest of England usually had square topped bench ends. About a third of the existing poppyheaded benches also have carved figures on the arm rests. These are mostly found in central and north-western Suffolk, where good supplies of timber enabled the carpenters to be extravagant. Of these figures, those in central Suffolk tend to represent the Seven Sacraments, or the Seven Deadly Sins, or else the Symbols of the Passion. But in the north-west, less highly populated and so perhaps less closely scrutinised by the archdeacon and other enforcers of orthodoxy, we find a greater interest in the fascinating bestiaries, such as the unicorn, or the pig with human feet, or the mermaid.

But the most arresting piece of carpentry was the rood and screen which divided the nave from the chancel. Rood is the Old English word for the Cross, and the rood comprised large carved figures, sometimes lifesize, of Christ on the Cross, with the Virgin Mary and St John on either side. It was placed on top of the screen, facing the nave. All the medieval roods of Suffolk were destroyed during the Reformation, but several of the screens remain. Here at Denston the dado (or lower part) of the screen is in place, and also, curiously, the rood beam up above, which may have been spared because it was supposed that it held the church together.

The Glem stream rises in the large parish of Wickhambrook (manor-brook), where a very scattered village is grouped around several former greens, and a profusion of old timber-framed halls. Giffords Hall is contemporaneous with its more substantial namesake near Hadleigh, both being built for the Giffords in the late fifteenth century. It is surrounded by its moat, and had deteriorated into an ill-kept farmhouse before being sensitively restored: the timber mouldings of the great bedchamber are particularly fine. Clopton Hall dates from the early sixteenth century, but made use of the timbers of a previous hall, whose moulded joists support the roof of the internal hall. Badmondisfield Hall is also moated and its restored great hall succeeds in recapturing much of its late-medieval atmosphere.

Pursuing the Stour further upstream, we next come to Cavendish, whose green is spoilt only by the busy road. The tower of the church (St Mary's) dates from the early fourteenth century, and is evidently designed to be lived in, since there is a fireplace on the first floor. When the peasants revolted in 1381, Sir John Cavendish secured his valuables in the tower, but to no avail, for he was caught and executed at Lakenheath, and his goods at Cavendish were seized. But in later centuries the Cavendish family prospered enormously, obtaining untold wealth and the dukedom of Devonshire.

It is a special pleasure to turn from the historical personalities associated with Suffolk to a living person who is incontestably a heroine of her own time – Sue Ryder. Her childhood was largely spent at Thurlow, where her father owned an estate, and where she was educated until the age of nine by her mother. This education included regular visits to the poor people who lived in the Elizabethan almshouses and the workhouse. In 1940 Sue, then aged seventeen, joined up for war service. After training in the First Aid Nursing Yeomanry, she was selected for highly secret work with the

Special Operations Executive, servicing the agents who were dropped into Nazi-occupied Europe ('the bods'). Here she came face to face with the reality of tyranny and persecution, particularly in Poland, and when the war ended she continued to help the Poles, especially those held in German prisons ('the boys'). In 1951 she decided to establish a charity to provide help for unfortunates of all sorts and in all countries. Her widowed mother had moved to a house in Cavendish, and this now became the headquarters of the Sue Ryder Foundation, which at first had very little money, and whose main resource was the galvanising personality of its founder. She inspired voluntary helpers to collect money and equipment and clothing. Armed with these, she would set out into the desolate and ravaged rural areas of eastern Europe in a two-ton Austin truck called Joshua. Meanwhile the house in Cavendish expanded to become a home with cosy rooms for thirty physically disabled or psychologically disturbed people, also affectionately referred to as 'bods'.

Like a heroine of romance, Sue also met a hero. Leonard Cheshire had been a bomber pilot and the youngest Group Captain in the Royal Air Force, and was awarded the Victoria Cross and, thrice, the Distinguished Service Order for exceptional bravery. In 1945 he was selected to observe the dropping of the atomic bomb on Nagasaki, and he emerged from the war determined to help in the relief of suffering. The result was the Cheshire Homes for the terminally ill, disabled and deprived. The union of two such dedicated people, bringing into practice the highest tenets of Christianity, has been an inspiration to many. As someone wrote in a letter to Sue Ryder, 'Your summons is a summons to seek and face the facts, to deny ourselves, to dedicate ourselves, to be there with those who are suffering. It is a challenge to all the young who find life insipid'.

Upstream of Cavendish (passing from the ancient hundred of Babergh into that of Risbridge) is Clare, whose pretty feminine name (it probably derives from the Latin *clarus* – clear) was adopted by the Norman to whom it was granted by William the Conqueror. From when Richard de Clare, as

Justiciar of the Realm, quashed a revolt in 1075 during William's absence abroad, to when his descendant Gilbert, Earl of Clare, as Regent of England (though only twenty-three years old), died at Bannockburn in 1314, rushing on the Scots 'like a wild boar, making his sword drunk with their blood', the de Clares were mighty feudal barons. Their territories were mainly in Wales and the Marches, where they picked up the Earldoms of Pembroke and Gloucester; and Richard 'Strongbow', Earl of Pembroke, also obtained lands in Ireland, and gave his name to County Clare. They intermarried with most of the leading families, helped by good looks: the sister of the first and second Earls was considered the most beautiful woman in England, a sensation at the court of Henry II. Joan, mother of the Bannockburn boar, was the daughter of Edward I. But Gilbert was the last of the male heirs of his house, and on his death the great estates were divided between his three sisters.

Elizabeth, the youngest of these, obtained the Honour of Clare, the feudal liberty which surrounded the castle and included estates in Essex. Three times widowed, she came to live at Clare. As a first cousin to Edward III she was a woman of influence, and this she put to good use by founding Clare College at Cambridge. When subsequently her granddaughter married Lionel, Edward III's son, the king created him Duke of Clarence as holder of the Honour of Clare.

Clarence is a wonderfully romantic title, but seems to have brought bad luck to its possessors. Since none of them produced heirs, it has always bounced back to the Crown as a dukedom in abeyance: indeed, it is still available – for Prince Edward, for instance. Lionel, after attempting to rule Ireland, negotiated a second marriage, to the daughter of Galeazzo Visconti, and died in Lombardy, aged thirty, soon after the wedding. Thomas, the next Duke of Clarence, was the second son of Henry IV: he supported his warlike brother in his campaigns in France, and was killed in action in 1421, aged thirty-three. George, the younger brother of Edward IV, was created Duke of Clarence at the age of twelve, and Lord Lieutenant of Ireland in the following year. He married the daughter of the all-powerful Earl of Warwick, and feebly followed his father-in-law when he turned against Edward and re-instated Henry VI as king. After Warwick's death George was reconciled to Edward, but not to their youngest brother Richard, Duke of Gloucester; and open quarrel broke out when Richard married Warwick's other daughter. 'False, fleeting, purjured Clarence' was done for, by tradition (and Shakespeare) drowned in a butt of malmsey wine, aged twenty-nine. The most recent Duke of Clarence was Albert Victor, heir to the throne as eldest son of Edward VII when Prince of Wales, a terribly retarded young man who died at twenty-eight. The only successful holder of the title was the third son of George III, who came to the throne as William IV. Meanwhile, for five centuries the title has been continually recognised in the person of Clarenceux, King of Arms.

The strength of the Norman castle at Clare is evident from the size of its mound and the stone fragments of the keep, approached by a maze-like path between the bushes. The outer defences have disappeared, though their line can be detected in the hemisphere of houses below. A railway station was built on the site of the castle bailey, but, with the closure of the railway, it has now been converted into a park. Just across the Stour, though in a tiny Suffolk enclave, is the site of Clare Priory, set in a grove of trees. This was founded in 1248 by Austin Friars brought over from France. It was the first Augustinian foundation in England, and the mother-house of many others. After the Dissolution, the former Prior's Lodging was preserved within the framework of a seventeenth-century house. Now, after over four centuries of secular use, Clare Priory is once again occupied by an Augustinian cell, a dignified conclusion to a long story.

The destruction of the castle and the priory must have been witnessed by many citizens of Clare with delight, as the symbols of outdated authority. But the present inhabitants of this former market town, now a large village, are deeply concerned about the conservation of their shops and houses, and of their spacious church (of St Peter and St Paul) which stands athwart the High Street. Nestling beside it is the former priest's house, built in 1473 and later decorated with exceptionally fine seventeenth-century plaster-work, known as pargetting. Pargetting is a peculiarly English decorative form, found especially in Essex and Suffolk on timber-framed buildings of the late-sixteenth and seventeenth centuries. Fanciful designs were worked in relief on to the external plaster cladding, developing into a specialised craft. The plaster was comprised of slaked lime, sand, cow hair, cow dung and scrapings which, after it had been washed, beaten, stirred and tested, was as tough as old leather.

At Stoke-by-Clare, two miles further up the Stour, the remains of a Benedictine priory, which became a college of secular priests in 1415, are to be found within the early eighteenth-century house called Stoke College, altered in 1897 by Lutyens. The personalities associated with it are not very edifying. John Elwes, its eighteenth-century owner, a long-standing Member of Parliament, was notorious as a miser. It was said that he refused to have his boots cleaned for fear of wearing them out, and that he would not reglaze his windows, but covered them with brown paper. As a result, he left half a million pounds. But such avarice seems less sinful than the disreputable conduct of Thomas Whitehead, who was the last prebendary of the priests' college before it was dissolved in 1548. He is said to have engaged in fraud and fornication, and was also accused of the manslaughter of a passing beggar, thus providing excellent ammunition for those who pressed for the suppression of such colleges.

Just upstream from Stoke-by-Clare is the hamlet of Wixoe, where the Stour takes a decisive right-angle bend. Wixoe means 'a spur of land', and this geographical feature is probably why it was the site of a major Romano-British settlement. Here, in the early stages of my walk down the valley, was where I first observed the way in which rivers such as the Stour are controlled by means of pumping stations and sluices. Beside a static channel bordered by water-lilies, a coarse-fisher told us that the Stour was only an afternoon river. But though it rather depressed us to think that this made it more like a canal, it is true to say that ever since the introduction of the water-mills, Suffolk's rivers have never flowed freely.

At the extreme south-west corner of Suffolk, and the nearest point to London, is Haverhill (oat-hill). It became industrialised in Victorian times, with two railway lines through it, and was noted for its production of horse-hair goods. It was greatly expanded during the 1960s, and Kedington, next door, has become one of its satellite villages. Kedington Hall was for centuries the seat of the Barnardiston family, though nothing now remains of it save a long lime avenue. It stood north of the village on a buff above the Stour, close by the church of St Peter and St Paul.

This church, whose setting is further enhanced by the huge elm trunks that have been preserved in its churchyard stands on a very ancient site. It contains the monuments of the family of Barnardiston (a cumbersome name, this, variously abbreviated in the past to Banson and suchlike), and no other church in Suffolk has such a collection. Several armoured Sir Thomases, soundly sleeping with their wives beside them, await in effigy the Day of Judgement. Sir Nathaniel and his lady, however, look a trifle impatient as they gaze out from their niche, their heads resting on their arms as if watching a boring play. As he was the most influential Barnardiston, and a leading Puritan at the time of the Civil War, his Catholic and Royalist enemies may have hoped he would have to wait a very long time, and might even go to the wrong place at the end, despite his pious life and thrice-daily prayer sessions. Other wall monuments commemorate his son Samuel, reputedly the original Roundhead (at any rate, his short haircut was noticed at Court), and his aunt Grissel, who was 'too wise, too choice, too old in youthful breath, Too deare to Frendes, too much of men desir'd, Therefore bereaft us with untymely death'. Ten heraldic Barnardiston hatchments line the walls, the family tree is displayed in a pew, and in the vault below are fifty-four Barnardiston coffins.

What makes Kedington church the jewel of this corner of Suffolk is that it never underwent a Victorian restoration. It seemed itself to go to sleep with the Barnardistons, and no succeeding Lord of the Manor came forward with the money to do it up. So it contains a full complement of mainly sixteenth-century furnishings, particularly the seating arrangements in which the population listened to the interminable sermons from the two-decker pulpit. The Barnardistons sat in their manorial pew, which has its own wooden ceiling and medieval screens for its frontage. In each aisle are the box pews of the families who maintained them. In the nave are the earlier benches for the ordinary people. At the west end of the aisles are tiered benches for the children, one for boys and one for girls; and between them the minstrels' gallery. Forward in the chancel are the communicants' pews. The general irregularity of all this furniture, and of the uneven flooring, reinforces the charm of this interior. But at the same time we can well understand the impulses that drove the Victorian reformers to sweep away such fossilisation of Erastian Protestantism, with its rigid class segregation and its plain preaching of the Word.

The stream of the Stour enters Suffolk from Cambridgeshire just above the Great and Little Thurlows and Bradleys (respectively, assembly-hill and broad-glade). Great Thurlow is the birthplace of Elizabeth Frink, the sculptress, whose most vivid childhood memory was of a damaged bomber crashing in flames at Stradishall airfield during the war. At Little Bradley there is a very early church, whose masonry and round tower are Saxon. In it is a brass to John Daye, the Puritan printer who published John Foxe's *Acts and Monuments*, or Book of Martyrs, which did more than anything else to flame the indignation of the people against the Henrican and Marian persecutions: the fourteen lines begin:

> Here lyes the Daye that darkness could not blynd,
> When popish fogges had overcast the sunne.

Though uncompromising, such phrases at any rate bear a historical clarity, and are undeniably appropriate here at this western corner of Suffolk, so near to Cambridge, that lodestar of Puritanism; though actually John Daye was born at the eastern extremity of the county, at Dunwich.

V

Orwell and Gipping

Before the construction of trunk roads and railway lines, the Orwell estuary was the main entry to Suffolk. Travellers were always impressed by the scenery as they sailed up to Ipswich. There was just enough rise on both banks to give an impression of a well-ordered landscape. 'These Hills on each side', wrote John Kirby in 1735, 'are enriched and adorned with almost every Object that can make a Landscape agreeable; such as Churches, Mills, Gentlemen's Seats, Villages and other Buildings, Woods, noble Avenues, Parks whose Pales reach down to the Water's Edge, well stored with Deer and other Cattle, feeding in fine Lawns . . .' Because of the easy accessibility to the sea and the county capital, the estates bordering the Orwell were particularly favoured by prominent people, including three redoubtable sea-dogs.

Grimston Hall, at Trimley St Martin on the north bank, was the home of the first of these, Thomas Cavendish. This adventurer had been with Sir Richard Grenville in his successful raid in the Caribbean in 1585. On his return he set about organising a raid of his own, into the remote Pacific. This involved a circumnavigation of the globe, such as had been undertaken by Sir Francis Drake a few years before. Cavendish himself provided the money for building a new ship, the *Desire*, of 140 tons, and for purchasing two escorting vessels, the *Content* (60 tons) and *Hugh Gallant* (40 tons). The *Desire* was built on the Medway, but on completion was brought to Harwich, where Cavendish (who signed his name Candish) visited his home and engaged some of the crew of 125 men. He then went around to Plymouth and set sail on 25 July 1586.

His aim was to grab the most valuable loot he could get, and his record (logged by Francis Pretty, of Eye, and written up by

93

Richard Hakluyt when Rector of Wetheringsett, near Eye) is one of unabashed piracy, and violence against anyone – native or Spaniard – who stood in his way. In February 1587 he passed through the Straits of Magellan and entered the Pacific. In the whole of this vast ocean the Spanish kept no warships because they thought they were safe. On 4 November came the moment for which he had so long been waiting. A galleon, the *Saint Anna the Great*, of 700 tons, was sighted off the coast of California, and he gave chase: the large crew surrendered after a feeble fight. Cavendish was unable to bring the galleon and its contents home, so once again he took what he could, including 22,000 gold pesos. Then it was across the Pacific to the Philippines, and thence to Java. The long journey home now began: in the Bay of Biscay they learnt of the destruction of the Spanish Armada, and they got back to Plymouth on 10 September 1588. Three years later the 'Trimley Hero', after squandering most of his booty, decided to repeat his performance. He left Plymouth with five ships in August 1591. But after once again passing through the Magellan Straits, everything went wrong, and Cavendish's ship disappeared at sea.

Philip Broke came from Broke Hall, Nacton, whose Georgian frontage can be seen from the Orwell. An exemplary naval officer, he was appointed to command the *Shannon*, a 38-gun frigate, in 1806. After the outbreak of war between England and the United States in 1812, the *Shannon* was sent to patrol the North American coast. In May 1813, while standing off Boston, desperately short of supplies and with an exhausted crew, the newly-built and larger American frigate, *Chesapeake*, unexpectedly sailed out of Boston harbour to attack him. In the short sharp engagement which ensued, the *Shannon*'s salvoes incapacitated the *Chesapeake*, which drifted foul of its foe, and was boarded by Broke ('Follow me who can') and about fifty men. The American crew surrendered ignominiously, in full sight of their horrified compatriots on the waterfront of Boston (which is, incidentally, in Suffolk County, Massachusetts). This victory was attributable to the sheer professionalism of Philip Broke and his crew, particularly to their gunnery standards. He returned home, was awarded high honours, but never fully recovered from his wounds. He is buried at Nacton.

Edward Vernon completes this trio of sea-dogs. Like Broke, he was also a naval officer, but of rather a different kind, as he combined his duties with a political career, as Member of Parliament for Penryn and then Ipswich. In 1739 he persuaded the government to allow him to lead a naval assault on the Spanish naval base at Porto Bello, in Panama. A fort, known as the Iron Castle, bristling with guns, barred the way. But Vernon gambled successfully on the Spanish garrison being completely unprepared, and his marines clambered into the fort through the embrasures and took the town. Vernon became a national hero and he purchased the estate at Nacton where he lived into old age. He is also remembered for instituting the practice of watering down the naval rum ration. The daily mixture was of one quart of water to half a pint of rum; and it was called grog after his nickname, 'Old Grogram', from his grogram boat-cloak.

Pin Mill, at Chelmondiston, on the south bank, is the heart of the Orwell and is frequented by scores of little boats in summer. This scene of busy leisure activity was once busy with real commerical work. The cargoes of ocean-going sailing ships, unable to get up to Ipswich, were transshipped here onto barges by gangs of dockers, while the river bed was dredged for septaria stone, used to make cement. A picture by Thomas Smythe, painted in the 1860s, shows the group of buildings at Pin Mill looking much the same as today, with much activity in ferrying people across to Nacton Quay. The Butt and Oyster public house is right on the water, and it used to be said that nifty sailors could manoeuvre their dinghies below its bay windows to order their drinks. Just beyond the pub, along the foreshore, is a collection of superannuated boats now used as moored dwellings. Barges, tugs and lighters, each with its railed gangplank, line the path along the lower edge of the wood against the shore, looking very inviting and prompting curiosity about the people who live in them. The most appealing is a Swiss cottage on a raft supported by metal drums, its approach decorated with bells.

When Arthur Ransome was exploring Suffolk waters, he was so enchanted by Pin Mill that he decided to leave his home in the Lake District and come to live permanently beside the Orwell. In 1934 he went to Broke Farm at Levington, on the opposite bank, and in 1939 for a short while to Harkstead Hall on the Shotley peninsula, after which the rigours of the war and his fading health forced him back to Cumbria. But Pin Mill itself was his spiritual home. Here were the King family of boat-builders, who built *Peter Duck* and *Selina King* for him. Also Annie Powell, who kept the tea shop; and the Altounyan, Busk, Young and Russell families, always in and out of boats and inspirational to his tales of childish heroism. At Pin Mill he kept his seven-ton cutter, the *Nancy Blackett*. His voyages in her, and the children who this childless man befriended at Pin Mill, were the inspiration for *We Didn't Mean to Go to Sea*.

This is surely his most thrilling novel, from the nautical point of view at any rate, involving as it does an accidental crossing of the North Sea, in which the young crew are in very real danger. All the details of the Orwell estuary are accurately described, including the view from Shotley Point, where the open sea can just be seen between Felixstowe and Harwich, and where the Orwell joins the Stour to form Harwich harbour. Today the great cranes of the Felixstowe Container Port dominate the scene across the water, and Harwich, by contrast, looks strangely old-fashioned, its silhouette dominated by its church tower: the big North Sea ferries use Parkeston Quay a mile to the east of Harwich. Here at Shotley the main activity used to be the training of naval cadets at the shore station, HMS *Ganges*, but it has now been developed into a sport and leisure centre, whose main facility is a marina where the finest ocean-going yachts are kept, and it glistens with stainless steel. Just here, in 884, Guthram the Dane witnessed the unexpected defeat of his ships by those of Alfred of Wessex, a humiliating experience for a Viking. Shotley Point is still remembered as Bloody Point.

The entire Orwell estuary is '*Margaret Catchpole* country', scene of the adventures of Richard Cobbold's romantic heroine. The story, about a spirited young woman whose life was ruined by her obsession with a handsome smuggler, William Laud, is only very loosely based on fact. Cobbold presents her as the daughter of Jonathan Catchpole, head ploughman on an estate at Nacton, and depicts her first adventure when, aged fourteen, she made the dash into Ipswich on a 'fiery little Suffolk pony' to summon the doctor to her ailing mistress. Down on the waterfront of Downham Reach, he describes how William Laud tried to abduct her. Some years later it was from the Cobbolds' house, overlooking the Orwell, that Margaret stole the sixteen-hand horse Rochford, and galloped away on him through the night to London in the expectation of meeting her lover.

One of the most memorable characters we encounter in *Margaret Catchpole* is Thomas Colson, the ancient fisherman of the Orwell, known as 'Robinson Crusoe', and widely recognised as being supremely eccentric, even in that age of eccentrics. He was haunted by the fear of evil spirits, and, to ward them off, he hung about him a weird collection of animal bones, rings, amulets, and magic words and verses, which almost covered his body. He rowed about in a boat studded with lucky horse-shoes. His habitat, the Orwell, was at that time teeming with birds. In winter, Richard Cobbold tells us, they 'used to come into the channel of the river in prodigious flights, covering hundreds of acres of water with their varieties of plumage': black coot, duck, mallard, divers, pin-tail, bar-geese and wild swans, in such numbers as would seem incredible today. It must have seemed a paradise, with all the natural life hardly touched by man; yet man's inhumanity to man was all too readily apparent at a time when the punishment for horse-theft was death.

One of the buildings bordering the Orwell, which must have been well known to Thomas Colson, is the Tudor tower at Freston. This narrow red-brick edifice of six stories was built with a partly practical purpose as a look-out for shipping. But with only one room on each storey, it has the appearance of a folly, and legend has it that it was built for a lord as the educative retreat for his daughter. It is said that he intended her to spend some time on each storey at successive moments of the day. The ground floor was for giving charity to the poor; the second storey, for needlework; the third, for music; the fourth, for painting; the fifth, for reading; and the sixth, for astronomy. I am only surprised that the legend didn't go a stage further and tell us how this top floor could also be used as her bedroom, from where she could let down her golden tresses at night, for her lover to climb up.

The Orwell Bridge, which lifts the A14 across the estuary to provide clearance for large freighters, is an elegant concrete structure whose tall flat piers elevate it towards the wide central arch. It cuts the skyline less obtrusively than a suspension bridge, and is an enhancement to the Orwell because it forms an emphatic division between the natural landscape and the industrial scenery past Cliff Quay to Ipswich Docks. It is an inherent feature of bridges that they can never be seen by those who pass over them, only by those who see them sideways on. The Orwell Bridge, quite properly, has walls which act as blinkers to prevent the motorists (but not the truck-drivers) from gawping at the Orwell; but the boats on the Orwell enjoy the confident sweep of the bridge from as far as five miles downstream.

The first obstacle to anyone who wants to appreciate Ipswich is its name, a sibilant lip-twister that is harder to mouth than Harwich or Sandwich and calls to mind a rail connection ('Which switch to Ipswich?') rather than a port. Ipswich began its life as Gipeswic, meaning, in concise Anglo-Saxon terms, a village at the corner of the mouth of a river. Ipswich has for long been the largest centre of population in Suffolk, and today nearly a fifth of the county's residents live there and many more come in to work there. But its history is one of commercial, rather than administrative, importance. No cathedral, castle or abbey was ever here to draw the visitor to Ipswich. It cannot compare with Norwich.

Perhaps because of this, Ipswich has been less careful than it should in preserving its old buildings, and as late as the 1960s was still destroying medieval structures such as the Half Moon Inn. This, together with the heavy Victorian Town Hall and

Corn Exchange, the enormous warehouses which dominate the lower part of the old town, and the ill-planned development around the Civic Centre, is the more serious obstacle to an appreciation of Ipswich, although some restitution has been made by banning traffic from the main shopping streets and the Tower Ramparts shopping centre. It is, in fact, in the layout of these streets that the centre of Ipswich really does have something special to offer, for it is still substantially that of the original Anglo-Saxon town, and dates from an earlier period than, for example, the Norman streets of Bury St Edmunds.

Ipswich was founded in the early seventh century, and soon became established as a port and as a base for the manufacture of pottery and other goods: 'Ipswich ware' was commonly used throughout East Anglia, and exported to other English kingdoms. The centre of Gipeswic was around the Market Place (the present Cornhill) and St Mildred's Church (on the site of the present Town Hall), and the greatest concentration of houses was between Tavern Street and Butter Market. This area, at the upper end of the alluvial gravels, was linked to the river bank by the same three street-sequences as today, with a bridge extending from Bridge Street. Along Carr Street and Cox Lane were the kilns of the potters.

In 879 the town was occupied by the Danes, though they surrendered control in 918 after Edward of Wessex had taken Colchester. Under the Normans a wooden castle was constructed, probably just to the west of Cornhill, but was demolished in 1176. In 1203 the Danish defences of the town were improved by deepening the ditch and raising the rampart. The growing prosperity of Ipswich is indicated by the sixteen churches, three hospitals and five religious houses that were founded there during the medieval period. The Augustinians were the first of the religious orders to settle in Ipswich. Their priory in the lower town, around the present church of St Peter and St Paul, was established in around 1130. A few decades later they also acquired the Priory of the Holy Trinity just outside the ramparts, on the site of the present Christchurch Mansion. In the ensuing century three large friaries were also built within the confines of the town: the Dominicans near the east ditch, the Franciscans by the western waterfront, and the Carmelites in the heart of the town by the Butter Market.

Apart from some fragments nothing is left of these substantial complexes. But a dozen medieval churches remain, in whole or in part, some of them redundant and most of them kept closed. Of these St Margaret's is the finest and most visited: the church of an affluent parish, it was much embellished in the eighteenth century. This surfeit of churches in so small an area serves as a reminder of the dominance of medieval religion and the traumatic changes brought about by the Reformation, when for over a century all worship was still confined within an enforced conformity, but one that altered in a contradictory and alarming way.

Ipswich was the strongest centre of Protestantism in Suffolk, not surprising in a port that had close links with the Netherlands and London. The radical new doctrines appealed particularly to the merchants and artisans of the specialised trades that had brought such prosperity to the county. They welcomed the changes in worship under Edward VI, and endured the five years of Marian Catholicism in sullen obedience, before emerging under Elizabeth I as Puritans, increasingly discontented with the episcopal and Catholic elements within the established church, and seething with indignation at the memory of the thirty-six Suffolk men and women whose death at the stake had been lovingly recorded in Foxe's Book of Martyrs. In the eyes of Matthew Wren, the Bishop of Norwich in the 1630s, Ipswich was the 'most refractory and styf place' in his diocese, fortified in its opposition to his authority by the redoubtable preacher at St Mary le Tower, Samuel Ward.

Obviously it was not just the influence of the merchants of Ipswich that caused the exceptionally strong support for Puritanism in Suffolk. Several of the leading county families, such as the Bacons, Jermyns and Barnardistons, converted to it under Elizabeth and they were joined by many others as the conflict intensified under her successors. But even these gentry, who financed preachers and appointed radical clergy, could not have swayed the county without the concurring sentiment of the ordinary population. The sense of independence induced by the dismantling of feudalism and the fluidity of labour; the natural common-sense instilled by generations of work on a tamed and level landscape; and the personal morality revealed by the translation of the Bible – all these came to give greater weight to the word of the preacher than to the mystery of the sacrament. The descendants of those who had built and embellished the churches were now stripping them of their ornaments, and beliefs and practices that had seemed eternal were now seen to be ephemeral.

This is not to say that Suffolk was wholeheartedly Puritan. Many people welcomed the reforms of Archbishop Laud whereby order and dignity had been restored to church services. They resented the enactments of the Long Parliament which overturned these reforms, together with the abolition of the episcopacy and the declaration that even the private use of the Prayer Book was to be a penal offence. But the Church had become inextricably bound up in the struggle between the King and Parliament, and Suffolk became increasingly supportive of the latter. In 1640 the Sheriff had been able to collect only a tenth of the Ship Money demanded from the county by the Crown, much less than in Norfolk.

In some ways, the most appealing ecclesiastical building in Ipswich is not one of the medieval churches, but the Unitarian Meeting House. This was erected for the Presbyterians in 1700. It is a wooden building, designed and constructed by a carpenter, Joseph Clarke. Its twin hipped roofs and its two storeys of windows effectively disguise its function, and distance it as far as possible from the architecture of a church. Within, the rectangular space of the Meeting House is broken by the box-pews, the galleries on three sides, and also, perforce, by the columns which support the flat ceiling. Against the south wall is the elevated pulpit, richly carved and furnished with a staircase with twisted balusters. The transference to the Unitarians was made easy by the absence of religious symbols, and it is not hard to imagine the Meeting House being put to use as a mosque, in which the pulpit fulfils an identical centrality, except that the box-pews would prevent prostration.

More than any other building, the Meeting House represents the long tradition of non-conformist worship in Suffolk. Under the Commonwealth, when the parish churches were Presbyterian, meetings of Congregationalists and Baptists were tolerated, though Quakers were roughly treated. After the Restoration in 1660, Anglican worship was re-imposed and non-conformists were all ejected. In 1672 a short-lived Declaration of Indulgence resulted in the licencing of twenty-eight Presbyterian and twenty-three Congregational ministers in Suffolk; but dissenters had to wait till the 1689 Act of Toleration for permanent acceptance of Protestant non-conformity. The number of people who adhered to these alternative denominations vastly increased with the arrival of Methodism in the late-eighteenth century, so much so that in 1829 there were more licenced meeting-places than parish churches. Such meeting places were generally in private houses or barns, but during the nineteenth century they were integrated into simple chapels, of which most Suffolk parishes eventually had at least one.

Several secular buildings dignify the architecture of Ipswich, most of them old, though the black glass Willis Faber Building should certainly be included among them. The Ancient House, in the Butter Market, is a sixteenth-century timber-framed structure which was improved in around 1670 and decorated with carved posts and brackets, and with the most elaborate example of pargetting in the county. Depicted in heavy relief are sympathetic figures which include a shepherd and shepherdess, a horseman and a nymph; and the four continents then known are represented by a Gothic church for Europe, a domed mosque for Asia, a crocodile for Africa and a tobacco-pipe for America. Down at the waterfront is the Custom House, a Classical building of 1844, with its main floor raised high up and approached by large twin stairways as if in precaution against a flood, and a bold portico and pediment.

Up on the site of the Priory of the Holy Trinity is the

Christchurch Mansion, set in its park just behind St Margaret's Church. This Tudor house, much restored and embellished, has always been the principal mansion of Ipswich, and Elizabeth I stayed here in 1561. It was later acquired by the Huguenot family of Fonnerau. In 1892, with Ipswich spreading in size, they decided to sell the estate for housing development. This disaster was averted by Felix Cobbold, who presented the mansion to Ipswich, and thus the grounds became a public park, and the house an art gallery and museum. Christchurch Park had always been an area of social activity; the Ipswich establishment used to parade there in summer, and in the mansion is a picture by John Duvall of the Suffolk Show in Christchurch Park in 1869, with Colonel Barlow proudly holding his prize-winning Suffolk Punch, Dalesman.

Ipswich was extremely prosperous during the sixteenth century, but thereafter it went into a long and heavy recession. It suffered from the dominance of London, both in ship-building and the control of the cloth trade. Ipswich shipowners found themselves less able to compete internationally with the Dutch, and the coastal trade also was sadly reduced when the merchants of the north-east of England began to ship their coal in locally-owned ships. All this was accurately observed by Daniel Defoe when he visited Ipswich in 1722. But he also noted what a pleasant place it was to live in, now that the pressure was off and property values were low: 'I take this town to be one of the most agreeable Places in England, for Families who have liv'd well, but may have suffered in our late Calamities of Stocks and Bubbles, to retreat to, where they may live within their own Compass'.

Defoe also predicted, with prescience, that the time would come when 'some peculiar beneficial Business may be found out, to make the Port of Ipswich as useful to the World, and the Town as flourishing, as Nature has made it proper and capable to be'. Nineteenth-century industry did indeed transform Ipswich, and one of the first to set this in motion was Robert Ransome. In 1803 he patented an improvement to the plough-share, whereby it was not worn away so rapidly on the underside, which led to further advances in cast-iron ploughs. Ransomes, Sims and Jefferies grew to be one of England's leading manufacturers of agricultural machinery, and Fison's, Ipswich's other major home-based industrial firm, developed agricultural fertilisers. And the docks were progressively improved by the construction of the Wet Dock in 1842. The Old Maltings alongside the Wet Dock testify to the former importance of the shipments of malt to the London breweries, and a mile downstream is the Cliff Brewery of Tolly Cobbold.

The Cliff Brewery dates from 1746, when Thomas Cobbold transferred his Harwich brewery to this site because it was close to the springs from which he obtained his water. At that time beer was brewed in innumerable inns and farmhouses, beer being the normal drink for ordinary people, some of whom never drank water. The commercial breweries, with their superior products, subsequently came to dominate the supply of beers and ales: by 1844 there were sixty-one of them in Suffolk. Cobbolds became the largest in Ipswich (as was Greene's in Bury St Edmunds), and eventually, in 1957, they merged with Tollemache to form Tolly Cobbold.

Until the Reform Bill of 1832, Suffolk's sixteen Members of Parliament comprised the two Knights of the Shire, plus two each for the boroughs of Aldeburgh, Bury, Dunwich, Eye, Ipswich, Orford and Sudbury. Of these, Ipswich has been the only borough to retain its own member, the remainder becoming incorporated into larger geographical constituencies. Though the franchise widened progressively, Suffolk was reduced to a nadir of only five members in 1948, increased by one in the 1983 boundary changes. Until the introduction of the secret ballot in 1872, all Parliamentary elections were partial, since it was not easy to vote against the wishes of one's landlord or employer. This obvious constraint had been made very evident in the hotly-contested election for the Knights of the Shire, held at Ipswich in the General Election of 1705. The main issue was the toleration of non-conformity, which the Tories opposed. There was an unprecedented turn-out, and both the Tory candidates got majorities. Analysis has shown that their support was mainly from electors who came from the smaller parishes, where the hold of the squire and the parson was strongest.

But perhaps the most heated elections in pre-Reform Bill Ipswich were those of 1820. The victory of the two Whig candidates was only announced after four days of polling, a scrutiny and a recount. One of them paid £30,000 in election expenses, which included the passage home of hundreds of non-resident voters, some from France and Holland, and handouts of up to £10 a head. Much of the cooping and stupefying of voters took place in the principal inn, the Great White Horse, whose long low frontages in Tavern Street and Northgate Street have been preserved, even though the interior is no longer as described by Dickens: 'Never were such labyrinths of uncarpeted passages, such clusters of mouldy, badly-lighted rooms, such huge numbers of small dens for eating or sleeping in, beneath any one roof, as are collected together between the four walls of the Great White Horse at Ipswich'. Here Mr Pickwick got lost in the middle of the night, with consequences that involved being carried next day through the streets in a Sedan Chair to appear before the magistrates.

In recent years the greatest single event for Ipswich was when its football team won the Cup Final in 1978. The crowning moment came with the triumphant arrival home of the victorious team next day. About a hundred thousand people lined the streets, or hung from the sides of buildings, and when the open-top bus inched its way to the Cornhill, the crowd erupted. Such an outbreak of civic enthusiasm had not been seen since the end of the Second World War, and it took place at a time when the expansion of the town and its general prosperity were at unprecedented levels. Ipswich may not have been granted the dignity of becoming a city, but it has undoubtedly succeeded in regaining the confidence which it had centuries ago.

Ipswich was the birthplace of Thomas Wolsey, the most powerful personage ever to have come from Suffolk. As Henry VIII's Lord Chancellor (1515–29) he was the virtual ruler of England at an exceptionally critical period, besides being Cardinal Archbishop of York. His father, Robert Wolsey (or Wulcy, as he spelt it), came from Sternfield, just south of

Saxmundham, and his mother, Joan Daundy, was also from a Suffolk family. Robert Wolsey moved to Ipswich, where he opened a butcher's shop in the St Nicholas ward, selling meat from his farm at Sternfield. He became a churchwarden of St Nicholas, though not a freeman of the borough of Ipswich. This may have been due to the brushes he had with the authorities, in such matters as being fined for allowing his pigs to roam the streets, for selling bad meat, and using his house for illegal purposes. But he was able to set his gifted son on the first steps of an extraordinary career by sending him first to the Ipswich Grammar School, and then, at the early age of eleven, to Magdalen College, Oxford. From then on, Thomas Wolsey owed his rise to power solely to his own personality and not to any family connections. In this he was following in the steps of several great medieval clerics, including the Thomas after whom he had been named, St Thomas à Becket, who had also been Chancellor of England.

In 1528 Wolsey obtained royal authority to found a college at Ipswich, in the same manner as he had done four years previously at Oxford with the foundation of Cardinal College. It was to be on the site of the suppressed Priory of St Peter and St Paul. But within a year he had fallen from power, and although Henry VIII was persuaded to refound Cardinal College as Christ Church, Ipswich College seemed to be too much of a memorial to the former chancellor; besides, its extensive property was coveted by the King and his courtiers, particularly the family of Wolsey's enemy, Anne Boleyn. So it was dissolved, and the Dean and the priests and choral scholars, who were already teaching and singing masses for the souls of Wolsey's parents, were dispersed. The only thing that remains of Ipswich College is a brick gateway, made filthy by the heavy dock traffic that thunders past it along the one-way College Street. This, and the foundation stone, which is preserved in the Chapter House of Christ Church, Oxford, is all there is to remind us of what might have become a great public school, comparable with Eton or Winchester; for it was certainly Wolsey's intention that the scholars of Ipswich should have preferential entry into Cardinal College.

When Wolsey died his faithful gentleman-usher, George Cavendish, was at his bedside. This Suffolk man had stayed with his master after his fall from power more than a year before, performing ever more menial tasks as the great household shrunk in size. It is a telling testimony to his character, so different from his kinsman Thomas Cavendish, that after some initial questioning, the Privy Council provided him with money and transport to return to his house at Glemsford. Here he occupied himself with writing a personal memoir, beginning with the simple sentence: 'Truth it is, Cardinal Wolsey, sometime Archbishop of York, was an honest poor man's son, born in Ipswich in the County of Suffolk'. When published in 1557 it helped rehabilitate the Cardinal as a statesman, and the moral tale of the humbling of such a proud and mighty man found eager readers, including Shakespeare.

Of all the Suffolk rivers the Gipping has suffered the worst environmental fate, because its little valley has been chosen as the route for the main line railway and the main cross-county road artery, the A14. These two, with all their cuttings and embankments and bridges, confine the Gipping on either side of its course from Stowmarket down to Ipswich. But I suppose there is some historical justice in this, since the Gipping was in early times an artery in its own right, and was made navigable for barges up to Stowmarket in 1793. It is merely a fortunate chance that the pattern of modern transport has generally kept away from the other Suffolk rivers.

Industrial Ipswich, with engineering plant, cement works, and conglomeration of pylons, extends upstream to Claydon. Here, well within the soundband of the A14, is Claydon Old Hall, known as Mockbeggers Hall, a charming Jacobean house. Its curious name inspired Matilda Betham-Edwards to write a novel about it, in which she asks 'What is life but a Mock Beggars' Hall, each of us getting a snub in turn?' Nearby, in the garden of a house called Lime Kiln, Humphrey Brooke in the 1960s created one of the most beautiful rose gardens in England, the first to revive the culture of old-fashioned roses with powerful scents. Upstream from Claydon is Shrubland Park. This is a large grey-brick Italianate mansion, mostly the creation of Sir Charles Barry in 1852. He also designed the extensive formal gardens, with terraces leading down the hillside in the manner of the Villa d'Este at Tivoli. Shrubland Park no longer serves as a private house, but has been put to a new purpose as a health clinic. Its clients generally come here to diet in luxury, after which they usually return to their self-indulgent eating, thereby finding themselves back at Shrublands the next year.

The Old Hall at Shrublands was the seat of a junior branch of the Bacon family until the eighteenth century, and at the time of the Civil War its owner, Nathaniel Bacon, together with his brother Francis, were prominent in the Parliamentary cause. The Suffolk gentry faced the prospect of conflict with great apprehension, and there was little enthusiasm for rebellion. They had close links with one another through their involvement in local government as magistrates, special commissioners, deputy lieutenants, and the like; and their sense of identity with their county was strong. Their natural solidarity as a social class was fortified by inter-marriage, even if this may not have been so prevalent as among their contemporaries in Norfolk or Kent. When civil war broke out in 1642, two of Suffolk's fourteen members declared for the King, four absented themselves from the Commons, and the remaining eight supported the Parliamentary cause with various degrees of eagerness. In the event, most of the county landowners managed to keep out of the war altogether, helped by the fact that, apart from an engagement at Lowestoft, no fighting took place in Suffolk. Of those who were actively involved, in either a civil or military capacity, the majority did indeed support Parliament. But a substantial minority, mainly Anglicans and mainly from among the large estates in West Suffolk and the coastal sandlings, dared to be Royalists.

All the same, since Suffolk was among the counties where Puritanism was strongest, it was bound to come in on the side of Parliament, even if at first reluctant to pay or to fight. Following an outbreak of Puritan violence in the Stour valley in August 1642, the authorities were obliged to execute the military legislation enacted by Parliament. East Anglia was secured from attack by the actions of Cromwell in ensuring the defence of its northern frontier: of his five troops of horse, one was from Suffolk. Thereafter, the county was increasingly constrained to join together with others in emergency measures for the prosecution of the war.

This resulted in the formation of the Eastern Association in February 1643, which came to include Norfolk, Suffolk, Essex, Cambridgeshire, Huntingdonshire, Hertfordshire and Lincolnshire. County committees were set up to finance the associated forces which were to supplant the individual county levies. In August of that year Parliament passed further ordinances whereby the Earl of Manchester, the Major-General of the Association, was granted authority to override the localism of the seven counties and establish a central financial organisation. With this he was able to form a fighting force that was superior to any of the other regional units in the Parliamentarian army, and was the precursor of Cromwell's New Model Army. He upset county interests by appointing officers on the basis of their military experience and energy, even if this meant promoting men from the ranks. He also required a general religious commitment from the whole army, though avoiding narrow sectarian confessions of faith. By the time of the decisive battle of Marston Moor, the courage, discipline and fighting spirit of Suffolk men, fortified by their belief in the rightness of their cause and by their sense of outrage at the depredations of the Cavaliers, was an important ingredient in the Parliamentarian army.

A little further up the Gipping corridor we come to Needham (needy-home) Market, in whose church of St John Baptist is the most ingenious of all the roofs in Suffolk churches, the 'culminating achievement of the medieval carpenter', as Munro Cautley calls it. The effect of this remarkable hammer-beam roof is enhanced by the plainness of the building itself, formerly a chapel-of-ease and not a parish church. The wooden roof embraces the entire clerestory, and it gives the impression of a whole church suspended in mid-air. Though its members were admittedly replaced in Victorian times, the design of this roof is entirely original, and represents the ultimate functional development in hammer-beam construction. It stands in complete contrast to the roof of St Mary's at Earl Stonham, only three miles north. Here is probably the most ornate of hammer-beams in the county, heavily decorated with pendants and pierced tracery. But in fact only half the hammer-beams are load-bearing, the others are just for show.

Meanwhile, several villages of note lie just outside the Gipping valley. To the south, where a monstrous web of pylons overlies the land, is Hintlesham. Hintlesham Hall was splendidly restored by the master-chef Robert Carrier, and has achieved fame as a gourmets' restaurant, the best known in Suffolk. The white-stucco Hall, as we see it, dates from 1720, and was built for Richard Powys. Its elegant frontage faces the park, with a central Venetian window and pediment. But it disguises the structure of an earlier Elizabethan house, built for Thomas Timperley. The drawing room of this house was redecorated with a magnificent plaster ceiling in the 1680s for Henry Timperley. Unfortunately for him, the Catholic Henry Timperley had hardly completed this splendid improvement to Hintlesham Hall before his patron James II was toppled from the throne, and he fled to join the exiled monarch at St Germain-en-Laye, outside Paris. For the remaining months of his short life in his uncomfortable lodgings he must often have thought regretfully of his lovely country house, never to be seen by him again, as in the lines from Macaulay's 'Epitaph to a Jacobite': 'Beheld each night my home in fevered sleep, Each morning started from that dream to weep'.

Just to the north of the Gipping is the parish of Coddenham. Here was one of the largest settlements of Roman Suffolk, Combretovium. It lay on the same main road as Stratford St Mary, close to where a military fort guarded the ford over the Gipping. Pottery and coins of the Claudian period and a statuette of the Emperor Nero have been found on the site. The settlement around it grew to become a commercial community, from which other roads radiated. Coddenham today is a small village perched on the edge of a hillock to the

north of Combretovium. This slope gives a special charm to
the group of houses with timber overhangs and plaster
pargetting which line the little street, some of them former
inns, and one dating from around 1500. The line of the hill is
also reflected in the design of the church, whose porch is set at
an angle, apparently so as to conform to the line of the path
from the village. The fine eighteenth-century hall, seen across
the stream from the village, was built as the rectory for one of
the Bacon family, surely one of the grandest of its time,
especially before its second storey was removed. It was indeed
a worthy residence for a 'squarson', and one imagines him,
perhaps unfairly, being driven in a carriage to the church
rather than walking.

Between Needham Market and Stowmarket we pass from
the ancient hundred of Bosmere and Claydon to that of Stow,
names which refer to the original meeting-places: the first
beside a mere, the second on a clay hill, and the third probably
a place by a ford. The twenty-five medieval hundreds of
Suffolk were grouped three ways. Those of the Liberties of St
Edmund and St Etheldreda, which were under Monastic
jurisdiction; and the remainder, which was under Royal
jurisdiction. These latter, including Bosmere and Stow, and
together with Ipswich and other Boroughs, were known as the
Geldable (or taxable). When it came to contributing to royal
taxation, a very simple allocation was made: half from the
Geldable, and, of the remaining half, two thirds from St
Edmund and one third from St Etheldreda. Petty Sessions of
justice continued to be held by hundreds till the nineteenth
century, but real administrative power moved towards the
County Courts and then, in Tudor times, to the Justices of the
Peace and to the Assize Judge at the Quarter Sessions. When
District Councils were first established they were based on
hundredal geography. But today only the name of one
hundred – Babergh – has survived successive rationalisations
into larger units.

As compared with Suffolk's other market towns,
Stowmarket has lost much of its historic core. This is partly
due to its nineteenth-century development as the chief

commercial centre for a great part of High Suffolk, with maltings and ironworks, helped by its excellent communications from canal and railway; and partly to some insensitive destruction more recently. As if in compensation, a large site at the centre of Stowmarket is now devoted to a Museum of East Anglian Life. The Abbot's Hall estate gets its name from the time when the manor of Stowmarket was owned by the Abbot of St Osyth's priory in Essex, who had his hall, or grange, close by the church and market place. Here also was his tithe barn, which is still standing, and is part of the extensive Museum, housed in various buildings and spreading over nearly thirty hectares. In it are exhibits of many aspects of life in Suffolk a century ago, providing a fascinating visual aid to an understanding of the past. A Suffolk Punch, a Suffolk Wagon, and a Suffolk steam-engine, provide references unique to the county. And, for the rest, a common theme is to be found in the manual toil of ordinary people, at work and in the home, beginning with domestic chores such as the daily emptying of chamber pots and the weekly clothes wash in the copper.

At Haughley (haw-wood), three miles from Stowmarket, the Normans built a castle with an earthwork that still looks formidable, emphasised by a towering cedar on the site of the keep. But it was only of timber construction, and was put to flames by the Earl of Leicester and his Flemish mercenaries in 1173. From about this time the Honour, or feudal Liberty, of Haughley began to decline in importance, though it survived to be awarded to Charles Brandon, Duke of Suffolk, in Tudor times. Haughley's market was lost to Stowmarket's, and was in disuse before the seventeenth century. At New Bells Farm at Haughley, the Soil Association set up its pioneering experiments in organic farming, making a scientific study of the comparative yields of fertilised and unfertilised land: much of the research has since been transferred to Bristol.

The Gipping rises just north of Stowmarket, and near its source is the parish of Gipping. The isolated little church of St Nicholas was formerly the private chapel of the Tyrell family, whose adjacent hall is now no more. Built in the 1480s for Sir James Tyrell, it is an exquisite example of the Perpendicular style, memorable without for the stone-and-flint panelling of its walls, and within for the high proportion of window-glass to wall space. A chaplain's dwelling is attached, with a beautiful chimney, and it and the chapel are decorated with various Tyrell devices: their motto, *Groyne que Vodroy* (let him complain who will); their crest, a peacock's tail in a boar's mouth; and the initials of Sir James Tyrell's wife, Anne.

The Tyrells had a curious association with the death of two English kings. Sir James himself was involved with the murder of the Princes in the Tower, the elder being the uncrowned Edward V. Shakespeare describes him as 'a discontented gentleman, whose humble means match not his haughty spirit', who arranges the dirty deed for Richard III. He managed to survive into the reign of Henry VII, but was eventually executed for treason. A distant ancestor, Sir Walter, accidentally killed William II (the red-headed 'Rufus') with an arrow when out hunting in the New Forest in 1100. Though, as the school-rhyme has it, 'No one will know if Sir Walter de Tyrell, Was aiming at Rufus or at a red squirrel' – an animal which, alas, has virtually disappeared from the Suffolk scene today.

VI
Deben

The Deben estuary is no longer a waterway for commercial traffic. The channel is not dredged, and the sedimentary muds are well preserved. Also, as a result of breaches in the sea walls, the area of salt marsh has greatly expanded in recent years, increasing the naturalistic impression of the tidal scenery. The sailing boats take over at weekends, from the Woodbridge marinas to the narrow mouth between Felixstowe Ferry and Bawdsey, and the entire estuary is bounded by farmland broken by occasional woods and villages. On the north bank is All Saints church at Ramsholt (wild-garlic wood), set among woods on cliffs of red crag, and with a remarkable buttressed round tower which gives an unusual profile. Waldringfield, on the south bank, is the main gathering point for the sailors, especially at the Maybush pub.

Further upstream a creek gives access to Martlesham, formerly on the main road: travellers often had to get out of their carts and carriages outside the Red Lion and walk up the steep hill to the heath. A Roman monument from Martlesham, now in the British Museum, reads with touching simplicity: 'To Mars Corotiacus: Simplicia herself willingly and deservedly set up this offering: Glaucus made it'. Martlesham Heath is today an important industrial site clustered around British Telecom's centre for research into high technology.

Into Martlesham Creek flows the little River Fynn, after running its course beside the railway line and under the mighty A12 viaduct. It flows past Playford (the ford where sports were held), with its fragmentary Elizabethan Hall, surrounded by a moat. Among the farmers of Playford during the early nineteenth century were the Biddells. Arthur Biddell, who married Jane Ransome, daughter of the founder of the engineering firm, was a most assiduous man. He farmed extensively, keeping copious day books recording all his transactions and accounts; and he also invented two agricultural devices, the Biddell's Scarifier and the Biddell's Extirpating Harrow. His son Herman followed his father as a farmer and decided to devote his surplus energies to a study of the breeding of the Suffolk Punch horses. In 1862 he summoned the best-informed horsemen of the leading farms to a meeting, and over the following fifteen years collated facts for *The Suffolk Stud Book*, a labour of love and still the classic authority on the subject.

Anyone who wants an impression of what old Ipswich once looked like should take a stroll round Woodbridge. In Elizabethan times both were busy estuarian ports, but Woodbridge failed to make it into the industrial age, to its great eventual benefit, the main reason being that large boats could not get up the Deben. The only obvious manifestation of the Victorian Age is the railway that runs beside the old quay, and even this has become an object of affection, providing almost as good a way of approaching Woodbridge as by boat. From boat or train, the first building to attract attention is the weatherboarded tide mill, recently restored to full working order: the tidal pool beside it is now a yacht marina. Woodbridge contains many elderly though vigorous people, and its reputation as a good place for longevity is longstanding: Cromwell's Excursions of 1819 noted its 'healthy and salubrious air, many of its inhabitants having lived to the advanced age of eighty, ninety, and some few to near a hundred years old'.

As well as being a port and a market town, Woodbridge was, from the time of the Reformation, the administrative centre for the Liberty of St Etheldreda, granted by the English King Edgar in 970 to the Abbey of Ely. When the abbey was dissolved in 1540, the Dean and Chapter of Ely Cathedral were permitted to retain its privileges, and derived benefits from the Liberty until it eventually became subsumed in the local government reforms of the nineteenth century. The Liberty, also known as the Wicklaw, extended over six hundreds, those of Plomesgate, Loes, Thredling, Carlford, Wilford and Colneis. (Incidentally, St Etheldreda, the royal founder and patron saint of Ely, was popularly known as St Audrey. St Audrey was held to have despised the wearing of jewelled necklaces, and so when, in Early Stuart times, ladies began to wear silk neckties, these were called 'St Audrey's Lace', soon abbreviated to 'Tawdry Lace'. When this became more generally worn, and of cheaper quality, 'tawdry' came into its present general use.)

The true centre of Woodbridge is up the hill at the Market Square, in which stands the Shire Hall, structurally Elizabethan but with most of its features early eighteenth-century Dutch, including gables with strapwork frills: it was originally open on the ground floor. To the side of the square stands St Mary's Church, happily secluded from the ceaseless traffic, so that its churchyard seems almost rural, and is, indeed, quieter than in the days of the Puritans, when it was freely used by traders and dealers. The great tower, thirty-three metres high, is embattled and pinnacled, and decorated with elaborate flushwork on the parapet and at the base. The arms on either side of the west door beneath the tower are those of the ancient families of Brotherton and Segrave, but the greater part of the money for the church came from the new merchants and ship-owners of the time, with names such as Kemp, Albrede, Spicer and Gooding.

Woodbridge flourished particularly in the time of Queen Elizabeth because of favours bestowed on it by one of its sons. Thomas Seckford, of Seckford Hall, Great Bealings, was a lawyer who became Master of the Court of Requests in the first year of the Queen's reign, and subsequently Surveyor of the Court of Wards and Liveries, both positions of enormous influence with great opportunities for personal enrichment. He acquired the Stewardship of the Liberty of St Etheldreda, he represented Ipswich in Parliament, and he purchased the estate of the former Augustinian priory of Woodbridge. In old age he found himself childless, and decided to found almshouses at Woodbridge, which he endowed with property in Clerkenwell in Middlesex. During the nineteenth century

The tomb of Sir Thomas Kytson at Hengrave. *Edmund Lovell/Suffolk Record Office, Ipswich.*

Holy Trinity Church, Blythburgh, standing above the water-meadows of the River Blyth. *Miles Jebb*.

St Mary's, Stoke by Nayland, and its mighty tower. *Suffolk Record Office, Ipswich*.

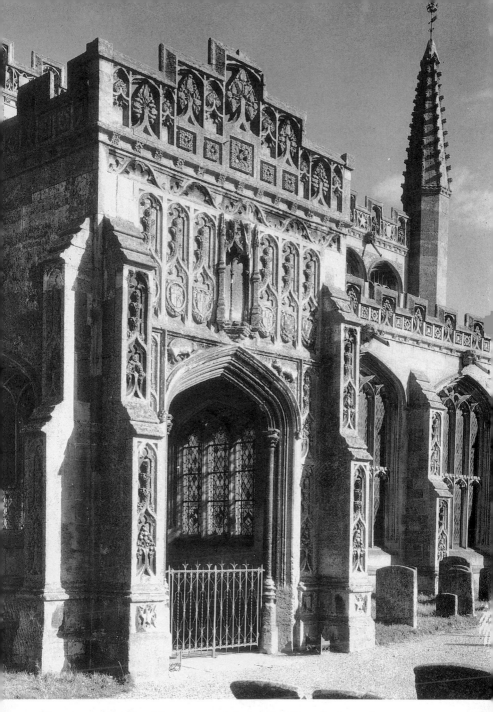

The ornate porch of St Peter and St Paul's Church, Lavenham.
National Monuments Record/RCHME Crown Copyright.

Sotterley Hall and Park. *Suffolk Record Office, Ipswich.*

The busy scene at Orford during the last century, overlooked by the keep of Henry II's castle. *Suffolk Record Office, Ipswich.*

The beach at Felixstowe a century ago: everyone fully clothed, and bathers protected by machines. *Suffolk Record Office, Ipswich.*

The sea-front at Aldeburgh, with the beach right up against the houses. *Images Colour Library.*

The colossal oval rotunda of Ickworth House. *Britain on View/Mirror Syndication International.*

Suffolk Punch horses at work. *Kit Houghton.*

Pre-mechanical harvest at Woodbridge. *Suffolk Record Office, Ipswich.*

Angel Hill, Bury St Edmund's in 1780, with monastery gates, Assembly Rooms, and Angel Inn. *Suffolk Record Office, Bury St Edmunds.*

The enormous Palladian frontage of Heveningham Hall. *National Monuments Record/RCHME Crown Copyright.*

The formidable curtain walls of Framlingham Castle, seat of the medieval Earls of Norfolk. *S. & O. Matthews Photography.*

this property became immensely valuable as London expanded, and the Seckford Foundation continues to benefit Woodbridge to this day.

Contemporary with Thomas Seckford was a Woodbridge man who became a hero of his time. John Fox was the master gunner in a trading ship, the *Three Half Moons*, which was attacked by Turkish galleys off Gibraltar in 1563. After a fight, the surviving crew were captured and put to work as galley slaves, and most died of the ordeal. During the winter months the galleys lay up in the harbour at Alexandria, where the slaves were shut in prisons, their legs, as always, shackled in irons. But Fox was a natural survivor, and was by now getting perks and privileges through his skills as a barber and allowed out of the prison on parole, together with a few others. In January 1577, he decided to organise a mass escape. The prison governor was enticed into a house where Fox murdered him. Together with his fellow trusties, Fox then overwhelmed some of the guards and released the prisoners, who were provided with files to cut their leg-irons. There was then a great rush to prepare a galley and scuttle the others, and soon they were sailing towards the harbour entrance, running the gauntlet between the two forts which fired ineffectually on them. There were 268 men on board, from sixteen Christian countries, with John Fox in command. Famished and exhausted, but with only eight lives lost, they eventually reached a monastery at Candia on Crete. Despite being a Protestant, John Fox was commended by the Pope and given a gunner's commission by the King of Spain. Two years later, however, he came home to England, where he was awarded a state pension, and for several years he sailed a ship in the coastal trade between Blythburgh and London.

Woodbridge and its surrounding district provide a literary hunting-ground for those in search of Edward Fitzgerald. For half a century after his death he enjoyed a fabulous popularity through his famous translation and adaptation of the Rubáiyát of the Persian poet, Omar Khayyám. This sensuous and aesthetic work became probably the most widely read poem in the English language, and went into hundreds of editions. There is much about Edward Fitzgerald's life to fascinate us, and his reclusion and eccentricity serve to enrich our conception of rural life in mid-nineteenth century Suffolk.

He was born at Bredfield (broad-field) House, just outside Woodbridge, from which his family then moved to Boulge House, a mile away (Boulge is from an Old French word meaning an uncultivated clearing). In 1837, at the age of twenty-eight, he removed himself to a cottage by the entrance to the drive in a half-hearted attempt to withdraw from the influence of his dominating mother. After her death, he found the proximity of his brother's family too much, and bought an old farmhouse at Melton (mill-place). At the age of forty-seven, he most unwisely decided to marry, but immediately realised his mistake ('I'm going to be married – don't congratulate me'); and after he and his wife had parted he went to live in lodgings in the Market Place at Woodbridge. As a boy he had attended the Grammar School at Bury. As an older man he often took lodgings at Lowestoft. He frequently stayed with his married sister at Geldeston, near Beccles. So he was splendidly steeped – one might say, fermented – in Suffolk, and his admiration for the county often strikes a chord today.

He delighted in bright colours, and the crops 'as they grow green, yellow, russet, and are finally carried away in the red and blue waggons with the sorrel horse'. He filled his garden with cottage flowers, anemonies, wallflowers, irises, poppies. Walking was for him a regular form of exercise, and he fulminated against the landlords who blocked the ancient footpaths, and deplored the intensification of agriculture – the squires who 'only use the Earth for an *Investment*: cut down every old Tree: level every Violet Bank: and make the old country of my Youth hideous to me in my decline'. This led him towards sailing. He bought a boat, the *Waveney*, which was succeeded by the specially-commissioned *Scandal*. Fitz didn't himself participate in the sailing, but sat and admired the scene, or read from Sophocles: 'I am happiest going in my little boat round the coast to Aldbro', with some Bottled Porter and some Bread and Cheese, and some good rough Soul who works the Boat and chews his Tobacco in peace'. In this way he came to know the Suffolk coast intimately.

In a rural community such as Woodbridge, social convention was paramount, and a man of means was expected to keep an appropriate establishment, dress correctly, and attend the services of the Church of England. Edward Fitzgerald, who enjoyed a substantial private income, especially after the death of his mother, decided to ignore convention. In Boulge Cottage his natural indolence and untidiness soon got the better of things. Visitors might be admitted by Fitz, unshaven, and in his dressing-gown and slippers. They would find his study littered with paintings propped against the walls, books and music scattered about, and boots, hats and sticks and other lumber cluttering everywhere. Against the wall was an upright piano at which he would play Handel and Mozart to himself, and to his black retriever, Bletsoe, and his parrot, Beauty Bob. As he got older he became increasingly slovenly. He would walk through the streets of Woodbridge in a seafarer's coat and trousers of baggy blue cloth, with a green and grey shawl over his shoulders; he wore a stand-up collar and black silk tie, and a battered top hat secured in windy weather by a large handkerchief knotted below his chin. His was a vegetarian and near-teetotaller, though he smoked his pipe incessantly. He ignored the services of the church. He spoke in a husky voice, with a melancholic deflection at the end of the sentence. He was capricious, and could be unpredictably courteous or abruptly rude. He was congenitally lazy.

For friends he had his Woodbridge cronies: George Crabbe, son of the poet; Thomas Churchyard, the solicitor better known for his landscape painting; Bernard Barton, bank-clerk and poet; and Francis Capper Brooke, an antiquarian. But for deeper emotions he envinced platonic infatuations for two men. The first of these was William Kenworthy Browne, the wealthy son of a Bedford merchant. After Browne's premature death, Fitz was desolated, but soon found a substitute in a much wilder figure, 'Posh' Fletcher, a Lowestoft fisherman. Fitz had taken to prowling around the quays with a bottle in his hand, searching for kindred spirits. Here was 'a man of the finest Saxon type, with a complexion *vif, mâle et flamboyant*, blue eyes, a nose less than Roman, more than Greek, and strictly auburn hair that any woman might sigh to possess'. He loved to go out sailing with Posh at the helm, while he sat in the stern, splashed by the spray. It was for Posh that he financed a new fishing lugger, named suggestively the *Meum and Tuum* (known locally as the *Mum and Tum*); but the venture was not a success, any hope of profit being destroyed by Posh's heavy drinking sessions.

Edward Fitzgerald's eccentricity was partly inherited: he and his mother were both the children of first cousins. He was of Irish descent and would, one feels, have been more at home in the streets of Dublin than Woodbridge. It was his disastrous relationship with his own flamboyant mother that directed him down the solitary path of his life, and made him into a profound misogynist. His natural kindliness was apt to evaporate in any bothersome encounters with women. What must have been the feelings of his wife when they met, for the first time in years, in Woodbridge? Fitz was walking with Posh: 'I said, "how d'ye do, Ma'am; how long have you been here?" I made off.' Beneath this sort of cruelty was a deeply melancholic man, whose life, as has been said, was 'a succession of sighs, each stifled ere half uttered'.

Beneath the tower of the lonely church of St Michael, Boulge, is his solitary grave, for he refused to be buried in the adjacent family mausoleum. On it is a Persian rose from the grave of Omar Khayyám at Naishapur; and on the stone are inscribed the words 'It is he that hath made us, and not we ourselves', which is the nearest Biblical equivalent to the Rubáiyát's 'We are helpless – thou hast made us what we are'.

Woodbridge is close to the head of the estuary into which the Deben flows at Melton. A few miles upstream is where the dynasty of the Wuffingas established their chief settlement. Rendlesham is now not even a village, just a few houses on a buff above the left bank of the river, but there is no doubt, from a reference to it in Bede's *History of the Anglo-Saxons*, that it was the seat of the King of the East Angles. No trace of the palace remains, although, tantalisingly, one of the fields was known as Great Woodenhall within the last two hundred years; and, as a further clue, the church is dedicated to St Gregory, which implies that it was one of the earliest in the kingdom. Across the river is Ufford, whose name is thought to derive from Uffa, the founder of the dynasty. And just downstream from Woodbridge is the manor of Kingston, also with royal implications.

The Wuffingas arrived during the mid-sixth century, and were themselves of Swedish origin, linked to the royal house of Uppsala. They created a unified kingdom of East Anglia and ruled it for two centuries. The most authoritative member of this dynasty was Raedwald, who died in 625. He was nominated as the presiding monarch (*bretwalda*) by his fellow Anglo-Saxon kings, an exceptional honour to bestow on the ruler of such a secondary and peripheral kingdom. His statesmanlike approach is evident from the way he hedged his bets at a time when the Christian gospel was first being preached in England. In his temple at Rendlesham he installed a Christian altar, but retained a smaller pagan altar beside it, letting it be known that he was persuaded to do so by his wife.

After the short reign of Raedwald's son, Eorpwald, East Anglia became Christian under Sigeberht, thought to be Raedwald's step-son. Sigeberht was an unworldly man who abdicated and retired to the monastery he had endowed at Beodricsworth (later St Edmundsbury). When East Anglia was invaded in 636 by Penda, the pagan king of Mercia, Sigeberht was pulled out of the monastery to bolster morale. But he refused to bear arms, and the sight of him wearing monk's robes and with his head tonsured, and carrying a white wand to symbolise peace, can hardly have inspired confidence at the ensuing battle, where he was killed. Penda acted with equal ruthlessness eighteen years later, when he once again overran East Anglia and slew Sigeberht's successor, Anna. Thereafter the Wuffingas were obliged to swear allegiance to the Mercian kings, though they remained unmolested for nearly a century, the last of the line being Aelfwald, who died in 740.

The wooden hall of the Wuffingas at Rendlesham may long ago have rotted into the ground, and our historical knowledge of this distant dynasty may only be slight. But their life-style has been most dramatically revealed by, of all things, their death-style, for one of their graves has miraculously survived intact to be uncovered by modern archaeologists. The death of a ruler in those closed and tribal societies symbolised the death of the entire people, so it is a most satisfactory paradox that the possessions buried with one of these rulers for the purposes of his journey into the world of the shades should be almost the only artefacts to have emerged into the modern world – unless maybe the Angles would have judged the Suffolk of today to be indeed a 'world of the shades' come true, a world of endless feasting and unimaginable comforts. Although we cannot be absolutely certain, it is quite likely that the grave is that of Raedwald, which would account for the particular splendour of his burial.

Sutton Hoo (the spur of land by the south place), the site of this ancient royal graveyard, is about half a mile inland from the banks of the Deben opposite Woodbridge. It is on higher ground and, denuded of intervening trees, would have stood out prominently against the horizon to all who travelled in boats on the tide to Rendlesham. To the Angles, their boats were more than just a convenient method of transport. They represented the skill, courage and discipline with which they had mastered the seas and migrated from the continent. So it was natural that the body of the king should be buried in a ship for his ghostly journey.

When the ground had been cleared away, a trench was dug that would exactly fit the ship. The ship selected was not, it seems, a new ship so much as a superannuated royal barge – in this particular respect, the tribe economised a bit – but it was of impressive proportions, being twenty-seven metres long and four and a half wide, and fitted with rowlocks for twenty oars on each side, and a large steering paddle, lashed to the starboard side. It must have been hauled up from the river on rollers and, seemingly, its stern was damaged as it was dropped into the trench. This ship was revealed to the archaeologists of 1939 and 1965 in the form of a shadow, for none of the wood had survived, and it was discernible only from its iron rivets and the sand cast of its planks and frames.

A burial chamber was then constructed amidships, and inside was laid the body of the king – at least, so it is supposed, although the acidic conditions of the soil at Sutton Hoo have destroyed virtually all organic material. He was surrounded by his regalia. His helmet was forged from a single piece of iron covered with plates of silvery foil with decorative motifs, some from Scandinavian mythology; and to it were attached deep ear-flaps and neck-guard, and an oval face-mask. His sword was pattern-welded and, together with its scabbard and belt, was mounted with superb gold and *cloisonné* garnet fittings. His circular shield of limewood and hide was bound with gilt-bronze clips and strips, and mounted with representations of a dragon and a bird of prey; at its centre was a highly decorated boss, with garnet-eyed animal heads. We may imagine that at great folk gatherings or important ceremonial occasions the king would have manifested himself in these glorious and awe-inspiring trappings, perhaps out of doors and on horseback, the silver of his helmet and his drawn sword flashing in the sun.

But this was not all that was buried with the king. There was a strange totem, a whetstone carved at either end with sombre, bearded faces. There were spears and angons and an axe-hammer and a coat of chain-mail. There was his hoard of silver, manufactured in the Eastern Roman Empire. This comprised a great dish with a deep foot-ring, and a fluted bowl with a female head at the centre, and a nest of shallow bowls, and a pair of spoons (inscribed with the Christian names of Paul and Saul); also, a bronze bowl. Then there were drinking horns with silver-gilt mounts; hanging bowls with Celtic decoration; a maplewood lyre; gaming pieces; and domestic equipment including a large bronze cauldron together with the chain from which it would have been suspended from the rafters of the hall.

From passages from the great Anglo-Saxon poem *Beowulf*, we can envisage the scenes that accompanied the burial of the king: the infilling of the grave and the heaping of the mound by the men, the ululation of the women, and finally the circling of the grave by the leading warriors in their full regalia on horseback. Surely there were robed priests who evoked the pagan gods and placated them with sacrifices – mutilated skeletons are much in evidence at Sutton Hoo. It is possible that this particular burial was the most splendid that had ever been seen by the East Angles, and it could have represented a defiance of the old Scandinavian customs and beliefs against the new ideas emanating from Gaul, as expressed in Christianity.

Though they would hardly have dared to express it, I cannot but suppose that Raedwald's sons – Eorpwald and Sigeberht – must have experienced a few mixed feelings as they watched all those prized possessions being consigned forever to the earth in what was in effect a pretty swingeing inheritance tax. The local Anglian craftsmen and embroiderers, however, must have looked forward to a welcome spate of royal orders: that is, to the extent that the grave treasures had actually been made in England. The central regalia at Sutton Hoo bears a close relationship to the near-contemporary hoards at Vendel and Valsgarde in Sweden. Undoubtedly the Wuffingas originated as a Scandinavian dynasty, and we cannot tell to what extent their kingdom had developed its own autonomous craftsmanship in the early seventh century.

For ten days the royal treasure of Raedwald was owned by Edith Pretty, the landowner of Sutton Hoo in 1939. The question for the local coroner's court was whether it was treasure trove, in which case it would have belonged to the Crown. In a controversial ruling, the court found that it was not treasure trove because it had been buried without any intention of recovery. Mrs Pretty decided of her own accord to give it to the nation. After spending the war buried even deeper against enemy bombs, the work of restoration began, and the Sutton Hoo treasure is now the most prized exhibit of Early Medieval Art in the British Museum. The East Angles may be one of the most obscure of the early English kingdoms, but they do indeed take pride of place when it comes to visual display, and it is good to think of this corner of the Suffolk sandlings – where archaeological activity still continues – yielding up such incomparable riches.

Rendlesham has undergone a strange metamorphosis in recent years. The wartime airfield at Bentwaters, right next door, became the large American Air Force base of the Cold War, and, now that the base is to close, who knows what further development will occur? Meanwhile, the Victorian mansion at Rendlesham has been pulled down and is commemorated only by two early Gothic-revival lodges of the previous hall, one a sham ruin and the other in the form of a medieval shrine, with flying buttresses supporting a central pinnacle which serves as the chimney. These two architectural relics seem appropriate reminders of the faded fortunes of the Thelluson family, who took their title from their estate at Rendlesham. Peter Isaac Thelluson, who died in 1797, had accumulated an immense fortune, and left a will in which £100,000 went to his wife and children, but with the remainder, which amounted to £600,000, being consigned to a trust which was destined for his eventual and as yet unborn eldest great-grandson. This unusual and eccentric designation of family affairs was the cause of two important legal processes. In 1800 an Act of Parliament forbade accumulations of more than twenty-one years. And in 1859, after many years of legal battling between rival contenders for the fortune, the House of Lords gave a final ruling which was to the benefit of the primogenitive great-grandson, rather than the eldest in birth; but the legal costs had been so enormous that nearly all the fortune was lost.

Time has been kind to Ufford, just across the valley, which retains its core of old houses, insulated from traffic by very narrow lanes. Ufford has also been lucky in the preservation of the medieval furnishings of St Mary's Church, now designated with Catholic emphasis 'The Church of the Assumption of Our Lady, Mother of God', where a daily eucharist has been celebrated for nearly a century. Perhaps this emphasises a continuing anti-Puritan tradition in Ufford, for in 1643 the churchwardens put up a commendable passive resistance to William Dowsing and his gang of image-smashers. Dowsing recorded that:

... we were kept out of the Church above 2 hours, and neither the Churchwardens, *William Brown*, nor *Roger Small*, that were enjoyned these things above three months afore, had not done them in May, and I sent one then to see it done, and they would not let him have the key. And now, neither the Churchwardens, nor *William Brown*, nor the Constable *James Tokelove*, and *William Gardener* the Sexton, would not let us have the key, in 2 hours time. New Churchwardens, *Thomas Stanard, Thomas Stroud*. And *Samuel Canham*, of the same town, said, 'I (i.e. Dowsing) sent men to rifle the Church;' – and *Will. Brown*, old Churchwarden, said, 'I went about to pull down the Church, and had carried away part of the Church'.

Though he did take the angels off the roof and swept the church clean of 'superstitious pictures' and inscriptions, he spared the star attraction of the church, the glorious wooden font-cover, despite taking all the statues off it. This work of art, suspended from the roof, rises for five and a half metres above the stone font. It soars in gracefully receding tiers, all decorated with elaborate pinnacles, canopies and tabernacle work, and the lower part is telescopic, and can be slid up over the superstructure when the font is to be used for baptism. The cover is surmounted by a carved pelican, a mystic symbol of Christ. The pelican need not feel lonely on his perch, because the contemporary bench-ends portray quite a menagerie of mythical and heraldic beasts. In few other Suffolk churches is the visual impact of fifteenth-century woodwork so strong as at Ufford. Into the small space of the nave are fitted the fascinating figure-ended benches, the strong roof with its tie beams, the remains of the rood screen – its dado and its beam across the chancel arch – and the great vertical font cover.

Rendlesham may well have been where the noble Wuffingas sired their princes, but Ufford is the birthplace of an even more pure-blooded dynasty. The entire breed of Suffolk Punches are descended from Mr Crisp's Horse of Ufford, which foaled here in 1768. The Suffolk Punch is Suffolk's most distinctive contribution to the animal kingdom, and he exemplifies the finest traditions of pre-mechanical farming. Merely to look at him is to perceive the dogged strength, the temperamental placidity, and the specialised skills, with which the farms were worked by men and horses. The Suffolk Punch was the ultimate draught animal: he not only replaced the oxen but outperformed all other draught-horses in application to heavy soils. No wonder that for many people the few remaining Suffolk Punches represent the old ways, and are the focus for those who deplore the total mechanisation of agriculture.

The Suffolk Punch today appears as a noble and beautiful creature in its own right: chestnut in colour, with a big forehead, a deep neck, long shoulders, well-rounded rib and deep carcass. But at first he was considered ill-proportioned, despite his merits as a draught horse. Arthur Young wrote that 'an uglier horse could not be viewed; sorrel colour, very low in the fore end, a large ill-shaped head, with slouching heavy ears, a great carcass and short legs' – features which earned him the contemptuous nickname 'Punch'. He was certainly at the opposite end of the scale to the fleet Arabian race-horses. His extraordinary shape was awesome, and Herman Biddell records that the Champion, Catlin's Duke 296, born in 1846, had a hollow in his back big enough to hold a pail of water: this horse was so placid that a child could manage him, but so potent that he booked more than 220 mares in a year. In spite of all the inbreeding, the Suffolk Punch is a supremely calm horse that will stand for hours immersed in deepest contemplation. But on the rare occasions that he does become nervous, the grooms are said to be able to calm him by the application of a time-honoured unguent, consisting of a frog's bone cured in a special mixture of herbs and chemicals, which is believed to immobilise the horse if rubbed on his shoulder.

The breed was developed in studs not far from Ufford – Rendlesham, Sudbourne, Butley, Newbourn and Melton – where extensive enclosures protected the mares from ill-bred stallions, and it was perfected by the 1840s. Soon the Suffolk Punches were becoming the normal horses on the farms, with Beauty, Captain, Brag, Duke and Prince as their most usual names. After feeding, they were turned out at half past six in the morning. They responded to the customary calls of 'cup-hey' for turning left and 'woosh' for turning right. Their seasonal work consisted of harvest in summer, moving on during the autumn to muck-spreading and carting off the mangels and cattle beet, and in the spring to drilling, then harrowing and hoeing. But their heaviest work was the winter ploughing. The fields were ploughed in 'stetches' of land, which allowed for the drainage of the field. One man and his team were usually reckoned to plough three quarters of an acre in one day. They worked on in one go, with only a twenty-minute break for elevenses, till half past two. They were then taken back to the stables, where they were fed a stone of corn for each working day, plus unlimited amounts of chaff. Great attention was paid to their grooming, with the coat being made to shine by the application of leaves of tansey, saffron or briony.

The horsemen who looked after the Suffolk Punches were superior to the ordinary farm labourers, and were paid a fixed weekly wage, unlike the 'daymen'. At the end of the last century their customary dress consisted of a cap, a red-spotted muffler, a sleeved waistcoat with a velvet front and cotton-cloth back and sleeves, cord breeches, sometimes lined with flannel, knee buskins and heavy boots. On Sundays it was a bowler hat, cord jacket and cord trousers whose outside edge was trimmed with steel-faced horse-shoe buttons.

Wickham (farm-home) Market is the next town above Woodbridge on the Deben, and it is where the main road has crossed the river from the earliest times. It was the home of John Kirby, an enthusiast who made a study of the entire county in 1732–4 and produced *The Suffolk Traveller*, a classic source of information for local historians. So his entry for Wickham Market is of interest. He begins by explaining that it is called Wickham Market to distinguish it from two other Wickhams, Wickham-Brook and Wickham-Skeith, but that it no longer had a market. Likewise the legal quarter sessions had been removed to Letheringham. Clearly, the town had seen better days. As if to find some compensation for this faded scene in his home town, Kirby goes on to boast that from the top of the tower fifty other churches can be seen on a clear day. This seems to be pardonable exaggeration and, so far as I know, no one has verified this claim, though maybe one could score the fifty by scaling to the top of the tall lead-covered spire above the tower, and certainly, since Kirby's day, at least fifty of the high-tension wire pylons that stride like giants past Wickham Market from Sizewell, can be all too clearly seen. He then explains that the manor of Wickham was originally owned by the family of Ufford, but then acquired by the nunnery at Campsey Ash: at the Dissolution of the Monasteries it was sold to Anthony Wingfield, and by him to the Earl of Rochford. The rectory of Wickham Market, together with those of Pettistree and Bing, so Kirby informs us, were vested in a trust for the benefit of the widows and orphans of the clergy around Ipswich. Finally, he tells us that the brick south aisle of the church (All Saints) was financed by Walter Fulburn, who was buried in it in 1489.

In the stretches above Wickham Market the Deben flows across weirs at the sites of several water-mills. Letheringham's mill has been partially restored, and has, one feels, exorcised the horror of the murder of the miller and his son that took place in 1696. Close by, the Easton Farm Park provides a fine display of farming methods past and present, with many rare breeds of animals, as well as old machinery. This is the former Home Farm of the estate at Easton, which was in Victorian times run on model lines, being owned by the ducal family of Douglas-Hamilton. They are no longer at Easton (east-place), and their house has been pulled down. But reminders of them are to be seen in the laundry and the dairy, and the kennels, still used by the local hunt, the Easton Harriers. Also in the quality of the cottages and the provision of a village hall and a school, all aspects of a privately-owned village, in contrast to the 'open' villages of the time, with their crowded hovels.

As a grand flourish, the Hamilton's entire park and grounds, comprising sixty hectares, were enclosed with a serpentine wall. Serpentine garden walls (also known as crinkle-crankle, or ribbon walls) orginated as a peculiarity in Suffolk during the late-eighteenth century, and at least fifteen remain from that time. Their purpose was mainly decorative, though fruit trees could be neatly trained into the concave bays. The wall at Easton, though now destroyed in many places, was the longest in East Anglia and probably in the world, and was built right up to the walls of All Saints church, enabling the aristocrats to enter privately for worship. Their privacy was also safeguarded within the church itself by boxed and canopied pews on either side of the altar, installed during the seventeenth century by the previous owners of the estate, the Wingfields.

By contrast, the great house at Helmingham, whose park is watered by a stream which flows into the Deben, is still occupied by the Tollemache family for whom it was built in Tudor times. Though embellished by architecture of the eighteenth and nineteenth centuries and the artistry of Nash and Salvin, it appears from a distance to be in its original state, with its moat and its gatehouse and its redbrick walls. This impression is all the more convincing when one surveys the park around it, in my view the finest piece of park landscaping in Suffolk, a wide sweep of grassland so large that its other side cannot be seen, dotted with clumps and groves of oaks, and grazed by red and fallow deer and highland cattle.

The monuments of the Tollemaches make the interior of St Mary's Helmingham more like a family chapel than a parish church. One of them is to the first four Tollemaches, that is to say, the first who had real wealth and power. The founder of this line was the Lionel Tollemache who died in 1550, a successful lawyer who was patronised by the Duke of Norfolk and married an heiress, though he felt it necessary to claim his Norman blood:

> Baptized Lyone Tollemache my Name
> Since Normans Conquest of unsoyled Fame
> Shews my Descent from Ancestors of Worth;
> And that my life might not belye my Birth,
> Their Virtues Track with heedful steps I trod,
> Rightful to Men, Religious towards God.
>
> Trained in the Law, I gain'd the Bar and Bench,
> Not bent to Kindle Strife, but rather Quench;
> Gentle to Clients, in my Counsels Just,
> With Norfolk's Great Duke in no little Trust;
> Sir Joyce his heir was my Fair Faithful Wife;
> Bently my Seat, and Sev'nty Years my Life.

Other memorials record the martial fortunes of later Tollemaches, who seem to have been unlucky in war. A Lionel Tollemache was killed at Valenciennes in 1793, 'the only British officer killed on that occasion'. His father, John, had been killed in a duel in New York. His uncle George was killed 'by falling from the mast-head of the *Modeste* man-of-war at sea'; and his uncle William was 'lost in the *Repulse* frigate, in a hurricane in the Atlantic Ocean'. But perhaps the most unlucky was Thomas Tollemache, a General who contended with John Churchill for military command in the days of William III. He was handed the poisoned chalice of leading an amphibious expedition to destroy the port of Brest, where he died at the head of his men, 'not without suspicion of being made a sacrifice in this desperate attempt, through the envy of some of his pretended friends'. Churchill went on to become the Duke of Marlborough.

The fortunes of the great seem out of place at Charsfield, midway between Helmingham and Easton, because this is the village most closely associated with Ronald Blythe's *Akenfield*, a social history based on the verbal accounts of local people. He portrays a community which was beginning to be sucked into the modern world, largely as the result of the two wars, but was still dreaming memories of the rustic, pre-mechanised age of earlier this century, and of the mysterious and intuitive side of country life, as against the literate and informed. The old people told him horror stories of the harshness of the farmers and the pretentions of the gentry (the under-gardener had been ordered to swing his arms as he went about his work, and the maids were told to face the wall when the lady passed them in the house), but some of them were still undeniably nostalgic about the old days. Their hardiness had been inherited from centuries of manual toil, and the ancient traditions of village thriftiness are admirably demonstrated in the cottage garden created at Charsfield by Peggy Cole, and called 'Akenfield'.

Life at Charsfield-Akenfield may have been tough, but it seldom degenerated into personal degradation or persecution. At Brandeston, just upstream on the left bank of the Deben, one of the most horrible instances of seventeenth-century cruelty was perpetrated on the eccentric and elderly vicar, John Lowes. He was accused of being a wizard. In order to obtain a confession, he was kept awake for several nights, and dragged backwards and forwards around a room until he was insensible to what he was saying. No clergyman was allowed to attend him before he was strung up on the gallows at Bury, so he had to read the Burial Service from the Prayer Book to himself.

The sources of the Deben converge into the eponymous Debenham (though, unlike the river, the town is pronounced with a short initial 'e'), a small town, or large village, with a long medieval street that rises in the middle and a church, St Mary's, whose tower may be pre-Norman. James Cornish, son of a late-Victorian vicar of Debenham, has left an engaging account of the parish he remembered as a boy. This was a time of improvements, at any rate to the church, to the schools, and to the roads. But it was also a time when farming declined from a period of prosperity to one of acute depression. During the 1860s the demand for arable had been so intense that isolated trees were felled, and woods and the wide grass verges of country lanes were annexed for ploughing. But during the 1880s fields lay fallow, hedges untrimmed and farmsteads unrepaired. After the freak wet summer of 1879, grass even stood unmown and barley unharvested. But, as today, the misfortunes of farmers were a boon to naturalists. James and his brothers were particularly well-informed on natural history, and roamed the parish, rough-shooting or bird-nesting or fossil-finding, but always observing. Their favourite spot was near the source of one of the headwater streams, where a wood loud with wrens and nightingales stood beside a meadow bright with cowslips and fritillaries, in which the stream had formed gulls in the blue clay.

For here, above Debenham, we have reached the centre of the great stretch of chalky boulder-clay, the ancient Woodland, also known as High Suffolk. Partially cleared in Roman times, it was intensively settled during the Anglo-Saxon period, so much so that by the time of the Norman

Conquest it bore, together with central Norfolk, a rural population that was denser than anywhere else in England. This settlement had spread from up the river valleys, with their loamy soils, onto the higher acreages of thicker clay. The progressive clearances for ploughland or pasture, hacked out of intervening woods or copses, decade by decade and century by century, together with the early establishment of small-holdings, had the effect of creating homesteads separated from each other, which became formed into scattered villages. Not only was the village itself – the settlement around the original 'ton' or 'ham' – comprised of houses standing apart from each other and at all angles, but most parishes also contained satellite hamlets, usually with names designating a Green, Tye, End or Street. Even the church sites were often at isolated places, determined by a rough centrality to a dispersed community. The manorial strip-fields became progressively enclosed even during the Middle Ages, and their hedges and ditches followed the lines of the twisting lanes. Thus was our ancient countryside formed, or as Kipling puts it, in a poem that extolls our history-haunted landscape, 'And so was England born!'

The diligent cultivation of the land in High Suffolk was primarily the achievement of innumerable small-holders within the feudal system. Already at the time of Domesday Book (1086) Suffolk had registered more freemen than the whole of the rest of England put together, and their influence was felt during the twelfth and thirteenth centuries, when demand for food intensified with a growing population. The natural pressure for the consolidation of smallholdings into integrated farms was subsequently achieved during the sixteenth century, and the yeomen of High Suffolk increased their efficiency by means of extensive enclosures. The hedges and ditches with which the farmers bounded their fields were always hated by the peasantry who thereby lost their common pastures and were restricted to farm labour. So it is ironical that what were once the symbols of human exploitation should now be regarded as the adornments of the landscape and the sanctuaries of natural life.

The ditches through which the streams trickle into Debenham have for centuries drained the heavy clay soil on which the water accumulates. In addition to the ditches there are, in this part of the county, several good examples of moated houses. There are between five and six hundred moated sites of farmsteads or halls in Suffolk, dating mostly from between the twelfth and fifteenth centuries. They were dug mainly for drainage, important on the clay soil, and some also served for stock control and general security. They could equally be used as fish ponds, even though they must inevitably have received slops, or even sewage. Perhaps with this in mind the great Sir Samuel Barnardiston, when he constructed his new house at Brightwell, overlooking the Deben estuary, in the mid-seventeenth century, adopted an innovation in fitting a rainwater tank on the roof, in which he kept his fish.

Aspall Hall and Crows Hall, on either side of Debenham, are both moated, and have frontages of red brick with blue-brick decoration. Crows Hall is the older and smaller, a fragment of a Tudor house, and seat of the lords of the manor of Debenham. Aspall (aspen-corner) Hall is Jacobean, but was renovated in the eighteenth century and purchased by the Chevalliers, a French Protestant family, whose descendants still live there. The immigrant Chevalliers were industrious and enterprising. From 1728 they produced cider which attained a special quality, not only from the intelligent cultivation of apples, but also from the acquisition of a special cider-press from Normandy, a great granite trough with a cylindrical stone for crushing the apples. That same uncarbonated cider is still produced at Aspall; the press was in use till 1971 and still stands in working order in the Cyder House. Another achievement was the cultivation of a specially fine malting barley. This had been discovered by John Chevallier in 1831, in the garden of one of his labourers who, some years before, had found an enormous ear of barley in his boot after threshing, and planted it with dramatic results. This John Chevallier, incidentally, was the grandfather of Field Marshal Kitchener, and was himself a most authoritative figure in the district.

The abundance of late-medieval woodwork hidden away inside the manor- and farm-houses of Suffolk was dramatically revealed to me when I was visiting the house of some friends near Debenham. Climbing up to the attic by means of a narrow corkscrew stair, the carved tie-beams of an original great hall are dramatically revealed: huge barriers across the dark attic space, a wonderful place of mystery for the children in the adjoining bedrooms. Here it can be seen that the central part of the house, converted into its present three levels in Elizabethan times, was formerly just a single space – a great hall some nine metres high. It was heated by a central brazier, whose smoke still blackens some of the roof timbers. And it was decorated with an elaborate cornice, visible on the present first floor, with angels, shields and banners worthy of any church. All this inside what appears from outside to be a simple farmhouse, albeit moated.

Just west of Debenham are Monk Soham (lake-home) and Earl Soham, once belonging respectively to the Bury Monastery and the Earl of Norfolk. The rector of Monk Soham for most of the reign of Queen Victoria was Robert Hindes Groome, whose father John had been rector there for twenty-six years previously. Robert and his son Francis, who edited the popular 'Suffolk Notes and Queries' for the *Ipswich Journal*, were great gatherers of rustic anecdotes, and in his account of Robert's life at Monk Soham Francis has left us some delightful sketches of the ordinary village folk. There was Tom Pepper, a plain-speaking yeoman and a Dissenter, who attended the Chapel and not the Church, but who maintained a relationship of mutual respect with the Groomes despite such remarks as 'The clargy, they're here, and they ain't here; they're like pigs in the garden, and yeou can't git 'em out'. There was Susan Kemp, of direct speech, who would recount her ailments to the rector, such as her bowel troubles: 'That fare to go round and round, and then out ta come a-raspin' and a-roarin' '. In her back room lived two poor men, one a half-wit and the other blind, who both seem to have benefited from her constant demands upon them, a sort of occupational therapy. Also squeezed into the same house as

Susan, on the upper floor, was Willam Ruffles and his wife. Will told the rector of how he and a friend had once cured a woman of the fits by witchcraft. They boiled some clippings of her hair and nails, and then 'we h'ard a loud shrike a-roarin' up the chimley; and yeou may depind upon it, she warn't niver bad no more'.

Francis Groome also tells of the changes in farming that altered the face of the land in this corner of High Suffolk during his father's time there, and they have a curiously modern ring about them. The small farms had been amalgamated and reduced to half their number. The small fields had been made into larger ones, with much hedgerow destruction. Of the two greens, one had been enclosed. So many trees were taken out that the only substantial group remaining were the oaks, elms, beeches and limes that the Groomes had planted around their rectory. And several made-up roads had been introduced into a parish that had consisted solely of green lanes. With these shades of ancient yeoman farming in our minds' eyes, this is an appropriate place to conclude a description of the Deben.

VII
Ore and Alde

The rivers Alde and Ore meet near Blaxhall, and from there conflow as the Alde until just short of Orford, where the river's name changes back to Ore. The Alde used to join the sea around Orford, and the seven-mile extension to its mouth only developed during the sixteenth century, due to a massive southward shift of Orford Beach. The lower Ore also receives another river, the Butley, which is really a tidal limb fed by a stream.

The area of land between the estuaries of the Deben and the Alde was once largely open heaths and sheep walks, known as the Sandlings, or Sandlands, and stretching right up the coast towards Lowestoft. These lighter soils of glacial sands and gravels had been cleared and cultivated by early settlers, but gradually deteriorated as the top soils blew away. They came to be used extensively for sheep. Great flocks of over a thousand head, watched over by shepherds in long cloth cloaks with crook in hand, moved slowly forwards across the open land, munching the turf and keeping back the bushes, and unconscious of the magical musical effect created by their bleating mingled with their tiny tinkling bells. Until the seventeenth century their main value was in their wool, but later they were bred mainly for their meat, and Suffolk became a prime supplier of mutton and lamb to the London market. The quality was perfected by the creation of the Suffolk Black Face sheep, a cross between the Norfolk horned ewes and the famous South Down rams.

The crucial importance of sheep is demonstrated as early as the eleventh century in this tally of animals recorded in the Suffolk entry in Domesday Book: 768 horses of various sorts, 3,092 cattle, 4,343 goats, 9,843 swine, and 37,522 sheep.

During the Middle Ages the intensive rearing of sheep was universal throughout the county, and a vital element in the prosperity of High Suffolk. But subsequently its emphasis shifted to the grasslands of east and west, bought up by large landowners. When one considers that wool was originally Suffolk's greatest export, and that Suffolk's greatest industry was the cloth trade, itself based on wool, and then that the great flocks of Suffolks dominated whole areas of the county, one realises that sheep were indeed at the heart of Suffolk's economy for centuries.

Today a great part of the coastal land between Deben and Alde is taken up by plantations of the Forestry Commission or their successors – the largest in East Suffolk. Tunstall (farm-stead) Forest and Rendlesham Forest have transformed the former sandy heathlands. Their earlier plantings, which tended towards regimental blocks of conifers, suffered astonishing damage in the 1987 hurricane, when in a single night much of the forest was blown down. But their subsequent replantings have been more sensitively planned, with many healthy clearings for wild-life. Situated between these recent afforestations is an utterly different piece of woodland at Staverton Park. Here are ancient coppiced oaks, probably emparked from wildwood in Saxon times, and with a remnant of primeval woodland known as the Staverton Thicks. 'Thicks' is the right word for this venerable place, an almost impenetrable undergrowth of holly, hawthorn, elder, ash and briar beneath the foliage of hundreds of medieval pollard oaks. Hugh Farmer, who has sensitively portrayed this area in *The Cottage in the Forest*, describes the hollies as 'out topping and strangling the oaks'. It is mysterious and wild, and we can perhaps sense the awe with which primitive man must have entered it. But it is also vulnerable and pathetic, and invokes feelings of guilt that such an exiguous fragment remains. Our only consolation must be that we have not entirely squandered the inheritance of the oak forests, thanks to the exceptional quantity of medieval timber that remains in Suffolk in the form of posts, trusses, beams and roofs in houses and churches.

The Augustinian Priory at Butley was once the richest

monastery in East Suffolk. Its buildings have long since vanished, or are barely traceable among the farm buildings, with the exception of its magnificent gatehouse, which was converted into an elegant dwelling in 1737 and then restored in 1926 for M.J. Rendall on his retirement as Headmaster of Winchester College. This gatehouse dates from the early fourteenth century and its frontage provides one of the earliest and finest displays of flushwork – that interplay of stone and flint so beloved of Suffolk's medieval masons. The stone had to be imported, and in this particular case it came from quarries south of Paris in the valley of the Yonne. With this material the masons carved all sorts of decorative devices, such as sham windows and statue-niches, and also a panel of thirty-five armorial shields of the powerful families. This acknowledge-ment to secular patronage became especially appropriate at Butley in Tudor times, and Princess Mary, Duchess of Suffolk, came twice to the Priory for lengthy summer visits, bringing her own furnishings. We catch a flavour of her life there from letters which refer to alfresco meals, dining under the oaks in Staverton forest and, on one occasion, taking refuge in a church when the rain came on. Since her marriage was a love-match, it all sounds most romantic, though actually her husband was only with her for some of the time, being otherwise much occupied in county and state affairs.

At the head of the Butley creek stands St Peter's, Chillesford (gravel-ford), whose tower is built, exceptionally, of Coralline Crag, light brown and roughly textured. To the east of it is Sudbourne (south-stream), whose large estate was once re-nowned for one of the finest partridge shoots in England; it was very nearly purchased by Edward VII (when Prince of Wales) rather than Sandringham. Kenneth Clark, whose parents came to own it, has given an amusing description of those grand shoots at the beginning of this century. An army of beaters, dressed in smocks with red lapels, drove the birds towards the guns, who included crack shots such as Lord Ripon and the Prince of Wales (the future George V). The competitiveness was such that if a good shot had an off day he went into a great sulk, and dinner had to be taken up to his room on a tray. Gluttony was never far away from the Edwardian shoots, and besides their cooked breakfasts and sumptuous dinners, the guests enjoyed heavy lunches in pavilions in the woods, where they ate oysters and liver pâté, steak and kidney pudding, cold turkey and ham, treacle tart, double Cottenham cheese, and plum cake 'to fill the corners'. Kenneth, the percipient son of the house, was able to view such follies with detachment, and to turn his acute visual sense instead to the beauty of the sandlings around Sudbourne, to the hazy lines of the Scotch Pines on foggy mornings, or the light reflected from the ponds and meres, all of which was to prove such a sound foundation for his life as an art critic and connoisseur, and, in particular, to the theories developed in his book *Landscape into Art*. Suffolk, he has written, offers 'the best kind of scenery for a landscape painter'.

During the early nineteenth century, the villages of the 'Butley peninsula' (such as Bawdsey, Hollesley, Eyke and Butley) were noted for the vigour and spirit with which they competed in games of 'camp'. Camp was a primitive version of Rugby football, specially popular in parishes near the coast, and several Suffolk villages still have Camp Fields, if only in name. Our earliest description of it is in Edward Moor's *Suffolk Words and Phrases*, published in 1823. He tells us that the goals, which were just gaps between discarded coats, were 150–200 yards apart, and there were no marked boundaries to the pitch. The teams were between ten and fifteen a side, and the ball was only the size of a cricket ball. The ball was caught and carried as in rugby, and if the man holding the ball was brought down with it, his side lost a *snotch*, as they also did if an opponent carried the ball through their goal. The players were stripped to the waist, and barefoot.

Just upstream on the Ore from its confluence with the Butley, is Havergate Island. Together with the southern part of Orford Beach, this is now a Nature Reserve, and a centre for the observation of waders and wildfowl. The most numerous of the birds wintering here are the wigeon and the lapwing, together with dunlin and gulls. But the most precious are surely the avocets, to be found in numbers only on this particular estuary, distinguishable by their curiously upturned beaks. From here the boats travelling upstream turn the corner at Cockold's Point and come in sight of Orford, with the towers of the castle and the church framing it on either side.

Orford (sea-ford) Castle faced the sea directly when it was built. Its purpose was to establish royal authority in East Anglia against the rebellious barons. Only the keep of this large castle remains; but it is enough, because its architecture is highly original and the bare space around accentuates its effect. Begun in 1165, it was the first in England to avoid rectangularity, being designed on the basis of a polygon. On to this polygon are clamped three tall towers. This was both efficient (it saved the need for a fourth tower) and effective (it reduced the danger of undermining or stone-slinging). What is more, the walls of the keep are made economically with septaria, a local limestone, though the quoins had to be shipped from Northamptonshire and the finer dressings from Normandy. Henry II got good value for the £1413. 10s. 10d recorded as its cost in the Pipe Rolls; and on its completion eight years later it was put to immediate use by the royal forces which landed at Orford to invade the territories of the Bigod Earl of Norfolk.

Like several other English castles, Orford never actually endured a siege, though it did surrender to the French Prince Louis in 1217. Not being associated with great events, it is remembered for speculative incidents of horror and imagination associated with the castellans. The cruel Hugh of Dennington, who terrorised the countryside around Orford in the late thirteenth century, scourged William of Butley to death in the dungeon. And Bartholomew de Glanville, the original castellan, is said to have kept as a prisoner a merman, who was 'like a human being in all his limbs'. He liked to eat raw fish, which he first wrung out with his hands until all the liquid had gone. His captors treated him severely for refusing to answer their questions, and were angered when he refrained from bowing his head to the sacred images when taken to see the church. At least, that is the story recorded by a monk, Ralph of Coggeshall, though, to be fair to him, he leaves his readers to speculate on the probability that this was merely a seal, conceding that 'many people tell such marvellous tales about this kind of event'.

The construction of Orford Castle involved the transformation of a small fishing village into an important port, and an appropriate church was needed for it. For reasons unknown, this large twelfth-century church fell into disrepair within a hundred and fifty years. The church which replaced it was larger in space but, unusually, shorter in length, and without a chancel arch; the ruins of the Norman chancel stand against it in the churchyard, with massive piers of varying designs. The tower of the church (St Bartholemew's) is also unusual because its upper part is the result of a recent reconstruction in which the buttresses extend above the parapet and terminate in flat tops. This gives the tower a fortified appearance, and because the church is on high ground and prominent from the road, and has no large upper windows, it is often mistaken for the castle.

Like Dunwich up the coast, Orford was represented by two members in Parliament till the Reform Bill of 1832; and it remained a borough till 1886. The castle itself had passed out of royal control in the fourteenth century, and eventually was abandoned; it was only saved from being dismantled because it was such a useful landmark from the sea. The lordship of the castle went with the manor of Sudbourne, whose aristocratic owners were the leading magnates in the neighbourhood. But when Sir Robert Walpole, the Prime Minister for over twenty years, was elevated to the House of Lords in 1742, he took the title of Earl of Orford, although he had no connection with the town or the locality, except that it was a typical example of the rotten boroughs by which he manipulated his patronage. By then Orford had become redundant as a port and was in decay. Delapidated houses were pulled down, streets were downgraded into tracks or paths, and the market-place was no longer busy. The surviving fishermen were reduced to dragging for oysters, and among the town regalia are three oyster measures, together with the Water Bailiff's silver oars.

Orford remained a backwater until quite recent times.

Unlike Aldeburgh, it could not profit from the attractions of the seaside because the river flowed between it and the shore. And from the 1930s till very recently, Orford Ness has been controlled by the military, and closed to public access. As a result, Orford has been spared insensitive development, and has the appearance of a village. The rows of red-brick Georgian cottages which line Quay Street, some of them set well back behind grass, lead the eye and the feet pleasantly down to the jetty, passing by the Jolly Sailor pub, which dates from Elizabethan times and preserves all sorts of mementos of seafarers and smugglers, floods and gales. The Jolly Sailor was awash in the 1953 floods, and so it was with personal experience of the effect of rising waters that some of the audience heard the very first performance of Benjamin Britten's *Noye's Fludde*, which took place in Orford Church five years later. And his *Curlew River*, which also was first performed here, is likewise particularly apposite to an Orford setting, with its theme of an encounter at a lonely ferry. Charon himself, who ferried dead souls across the Styx, would have felt entirely at home on Orford jetty.

From the Orford jetty, with its optimistic complement of little sailing boats, an incoming tide will waft us up river to the hairpin bend by Slaughden Quay at Aldeburgh, where the Alde ought by rights to enter the sea, but doesn't. The tide penetrates for yet another seven miles up to the bridge at Snape, and on the way it passes through the broad expanse of water in the Iken Flats, surely the most beautiful part of this estuary. To the north is the entirely naturalistic stretch of tidal river-bank in front of Snape Warren and Blackheath Wood. To the south, the grass-covered river wall which bounds the Iken marshes and the copses beyond. At low tide the great expanse of inter-tidal mud-flats is revealed, and its twice-daily action ensures that these oozy accretions are in a continual state of flux. They are subject to the gradual process of silting, as well as to seasonal fluctuations, and they provide a rich habitat for those estuarian organisms which have specialised in overcoming the problem of the fluctuating salinity: the molluscs, crustacea and worms, consumed by various species of birds and fish, the long-billed waders probing for the deepest-burrowing invertebrates.

This scene-changing scenery, alternately watery or muddy, was the playground for one of Suffolk's finest admirers, Julian Tennyson, the author of *Suffolk Scene*. His life was cut short in the last war, and so his youthful enthusiasm for the Suffolk countryside of the 1930s, the countryside that seemed to have gone to sleep, is all the more poignant. At least he has been spared from seeing the changes of the last half century. In those days wildfowl were less protected, and shooting was a free-for-all up to the high-water mark, with many a scuffle between the wildfowlers and the gamekeepers around the embankment boundaries. Julian Tennyson and his brother used to go out duck-shooting on the Iken Flats from a punt, which inevitably capsized. On one such occasion they abandoned the punt and attempted to wade to shore across the mud; but his brother very nearly got swallowed up, sinking, as Julian, a master of the droll analogy, put it 'like the periscope of a submarine'. Another time they clung to the overturned punt, and called for Old Sam, who was eel-fishing from a nearby boat, to rescue them. He affected not to hear their cries, and only after a long while did he approach them, with the words 'Them eels carn't wait, yew barstids can!' Julian also capsized in a boat on the Ore, when in the care of Harry, an Aldeburgh fisherman who had 'seen the Light' after being swept overboard, and had joined the Plymouth Brethren: they spent a cold night on Havergate Island. Here is his description of the dawn chorus on the banks of the Alde:

. . . an old cock pheasant, breaking upon the world like the ringing of an alarm-bell in a sleeping town. It is a signal. At once there bursts forth the most wonderful and tremendous clamour ever heard in Suffolk's quiet countryside. In front of you the triumphant crow of pheasants, the urgent caw of rooks, the gentle plaint of wood pigeons, the staccato jukking of partridges; behind you the scream of gulls, the nervous chatter of dunlin, the shrill pipe of redshank, the querulous wail of curlew and whimbrel, the throaty cackle of mallard and shelduck, the hoarse bark of ill-tempered old herons; all these and a score of other voices are mingled together in a mighty concert, and the whole air throbs with the beauty and amazement of it.

Thirteen hundred and fifty years ago the early Christian missionary, Botolph, was looking for a site at which to found a religious community. The old chronicle tells us that 'the unwearied man of God looked about him everywhere till at last he found by the mercy of God such a spot, Ikano, which was just the God-foresaken devil-possessed place he was in search of'. Scholars have identified this as Iken; and since it is one of the finest sites in the county, overlooking the Alde estuary and the low-lying land around, I cannot but suppose that Botolph likewise found it lovely, and that the chronicler's epithets were merely the conventional forms of description for a wilderness, or, as we would call it nowadays, a nature reserve. Botolph, like Julian Tennyson, must have marvelled at the dawn chorus, which assumedly interrupted his early morning prayers in summer, and likewise he surely would have had difficulties with the mud-flats. The present church, thatched and pewless, is dedicated to him. It stands prominently on a corner of the higher ground beside the estuary, and its fifteenth-century tower, draped by trees, is visible from across the water in three directions, including the view from Snape Maltings. Botolph's original church was in all probability on this site, as is indicated by the dedication, the remains of a Saxon cross in the rubble-walling of the tower, and the timbers of a wooden church found below the nave.

The Alde estuary concludes at Snape Bridge. A tall masted ship is moored at the quayside, as if to emphasise that this is as far as it can go. It provides a nautical touch to the lawns and reeds and rushes that surround the Snape Maltings, which have been transformed into Suffolk's delightful musical centre. The enjoyment of music – or, for that matter, any form of art – is always enhanced by its visual background, and a rural setting which offsets the intellectual and emotional demands of music by the simplicity of the natural scene is particularly satisfying in an age of urban disillusion.

At Snape an old industrial complex of buildings existed for the purpose of producing malt, the main ingredient of beer. In front were the warehouses where the barley and coal were stored. These we still see, weatherbeaten and irregular, jumbled up with bricks of different colours and with wooden boardings, lofts and staircases. Behind them was the building where the barley was germinated, comprising several floors and chambers, and heated from below. This is the old malting house that has been converted into a concert hall. Designed by Ove Arup, it is acoustically sensitive but visually simple, with the old bare brick walls supporting an unceiled wooden roof, and with new but vernacular ranges attached to it. The four prominent ventilator shafts atop the roof simulate the vents of the maltings. In 1969, two years after it opened, it was gutted by fire, but was rebuilt within a year. It is in regular use for the Aldeburgh Festival and for other musical events round the year, as well as providing a home for the Britten-Pears School for Advanced Musical Studies. The rambling village of Snape lies half a mile to the north of the Maltings, and in it is the old windmill where Benjamin Britten lived when he was composing *Peter Grimes*, and the circular brick room in which he worked must have been as curious a dwelling as Grimes' upturned boat.

I now pass rapidly upstream to divert attention from the high tension wires, railway and A12 road which all cross the Alde within a few miles of Snape, but before doing so I must mention two places. The first is Blaxhall, just to the south. It seems that early in this century this small village contained an inordinate number of people by the name of Ling; and since it would have been inappropriate to refer to them by their Christian names, they all had nicknames, such as Skilly Ling, Mory Ling, Ludy Ling, Croppy Ling, Rook Ling, Straight Ling, Wag Ling, Pessy Ling, Finney Ling and Nacker Ling. Such real characters would, I feel sure, have felt affinity to the very human ones in Britten's *Albert Herring*, since Loxford, the fictional village where these lived, must have been quite close to Blaxhall. It is true that its name is an alliteration of Yoxford, nine miles north. But Albert's wreath is found on the road to Campsey Ash, the village next to Blaxhall, and his bucolic night out is spent at Wickham Market, conveniently close to Blaxhall. The inspiration for Albert Herring's name came from that of the owner of a grocery store at Tunstall, immediately south of Blaxhall.

The second place to mention here is Saxmundham, on a stream which drains into the Alde from the north. This small market town thrived as a staging post on the Yarmouth road, and the Bell Inn for long retained in its yard a memento of those days – the 'Old Blue' stagecoach. The Old Blue's run began at the Great White Horse at Ipswich, and it halted at the Crown at Woodbridge, the White Hart at Wickham Market, the Bell at Saxmundham, the Three Tuns at Yoxford, the White Hart at Blythburgh, and the White Lion at Beccles. The coming of the railways spelt the end of the stagecoaches, and when James Hissey and his wife toured this way in a phaeton (a light open carriage drawn by two horses) in the 1880s, they drove from Woodbridge without encountering a single other vehicle before arriving at Saxmundham, 'a slumbrous town that wakes into some semblance of activity one day in seven'. To me the best thing about Saxmundham is its name, so deeply resonant of the Anglo-Saxon settlement. 'This is Saxmund's home: Keep Out', seems to be the message.

The towers of Stratford St Andrew and Farnham (fern-home) glower at each other from only a few hundred metres across the Alde, and in the old days the two communities were equally suspicious of each other. Upstream of them the Alde passes between the parishes of Benhall and Great Glemham. Each is associated with a nineteenth-century clergyman whose ministry was only secondary to his literary interests. John Mitford, at one time vicar of Benhall (bean-hall), was a miscellaneous writer who for seventeen years edited the *Gentlemen's Magazine*, that repository of antiquarian ephemera and country tit-bits which was as much the required reading of the country gents as *Country Life* is today. His great merit was that he was deeply interested in natural history, but he had unfortunate sexual predelictions, and caused a scandal, when he was a curate at nearby Kelsale, by interfering with children. The poet Samuel Rogers wrote of him: 'He is no more fit to be a parson than I am to be the Angel Gabriel'.

At Great Glemham we encounter the poet George Crabbe in an altogether different guise from the angry misfit we observed at Aldeburgh. By now he had settled down in a house in what is today the park of Glemham House. Through the influence of his wife's uncle, who lived at Ducking Hall in next-door Parham, he had acquired the curacies of Great Glemham and Sweffling; and he was also earning royalties from his published poems. His son (also George) has given a nostalgic account of their family life here. They would wander along the green lanes on summer evenings to the sound of the nightingales. The poet would read aloud from a novel as he walked, whilst his sons ran about netting moths and butterflies and catching glow-worms. Each child was given his own patch of garden to cultivate, and their father was their schoolteacher.

George Crabbe would surely have recognised a kindred spirit in another cultivated and benign father who lived at Glemham House in our own day, Jock Gathorne-Hardy, Earl of Cranbrook. Jock, besides being a practical farmer, was a self-taught naturalist who became one of the greatest experts on bats. He wrote perceptively about the countryside and the need for conservation long before it became fashionable to do so, and was steeped in Suffolk lore and poetry. His wife, Fidelity, has played an important part in the origins and development of the Aldeburgh Festival. As a couple they were renowned and admired for their complete unpretentiousness, and Glemham House remains a home from which their family continues to promote those worthy causes which so enhance the delectable little valley of the Alde. Most appropriately, Glemham means 'happy-home'.

Next upstream is Rendham, where in 1907 a boy recovered from the river a life-size bronze head of the Emperor Claudius, presumed to have been looted from Camulodunum in 61 AD. Then, beyond Bruisyard, with its fine Elizabethan manor house, built on the site of a nunnery, and its substantial vineyard, we come to Badingham.

The southern end of this pretty village is at the foot of a steep rise and turn of the main road, where it lurches away from its original Roman course, a good example of Chesterton's allegation that 'the rolling English drunkard made the rolling English road', especially as the White Horse pub lies enticingly at the foot of the hill. On entering the church at Badingham, the eye is immediately drawn to the magnificent hammerbeam roof, dating from the early sixteenth century or earlier, though with replacement angels. It seems to soar because the whole church slopes upward towards the altar, which must have annoyed the Puritans. But then, perhaps Catholics might have been equally disturbed by the alignment of this church. It faces north-east rather than east, with the result that the sun shines directly through it on midsummer day. The church is dedicated to John the Baptist, whose name day is 24 June; but there are some who suspect that this acknowledgement of the summer solstice has to do with pre-Christian celebrations. Meanwhile the quest for experimentation in spiritual matters has recently been revived at Badingham with the installation of a Centre for Transcendental Meditation in the Old Rectory.

Badingham was where H.W. Freeman lived, and the farm described in his novel *Joseph and his Brethren* was based on Okenhill in this parish. This book dwells lovingly on the tyranny of some of the old farmers towards their families, and their unimaginative peasant cunning. Benjamin Geaiter, the dreadful patriarch conjured up by Freeman, has five bovine sons to command – Ben, Hiram, Bob, Ern and Harry – who are really his slaves, and by whose sweated labour 'the dirtiest, sourest, hardest, damnest bit of land' is turned round into a profit at a time of agricultural depression.

The Alde does not extend far above Badingham, but three miles to the south west, at Saxtead, we find the River Ore again, which flows down through Framlingham on past Parham, Marlesford and Little Glemham to join the Alde near Blaxhall. These sister-rivers flow for nearly all their courses through the hundred of Plomesgate, whose name implies that the original meeting-place was at the gate of an orchard of plum-trees, and has been tentatively identified as being in the parish of Parham, which means a place where the pear-trees grow. The Anglian tribal elders who gathered in this idyllic spot seem to have made a better choice than those in the adjacent hundred of Loes, who, to judge from its name, met in a pig-sty!

At Saxtead Green, a post windmill (successor to an original

one of 1287) has been preserved in working order. That is to say, the open sails revolve with the wind, thereby always facing it and turning the upper part of the mill with them as they do so. At Parham, Moat Hall displays one of the finest fragments of early Tudor brickwork in the county. Before the days of 'listing' ancient buildings, a fifteenth-century stone archway from Moat Hall was sold to America, provoking an indignant, if chauvinistic, comment from M.R. James: 'Language fails me when I think of it forming the portal perhaps of the stately Buggins home in – no, on – Plutoria Avenue, Zenith City, flanked, it may be, by Assyrian base reliefs and surmounted by a mosaic from Sicily'. At Little Glemham, the large Early Georgian frontage of Glemham Hall stands for all to see in its spacious park.

Between Badingham and Saxstead is Dennington, whose church interior is perhaps the most attractive in the whole catchment of the Alde. On opening the medieval door, we find a rich mixture of furnishings. The eighteenth-century box pews, arranged around the three-decker pulpit, only fill the front of the nave: behind them are the medieval pews, with exceptionally intricate tracery, and the depiction of various strange animals. These include a sciapod, a fabulous inhabitant of Libya, who was entirely human except that he had enormous feet. When he felt tired he lay on his back in the shade of his feet (sciapod being Greek for shadow-foot). The rood screen under the chancel arch has been reduced to its base, but its extensions around the chantry chapels on either side remain, complete with their elaborate lofts. Within the south chapel are the luminous fifteenth-century alabaster effigies of Lord Bardolph, an Agincourt veteran, and his wife: he in armour, with his feet resting on an 'eagle; she with a mitred headdress, her feet on a wyvern.

Framlingham was for many centuries a seat of power of the Earls, and later, Dukes, of Norfolk, whose territories always included important estates in Suffolk. The first family to hold this title was called Bigod, and this unattractive name, possibly acquired because of their frequent 'by God' expletives (though probably pronounced in Norman French, 'bec-go'), seems entirely appropriate for what Julian Tennyson has called 'about the toughest brood ever hatched in England'. Successive Bigod Earls considered themselves the rulers of East Anglia, and defied the 'King of Cockney' when he tried to restrain them. The founder of their house was Roger Bigod, Steward to William II and Henry I, who came into the possession of 117 manors in Suffolk. After his eldest son, William, was drowned in the tragic wreck of the White Ship in 1120, the Bigod estates went to his second son, Hugh.

Hugh Bigod was soon embroiled in the anarchical contest between Stephen and Matilda for the throne. He was not the only baron to change sides opportunistically, but he certainly did so in a big way. In 1135 he declared for Stephen, who rewarded him with the Earldom of Norfolk. But his resistance to any royal authority twice brought Stephen with an army against him, and he twice had to surrender after a siege, at Norwich in 1136 and Bungay in 1140. He was at the side of Stephen at the disastrous Battle of Lincoln, but soon after-wards he reverted to the support of Matilda, though on the accession of her son, Henry II, he was obliged to surrender all his castles. In 1165 the king restored to him Framlingham and Bungay, but at the same time he began work on the first royal castle in East Anglia, that at Orford. Faced with tighter royal control in his fiefdom, Hugh joined forces with the Earl of Leicester who invaded Suffolk with a Flemish army in 1173. Though they were soon defeated outside Bury, Hugh Bigod continued his defiance till the king himself entered Suffolk in the following year. Even then this redoubtable survivor succeeded in making peace and retaining his estates by means of heavy payments to the crown, but he was obliged to surrender Framlingham and Walton Castles once again. Though by now an old man, his martial ardour was as strong as ever, for he set off to Palestine on a Crusade. This was a different sort of contest, in which there was no side swapping, and it is thought that he met his death there.

Hugh's son, Roger, the 2nd Bigod Earl, secured himself in power by loyalty to Richard I during his exile, and regained possession of Framlingham. Under the reign of John, Roger

Bigod was in and out of favour. In 1213 he was disgraced and imprisoned; in 1214 he was campaigning with the king in France; and in 1215 he was one of the twenty-five barons who forced John to sign Magna Carta. The humiliation of the king provided the opportunity for Prince Louis of France to invade East Anglia, pillaging the coastal towns and marching towards London laden with booty. Roger's grandson, also Roger, the 4th Earl, maintained the Bigod tradition by changing allegiance during the struggles between the barons and Henry III. The rapidity with which the barons moved from opposition to acquiescence, and the kings from denunciations to pardons was, of course, all part of a political game in which the payment of fines was delicately balanced against military strength: the Bigods' power rested on their exceptionally large revenues rather than on their castles.

The short-tempered disrespect with which the Bigods and other feudal barons treated their monarchs is nicely demonstrated in the famous interchange between Roger, the 5th and last Bigod Earl, and Edward I at the Council of Salisbury in 1297. The plan was for the king to lead a campaign in Flanders, whilst a second force, including Bigod, went to Gascony. Roger Bigod refused to go on this unless the king came too. 'But without me,' said Edward, 'you will go with the rest'. 'Without you, O King, I am not bound to go, and I will not'. 'By God, Earl, you will either go or hang'. 'By God, O King, I will neither go or hang'. He didn't go – or hang.

The inability of the Angevin and Plantagenet kings to impose firm rule on England was never more apparent than during the collapse of authority under Edward II. The Earldom of Norfolk was at that time held by Thomas of Brotherton, who was loyal to the king, and controlled most of north-east Suffolk, including Framlingham. The remainder of the county was held by lords who supported the Duke of Lancaster. On the death of the Duke in 1322 the king was bold enough to outlaw several, but obliged to pardon them soon after, when his estranged Queen Isabella and her lover Mortimer threatened to invade. They landed, probably at the Landguard Point, and proceeded unopposed to Bury. The utter lawlessness of the county persisted for some time more, with the magnates squabbling over feudal rights and dues, and armed robbers dominating the countryside, even kidnapping the Abbot of Bury for several days. And it was followed soon afterwards by something far more terrible, the natural disaster of the Black Death of 1349, which is supposed to have killed over a third of the total population of Suffolk.

Framlingham Castle was built towards the end of the twelfth century by Roger Bigod, the 2nd Earl of Norfolk, on the site of one which had been demolished in 1174 on the orders of Henry II. Roger's castle was made to a radical new design, namely, that the curtain wall and not the keep should form the principal defence. This enabled a larger area to be made safe, where the whole garrison could conveniently sit out a siege. Fortified curtain walls had been found by the Crusaders in the Levant, and the new royal castles of Dover and Windsor had been provided with them. So Roger Bigod required his also. Labour was no problem for him, and, as to materials, he could afford to import large quantities of Northamptonshire oolite limestone, brought all the way up the Ore in barges.

So it is entirely befitting that these great walls, with their thirteen towers, are all that now remain of the medieval castle, since the interior has been entirely cleared away. Their size and strength have proved their ultimate salvation, just as the wellnigh impregnable keep at Orford has survived while all its lesser containing walls have gone. In both instances, the essence of the defensive system has become completely exposed, the one a continuous screen, the other a solitary block. Framlingham Castle cannot be seen from afar, being set on a piece of ground that can hardly be called a hill. The best view of it is from across the marsh to the north, where it stands high on its grass mound. This is the place to imagine the time when it was besieged by the forces of King John. When it surrendered, incidentally, the garrison comprised twenty-six knights, twenty men-at-arms, seven crossbowmen, and a chaplain, confirming that a large castle could be held by quite small numbers in that pre-gunpowder age.

The space within the walls of Framlingham bears traces of

the Bigods' hall and chapel, and also of the subsequent buildings erected there by the Mowbray and Howard Dukes of Norfolk, with brick chimneys, some of them apparently put there just for show, and the proud coat-of-arms over the gateway. After these aristocrats had fallen foul of the despotic Henry VIII, Framlingham became a royal castle. Under Elizabeth I it was used as a prison for Catholic priests. It was later returned to the Howards, but they then had no use for it as a seat and sold it to Sir Robert Hitcham, who effected the demolition. Subsequently the poor-house that we see was erected on the empty site, and though life in it must have been rather like a prison, at least it is satisfactory to think that the poor came to inhabit Framlingham Castle, whose history calls to mind the consoling phrase of the Magnificat, *Deposuit superbos* – He hath put down the mighty from their seat.

Though nothing remains in the castle, the church of St Michael at Framlingham contains the tombs of the Ducal and semi-royal Howards, which comprise perhaps the finest group of early sixteenth-century monuments in England. Thomas, the 3rd Duke, ordered the construction of what is in effect a family mausoleum in the chancel of this church, and he lies here surrounded by his most important relatives, though the series did not thereafter continue because, after the alliance with the Fitzalans, the Dukes went to live at Arundel in Sussex.

The 3rd Duke's tomb is a masterpiece of Renaissance sculpture, with the figures of the apostles in niches all around. It celebrates a proud and lucky life, for he lived to over eighty, having survived a sentence of death a few years earlier only because Henry VIII died the day before the execution. High on the wall above him is the helmet worn by his father, the 2nd Duke, at the battle of Flodden. The 2nd Duke had commanded the English army which decisively beat the Scots, and so brought great power and prestige to the House of Howard. The others around the 3rd Duke were not so lucky. A monument of subsequent date, of painted alabaster, records his son, the Earl of Surrey, beheaded by Henry in 1547: to signify this, his coronet is placed beside him. On a large tomb chest with shields and fluted pilasters is the Duke's son-in-law, the Duke of Richmond, the illegitimate son of the King, who died at the age of seventeen. And here are also the tombs of the two wives of his grandson, the 4th Duke: he was executed for treason by Elizabeth, because it was thought he was planning to marry Mary, Queen of Scots, as his third wife.

Together these tombs provide a sculpted record of the Howards' unsuccessful challenge to Tudor despotism. The nearest they got to the throne was in the provision of Henry VIII's second and fifth wives, Queens Anne Boleyn and Catherine Howard, both nieces of the 3rd Duke. But I think they can rest easy in the knowledge that the Tudors very soon died out, whereas the prolific Howards have held on to the dukedom of Norfolk, founded for them in 1483, through six royal dynasties – Plantagenet, Tudor, Stuart, Hanover, Saxe-Coburg-Gotha, and Windsor. When the present (and 17th) Duke came to Framlingham to celebrate the quincentenary of the dukedom, there were some who detected a distinct similarity to the thin-nosed effigy of the 3rd Duke.

It is doubly ironic that Framlingham should have been the place where Mary Tudor launched her campaign to gain the throne in 1553. No family had been more anti-Tudor than the Howards. No county was more strongly Protestant than Suffolk, and it was obvious that her accession would restore Catholicism. Besides, the Protestant claimant, Jane Grey, had links with the county through her grandfather, Charles Brandon, Duke of Suffolk. Mary and her entourage were on the run when they fled to Framlingham, and fully expected to have to get away by sea. But in the event East Anglia rallied to her support. Apprehension about religious change proved secondary to the general discontent at the appalling economic deterioration that had occurred during the reign of Edward VI. Inflation was rampant; the cloth trade was languishing in the face of foreign competition; landowners were turning their estates over to sheep-rearing and enclosing common land; rents went up and wages went down. The general mood was to oust the rotten government in London and install Mary, the legitimate heiress, as Queen. So she progressed from Framlingham through Suffolk and Essex and the capital fell without a fight. The euphoria in Suffolk was short lived when it was realised how bigotted her rule would be.

Framlingham today is a most attractive market town. Castle Street leads down the hill past the church to the triangular and sloping Market Place. It bears no mementoes of the times when the Earls and Dukes lived in the castle, but its shape was dictated by the medieval defences, which included a ditch around the town. Its most noteworthy buildings are the old almshouses – those of Sir Thomas Hitcham, the successful lawyer, and those of Thomas Mills, who managed to acquire the money for his through his skill as a popular non-conformist preacher. This philanthropic tradition at Framlingham was amplified with the foundation of Framlingham College by public subscription in the middle of the last century, intended to provide 'a scientific education for the middle classes at a moderate cost'. This large Gothic red-brick structure incongruously faces the castle from only five hundred metres across the intervening marsh, and each provides the perfect viewing platform for the other.

Coincident with the founding of the college was the building of a railway line from Wickham Market to Framlingham, closed to passenger services in 1952. Rustic termini such as Framlingham and Laxfield provided the setting for John Hadfield's *Love on a Branch Line*, in which an eccentric Suffolk earl owns a small line abandoned by British Rail, and runs it entirely for his private use. He is so obsessed by the venture that he relinquishes his mansion in order to reside in the train, with its dining-car, sleepers and saloon, and to be hauled up and down the line daily by a steam engine operated by his very attractive daughters, while 'in imperturbable calm the sober Suffolk landscape was gliding by'.

VIII
Blyth

The Blyth is Suffolk's smallest estuarine river, but the Blything hundred, the ancient district which surrounds the Blyth, is the largest in the county. So my description of this river includes the whole of the hundred, which is appropriately bounded by two Hundred Rivers – one to the north, coming out south of Kessingland, and one to the south, flowing into the mere at Thorpeness – both of them gaining the sea through sluices.

There are reasons for supposing that this large coastal hundred was an administrative unit before the Danish invasions, and its boundaries may even be those of some particular clan of the Angles. The hundred court was at Blythburgh, which must have been an important place from Early English times. It was to Blythburgh that the slain bodies of King Anna and his son were brought in 654. By the time of Edward the Confessor, Blythburgh was part of the king's hereditary possessions. Throughout the Middle Ages it enjoyed privileges denied to nearby Dunwich, such as minting and gaoling, and it held three annual fairs. An Augustinian priory was established at Blythburgh in the twelfth century, and the town attained a peak of prosperity in the early fifteenth, helped by the decline of Dunwich. Its quays were busy with fishing boats and trading ships that sailed up the Blyth, and its pastures were well stocked with sheep.

Holy Trinity Church at Blythburgh was built during the second half of the fifteenth century, replacing the previous church although retaining its great doorless west tower. The licence to build was granted to the priory, but there must have been a major involvement by the local landowners and merchants, and in particular from John Hopton, the Lord of the Manor, for whom a chantry chapel was built to the north of the chancel, where his marble tomb-slab is set in the wall.

But hard times were ahead for Blythburgh and its new church. Already the shipping trade was declining. Then came the Reformation and the dissolution of the priory, which, as the impropriator, had paid for the running and upkeep of the church. In 1577 there was a natural disaster, as described in Stow's *Annals*:

> On Sunday 4 Aug 1577, between the Hours of nine and ten a Clock in the Forenoon, whilst the minister was reading the second Lesson in the Parish-Church of Blithburgh, a Town in Suffolk, a strange and terrible Tempest of Lightning and Thunder struck through the Wall of the same Church into the ground, almost a Yard deep; drove down all the people on that Side of the Church, above twenty persons; then renting the Wall up to the Revestry, cleft the Door, and returned to the Steeple, rent the Timber, brake the Chains, and fled towards Bungay. The People that were stricken down were found groveling more than half an Hour after, whereof a Man and a Boy were found dead; the others were scorched.

In 1644 Blythburgh Church suffered badly from the attentions of the image-breakers, who fired bullets into the doors and the sculpted angels. The population declined, and for several years under the Commonwealth no services at all were held in the church. After a disastrous fire in 1676 many of the inhabitants removed to Southwold, and Blythburgh was reduced to a small village, though the court of the hundred continued to meet in the gabled building that is now the White Hart. The church must have looked a sorry sight in the early nineteenth century, with several of the aisle windows bricked up and the small stove for winter services being lit with the old parish documents. The congregation raised umbrellas when the rain poured through the holes in the roof. Fallen angels were ignominiously dumped on a heap of lumber in the churchyard, for them a far worse fate than their theological destiny, which was to join the rather agreeable ranks of Lucifer.

The slow process of repair since then, initiated by William Morris's Society for the Protection of Ancient Buildings, has conserved the precious remains without introducing Victorian forms of restoration. The result has been to give the interior of Blythburgh a special charm. The floor is still of rough old flagstones and bricks; the nave is mostly empty of pews; and the windows are of plain glass. The roof retains its delicate original paint, and some of its original angels. A small spiral staircase leads to the former rood loft, and priests' doors cause buttresses to fly. The figured bench ends of the medieval pews provide a visual morality lesson in seven common sins. Avarice sits on his money chest; Hypocrisy prays with open eyes; Greed exposes his distended stomach; Pride, his fine clothes; Drunkenness is in the stocks; Sloth is in bed; and Slander shows his slit and protruding tongue. The choir benches in the chancel bear carved frontals with figures of the Saints; and their book rests are pierced with the deep holes of inkwells, from the time when they were placed in the Hopton Chantry for the use of the village school.

Outside, the church displays great elaboration, with a perforated parapet along the top of the south aisle, and grotesque figures sitting atop the buttresses, and exceptional flushwork on the south porch. But the real reason why Blythburgh is the cynosure of north-east Suffolk – as against the equally wonderful Perpendicular church at Southwold, for instance – is its incomparable position in the landscape, especially as seen from the A12 road. From the south, across a patch of heathland known as Toby's Walks (Toby was a drummer-boy who murdered a girl here), and from the north, along the line of the causeway that bounds a wide stretch of water (not part of the estuary, but formed by the breaking of the river embankment), the long church with its eighteen clerestory windows is seen to best advantage. But there is also another way, from the west and along the river-bank, known only to walkers, where the tower is revealed above the reeds and rushes, closely protected by the protruding hill across the narrow valley.

Each of these various aspects of Blythburgh induces a feeling of loneliness and wildness, as in this lovely evocation written by George Gissing nearly a hundred years ago:

This is the valley of the Blyth. The stream ripples and glances over its brown bed warmed with sunbeams; by its bank the green flags wave and rustle, and, all about, the meadows shine in pure gold of buttercups. The hawthorn hedges are a mass of gleaming blossom, which scents the breeze. There above rises the heath, yellow-mantled with gorse, and beyond, if I walk for an hour or two, I shall come out upon the sandy cliffs of Suffolk, and look over the northern sea.

The Dunwich River now drains into the River Blyth at Walberswick, and in between the two is an area, half forest and half marsh, which, together with the land immediately to the south around the Minsmere River (described below) comprises the finest stretch of natural landscape along the shores of Suffolk. The forest is mostly of conifers belonging to the Forestry Commission; and although we may regret the heathland that they took over in the 1930s, at least they give a sense of peacefulness to anyone walking through them, and offset the marshes around them. These were all open to the sea in the Middle Ages, and may become so again. Meanwhile, they are safely protected from human interference by all manner of legislation, and large areas comprise nature reserves and bird sanctuaries. The walk through the Westwood Marsh, from the appropriately named Newdelight Corner to the sea, must be one of the finest experiences for lovers of the natural scene. After a brief section of heath, we walk on duckboards right through the middle of an otherwise impenetrable quagmire covered with growing or rotting alders, whose lush undergrowth gives an almost tropical appearance. From this we emerge on to the open marsh and continue along a dyke between the bird-busy rushes. A derelict brick wind-pump provides a marker, and when we reach it we can see the long line of shingle and hear the breakers and smell the salt. Otherwise, the only buildings visible are the tower of Walberswick church and the house at Westwood.

This house is on the site of the hall of John Hopton. Like his contemporary, John Paston of Oxnead in Norfolk, whose family letters provide such a fascinating insight into the life of the East Anglian gentry during the uncertain political times of the Wars of the Roses, Hopton kept his head down and concentrated on managing his own affairs. Westwood must have been a most congenial house. It was thatched (with rushes of the marsh), and around it were its bakehouse, barn, dovecot, fishpond, garden and park. Another great advantage of living so close to the sea was that fresh fish were easily come by – herrings and cod, and also salmon. During the eighteenth century Westwood became the centre of a large and profitable farm, and much of the natural landscape that we see today dates only from the abandonment of this agricultural enterprise.

Upstream from Blythburgh, towards Halesworth, we pass Blyford to the north and Wenhaston to the south. Just before Blyford is a piece of land called Bulcamp. Camden, the seventeenth-century historian, decided that this was where Anna put up his last ditch stand against Penda and his Mercian horde in 654. But there is no evidence for this, and it would anyway be odd for Anna to have chosen a site with his back to the Blyth, since his main concern must have been to save the land to the south – Dunwich, and the estuaries of the Alde and the Deben. The only certain battle of Bulcamp was when the eighteenth-century poor house was attacked by an angry mob in 1765. In St Peter's, Wenhaston, is a large early-sixteenth century panel depicting the Last Judgement, known as the Wenhaston Doom. Whitewashed by the Protestants, it was eventually thrown out of the church for burning, but overnight the rain revealed a small corner of the painting, and it was saved just in time. The medieval conception of hell is imaginatively portrayed, and the wearing of a crown or mitre seems to be a passport to heaven.

Halesworth is a fine example of an old Suffolk market town. Its heart has been happily restored to good working order by a satisfactory internal bypass (technically, an inner relief road) operation, which has driven all polluting traffic from its sinuous artery, the Thoroughfare. Halesworth has for long had a reputation for practical innovation. Sir William Jackson Hooker, who lived in what is now called the Brewery House, established an extensive herbarium here, an inspiration for his son, Sir Joseph, the famous botanist who developed Kew Gardens, and who was born in Halesworth in 1817. Patrick Stead, a Scotsman whose mercantile activities brought him to settle in Halesworth, was the first to develop the mechanisation of the processes of malting. Alfred Suckling, in his *History and Antiquities of the County of Suffolk*, describes Halesworth as lying 'at the bottom of an amphitheatre of hills which entirely exclude it from the distant view'; and informs us that the Manor of Halesworth was held for centuries by the families of de Argentien and then Allington, who successively held the privilege of serving the monarch with his first cup of wine on the day of the Coronation. (A more dignified task than that of Baldwin le Petteur of Hemingstone who, according to Suckling, had to perform a dance and a fart before the King at Christmastide.)

Barges brought goods from the sea up to Halesworth until the coming of the railway; and then a narrow gauge line was built from Halesworth to Southwold. How delightful it must have been to travel on this intimate railway! Passengers at Halesworth Station boarded a mixed train of goods wagons, vans and maroon-coloured carriages, hauled by a locomotive painted blue but bright with burnished brass. Once on its way, the miniature scale gave a great impression of speed as the engine drew the train along the valley towards the halts at Wenhaston and Blythburgh, and then through the sandy heaths to Walberswick, to the swing bridge across the Blyth and the terminus at Southwold, where luggage and hampers were unloaded on to the neat tree-lined platform.

Just south of Halesworth is Bramfield (broom-field). I shall describe this village in rather more detail than the others because it is the one I know best and where I have lived, off and on, for nearly half a century. In those days there was very little traffic. In this simple statement lies the greatest change that has occurred in Bramfield, greater even than the building of the former council houses. The population has by no means risen proportionate to the houses, but the traffic is unimaginable, for the High Street has the misfortune to be on an A road. As everywhere else, village life has also changed out of recognition, but a few sterling characters preserve the old tradition and refuse to bow to contemporary trends. Bramfield is a happy village, a village of achievement. At the time of writing, it still has a school, a general store, a garage, a butcher, two pubs, and a chapel as well as its church. Spare-time activity abounds, including dyeing and spinning wool, creating artificial flowers from sugar-paste icing, working pewter into embellished glass-surrounds, devising amateur dramatic productions, painting pictures, writing books, composing speeches, and researching village history.

Bramfield was one of 442 manors granted by William the Conqueror to his son-in-law Alan, Earl of Richmond, and at the time of Domesday Book it contained thirty-five villagers and seven smallholders, that is to say, forty-two bread-winning peasants and so a total population of around a hundred and fifty. There were thirty goats, twenty-four pigs, eight cattle and a draught horse. The church was endowed with twenty-eight acres. The manor passed into the possession of the religious college at Mettingham in the fourteenth century, and then, after the Reformation, to the Bacon family and then to the Rous family, Earls of Stradbroke. The ecclesiastical poll tax continued to be levied at Bramfield till 1805, when it stood at 4d a head on everyone over twelve years old, paid annually to the vicar.

Bramfield Hall was for long the residence of the family of Rabett, Dunwich traders who gentrified themselves at Bramfield in the sixteenth century. Though they had never been Rabbits (their name derives from an old word meaning a messenger), their coat-of-arms featured homely rabbits' heads – 'Argent a chevron sable charged with five guttees d'or, between three rabbits' heads couped of the second'. The Rabetts (usually called Reginald, and never Peter) variously fulfilled their appointed roles in local affairs as magistrates and clergymen, and even once a High Sheriff and a Member of Parliament: but they never held the Lordship of the Manor.

The Hall was built in late Elizabethan times, on the site of a timber-framed building which had housed clerics before the Reformation. It was renovated during the late-eighteenth century, when rows of new sash windows were inserted into the Tudor bricks. In the park is a remnant of a famous tree, the Bramfield Oak which fell in 1843. This was a mighty landmark, and I like to think of travellers recognising where they were when reaching it, in the days before road signs, for it stood a little way to the south of the village on the line of the lane that led in from Saxmundham and Framlingham, a lane appropriately called Earlsway. When, some two hundred years ago, a local poet was inspired to write a ballad about Hugh Bigod, Earl of Norfolk, being chased by the King's bailiff, he fancifully featured the Bramfield oak, thereby creating a myth about its legendary age:

> When the Baily had ridden to Bramfield oak,
>   Sir Hugh was at Ilksall bower;
> When the Baily had ridden to Halesworth cross,
>   He was singing in Bungay tower –
>   'Now that I am in my Castle of Bungay,
>   Upon the river of Waveney,
> I will ne care for the King of Cockney'.

This venerable tree survived, though mutilated and scarred, till 1843. On 15 June, an absolutely still day, it collapsed with a terrible crash, and its prostrate form was enveloped in clouds of dust. Then came the village, like hyenas to the corpse of an elephant, and cut it up for firewood. Beside its stump is the 'Son of the Bramfield Oak', which lost its higher branches when it took the full force of the 1987 hurricane.

The Hall park and fields, together with those opposite on Castle Hill, have been 'set aside' for half a century, and together comprise a most beautiful parkland right on the southern edge of the old centre of Bramfield. At the highest point on Castle Hill is a circular ditch around a thorn hedge enclosing a grass space, an ancient defensive enclosure. This is thought to have been an unlicensed (or 'adulterine') castle of earth rampart and wooden palisades, put up during the anarchy of the early twelfth century. The only aspect of the scene that is missing is the row of Thomas Neale's early eighteenth-century almshouses which were iniquitously pulled down by developers just before the years when building conservation became popular.

Looking up the Walpole Lane from the centre of the village, between the Queen's Head (Queen Elizabeth has been displaced by Boadicea) and one of the oldest of the cottages, we see the long serpentine wall of the Hall facing St Andrew's Church and its round tower. This round tower is the only one in Suffolk to stand entirely by itself, separate from the church. Together with another of similar date at the hamlet of Thorington (thorn-bush farm) only a mile away, it is by far and away the oldest building in the neighbourhood. The extreme simplicity of its cornerless rubble wall, though broken in places by subsequent windows and a door, provides a forceful statement of primitive defence and defiance. I like to see it flying St George's flag, and reminding the inhabitants of Bramfield that a thousand years of village life watch over their contemporary preoccupations. I also like to think that it may still be there after all the other buildings in the village have eventually collapsed, rotted away, or been variously destroyed during the forthcoming millenium.

Such round towers were erected during the eleventh century, mainly for defence; and it can be no coincidence that they are mostly near the coast, prey to Danish raids. Defence towers were built elsewhere in England, of course, but were usually square, not round. The reason why the round towers are peculiar to East Anglia is obviously because of the lack of freestone with which to make the quoins, or corners. There are 125 in Norfolk, forty-two in Suffolk, and only thirteen in the rest of England. They were originally roofed with conical caps of thatch. Their relationship to the churches of the time is a matter of conjecture. They cannot have been attached to the churches if they were built for defence, and their door arrangements strongly suggest that they stood alone. Such as survived usually came to be used as church towers, with doors inserted into them at ground level and windows cut for the bells, and new churches were then built up against them. Among the many theories that have been held about the East Anglian round towers, the most fanciful is that they are ancient wells left high and dry by the erosion of the surrounding earth – a fancy probably inspired by the sight of wells exposed to the sea by the eroding cliffs around Dunwich and other coastal towns, together with a loose interpretation of the biblical story of the flood, whereby the earth found new levels after the flood subsided.

The church at Bramfield is one of the finest in Suffolk. Its thatched roof, cream-washed walls and impressive Gothic windows look most appealing, offset from the rugged round tower. But I have worshipped in it for so many years that I find it hard to describe in purely aesthetic terms. To me it represents the spirituality of all Suffolk churches. Looking at its delicate medieval rood-screen, I hear snatches of the psalms; and the five painted figures of Saints in the panels of its dado are familiar friends. The pulpit and lectern call to mind the homilies of our vicars. Memories of family weddings pervade the altar, baptisms the font, and funerals the lychgate. The nave is bright with the candle-lit services of Christmas and the decorations of Easter and Harvest-time, and it resounds with the dignified vocabulary of the Prayer Book. The much admired alabaster monument to Elizabeth Coke, sculpted by Nicholas Stone, is a moving reminder of the deaths of so many other seventeenth-century mothers in childbirth. However, all such elevating thoughts are always brought down to earth by the flowery eighteenth-century inscriptions on the chancel floor, which record the squabbles between the Nelson and Applewhaite families. When the local heiress Bridgett Nelson married Arthur Applewhaite, her fortune became his by law; but it was to be expected that he would return it to her in his will. This he failed to do, so the Nelsons got their own back by inscribing his iniquity on his tombstone and, on Bridgett's adjoining stone, describing her 'fatigues of a married life, born by her with incredible patience', followed by 'the enjoyment of the glorious freedom of an easy and unblemished widowhood'.

About the only elderly inhabitant of Bramfield who has lived there all his life is Kenneth Clarke, and to me he personifies the old ways and attitudes of the early decades of this century, at the time when Bramfield was still an agricultural village. His innate cheerfulness, sorely tried by family tragedy, is infectious; and his once-fair hair and blue eyes bespeak of a native ancestry of many centuries. Kenneth's father undertook a variety of local enterprises at Bramfield. He ran a pub called The Swan, at the corner of Bridge Street; he dealt in horses; he bought a small farmholding; he opened a butcher's shop, and ran a slaughter-house. Kenneth's formal education was brief: he attended Bramfield School (still functioning as a Primary School) until the age of fourteen, and after that he helped his father and occupied himself with country pursuits, such as shooting and ferreting the ever-present rabbits. When he was a boy there was only one motor-car in the village. This was owned by the elderly Miss Tatlock, who lived at Bramfield House and was the undisputed Queen of Bramfield; at the age of only twenty-four she had provided the village with its school. For everyone else, horses were the only form of locomotion, other than walking. None of the lanes was surfaced – even the main road was only grit-covered, not asphalted – and cattle and pigs were driven along them on the hoof to market. Kenneth retains affectionate memories of old village characters such as Don Watts, the wheelwright, Tom Borrit, the tailor, and Bill Foster, the carpenter. His garden is over-run with flocks of muscovy duck and bantam hens, and he and his wife have never been concerned about renovating their house.

Upstream of Halesworth the little Blyth flows past Walpole. Its name means Welsh-pool, which might imply that a community of British peasants continued to live there after the English invasions, tolerated or ignored, one may suppose, by the ancestors of Kenneth Clarke. But Walpole's more authenticated claim to distinction is of more recent date, and is religious rather than racial. One of its buildings has been used as a Congregational Chapel, formerly called a Meeting-House of the Dissenters, since the days of the Commonwealth in the mid-seventeenth century. Sitting in the wooden gallery and looking toward the centrally-placed pulpit with its sounding-board, it is salutory to reflect on the long tradition of alternative services (alternative to those of the established church, that is) by which the consciences of the non-conformists were assuaged. Such services provided a sort of social safety-valve, for if they had been banned the consequences would surely have been revolutionary.

The water-meadows bordering the Blyth just up from

Walpole Bridge were extensively planted with poplars in the 1960s. These woods received the full force of one of the strongest gusts of the 1987 hurricane, and the sight of the seemingly impenetrable mass of trunks, branches and leaves, reminiscent of old photographs of First World War battle-fields, is one I shall never forget. The man who had planted these poplars was Andrew Vanneck, owner of Heveningham Hall, the palatial mansion which overlooks the Blyth a mile upstream; or, to be more exact, it overlooks a lake, formed by the damming of the river, part of a naturalistic scenario devised by the ubiquitous Capability Brown for the original owner, Sir Gerard Vanneck.

It is an encouraging phenomenon to those who still believe in the influence of heredity that the characteristics of contemporary people can sometimes be recognised in those of their quite distant ancestors. Andrew Vanneck was a gruff, short-tempered man who had made a stockbroker's fortune in the 1920s, particularly by means of late night telephone calls to Wall Street when the rest of the City had retired for the evening. When his older brother, Lord Huntingfield, put Heveningham up for sale, he decided to buy it. His no-nonsense attitude to everyone was commendable, if un-popular; and he certainly dedicated himself to the upkeep of an impossibly impractical house through decades of national crisis and austerity, keeping the most bitter frosts away from the state rooms by feeding enormous quantities of wood into the central-heating furnaces. Therefore it was with a feeling of recognition that I read, in François de La Rochefoucauld's description of his visit to Heveningham in 1784, that Sir Gerard, the original owner, received his French visitors very coldly, omitting to take off his hat to them; they duly went back to their carriage to put on their own hats before entering the house. Only after a while did the crusty bachelor thaw, and then they found in him a most intelligent host and guide to the newly-completed house.

What Sir Gerard showed his visitors is what we still see today, that is, if we can gain access. Heveningham Hall is Suffolk's grandest house, grander even than Ickworth, which sacrifices all its external and internal effects to its eccentric oval drum. The north front of Heveningham is twenty-three bays in width, and its seven-bay centre is supported by giant Corinthian columns, carrying a great frontispiece; at each end are three-bay pavilions, also columned, and with pediments. This enormous Palladian achievement by Sir Robert Taylor is all the more exceptional because it stands in a part of the county where there are plenty of red-brick manor houses but few other great houses. It also seems to be out of place at first sight, seemingly constructed of alien stone; but actually it is of brick, covered with stucco. Facing north, it often looks dark, and indeed the entire house suffers from a lack of sun because the ground to the south, where a much plainer facade overlooks a formal garden, rises sharply, and the winter sun confines its attention to the great glass-framed orangery which stands at the top of the hill amid cedars.

The interior of Heveningham is by James Wyatt, a youthful genius who here excelled himself, most especially in the entrance hall, which is entered immediately from the rustic surroundings of the park without any intervening porch; perhaps Sir Gerard Vanneck had good reason to keep his hat on indoors. The hall, decorated in subtle shades of green, has a most elaborate ceiling, in the form of a tunnel vault divided into bays, whose lines are reflected in the marble floor below. Columns of yellow scagliola form screens at either end, and busts of emperors stand in niches. The hall is devoid of furniture, thus enforcing one's sensation of being transported into the world of Ancient Rome, though surely the Romans never built so fine a room as this in East Anglia in all their centuries of rule. Besides the other state rooms – the elegant dining-room with its painted reliefs, the columned library with its oval medallions, the ballroom with its four corner alcoves – Wyatt included two exquisite miniature rooms: the Etruscan Room, and the Print Room, which has prints simply stuck onto the walls in decorative surrounds, and where generations of Vannecks ate their meals.

Heveningham Hall has been in the headlines for years with national debate about its state of preservation and its future ownership. The government purchased it from the Vanneck family, but after some years sold it to an owner whose stewardship was controversial. During his tenure a fire broke out and gutted the east wing, a marble fireplace was stolen, and a security wire barrier was erected around the house as a protest against the legal right of the public to walk across the park on a footpath. Whatever its future, I cannot feel that Heveningham could ever have made a pleasant house to live in, as it is extremely inconvenient and everything is sacrificed to the state rooms, so much so that the first floor becomes a sort of attic. I am reminded of the lines written by a visitor to Blenheim Palace soon after it was built: ' "Thanks, sir," cried I, "tis very fine, But where d'ye sleep, or where d'ye dine? I find, by all you have been telling, That 'tis a house, but not a dwelling" '.

The Heveningham Hall estate was largely in the neighbouring parish of Huntingfield, from which the Vannecks took their title. This estate had previously been held by the Coke family. The founder of this dynasty was Sir Edward Coke, the authoritarian Lord Chief Justice of England under James I. He and his sons had a talent for advantageous marriages. His first wife – one of the Norfolk Pastons – inherited an estate at Huntingfield, and his second was a sister of the redoubtable Robert Cecil, Lord Burleigh. It was to Huntingfield that Sir Edward retreated in 1592 to escape the plague in London, and we may imagine important legal decisions being made in this quiet upper valley of the Blyth. He settled his sons around him: Robert at Cookley, Arthur at Bramfield, and Henry at Thorington. Robert married the heiress to the Manor of Huntingfield, but subsequent generations of Cokes ceased to live here because they acquired the Holkham estate in Norfolk, and the Earldom of Leicester.

St Mary's church at Huntingfield is remarkable for its roof, laboriously and effectively repainted in the medieval style by the wife of a nineteenth-century vicar, with lots of angels and saintly figures and sacred monograms. A famous oak stood in the grounds of the former Huntingfield Hall, called the Queen's Oak because it was fallaciously supposed that

Elizabeth I had stayed here. Alfred Suckling quotes a memorable description of it: 'The principal arm, now "bald with dry antiquity", shoots up to a great height above the leafage, and being hollow and truncated at the top, with cracks resembling loop-holes, through which the light shines into its cavity, it gives us an idea of the winding staircase in a lofty Gothic turret, which, detached from the other ruins of some venerable pile, hangs tottering to its fall . . .'

The Blyth rises outside the Blything Hundred in the parish of Laxfield, a former market town with a broad street which concludes beside the church and the timber-framed guildhall, once the meeting-place of the parish guild. The church, of All Saints, has a particularly fine flushworked and buttressed tower. There can be no more benign a scene than here. But to me it is haunted by the horrible details of the death of the Puritan, John Noyes, as recounted by the martyrologist, John Foxe. Noyes had been condemned to death in 1557 by the Catholic court in Norwich, but since he came from Laxfield the authorities decided to put the fear of God in the neighbourhood by bringing him back to his home town to be burnt.

Knowing what was coming, the miserable inhabitants of Laxfield extinguished their hearths, so that the fire should not be acquired from their own houses. But the Constable and his assistant spotted a wisp of smoke mounting from a house, and broke down the door to get the fire. John Noyes was then brought forward. He knelt down and prayed, and then was bound to the stake. As the faggots were being placed around him, he said, 'They say, they can make God of a piece of bread: believe them not'; and then, 'Good people, bear witness that I do believe to be saved by the merits and passion of Jesus Christ, and not by my own deeds'. During the terrible minutes while he was burning and screaming with pain, one of the unwilling witnesses exclaimed in horror, 'Good Lord, how the sinews of his arms shrink up!' The Sheriff's men chose to interpret his words as 'What vile wretches are these!', and he was seized and taken before the magistrates at Fressingfield. He was sentenced to be put in the stocks and whipped around the market place the following Sunday.

So as not to leave Laxfield on such a gloomy note, I turn to the pages of a minor Elizabethan poet, Robert Greene, who, twenty-five years after John Noyes' death, composed a short drama called 'Friar Bacon and Friar Bungay'. In it the heroine, Margaret, a beautiful girl of humble birth, is courted by Lambert of Fressingfield and Serlsby of Laxfield. In the event, she refuses them both, for she has a better catch in Lacy, Earl of Lincoln: but here is Serlsby's down-to-earth proposal:

> I cannot trick it up with poesies,
> Nor paint my passions with comparisons,
> Nor tell a tale of Phoebus and his loves:
> But this believe me, – Laxfield here is mine,
> Of ancient rent seven hundred pounds a year,
> And if thou canst but love a country squire,
> I will enfeoff thee, Margaret, in all:
> I cannot flatter; try me, if thou please.

From Laxfield I shall return to the coast down the exquisite valley of the Yox, dubbed 'The Garden of Suffolk' by the Victorian nature-writer, Clement Scott, who also gave a memorable sobriquet to the North Norfolk coastline around Cromer – 'Poppy-Land'. The first village we come to is Peasenhall (pea-corner), whose long main street, approached along the line of the Roman road from Badingham, has houses on one side and the Yox ditch on the other. A range of cottages, splendidly converted by the Landmark Trust, have at their centre a late medieval wooden hall, complete with its carved door-heads for the service entrances, and the crown posts of hall and solar. It had been in use as an inn, or perhaps a hostelry for Sibton Abbey, by 1478. During the nineteenth century the village thrived on the Peasenhall Drill Works of James Smyth and Sons, who made agricultural implements and were the original inventors of the Suffolk Seed Drill.

Peasenhall, like Laxfield, is haunted by a death: not a public burning but a private murder. On the night of 31 May 1902, Rose Harsent, the twenty-three-year-old servant of William and Georgina Crisp of Providence House, just by the church, was strangled. William Gardiner, an older man and a foreman in Smyth and Sons, was accused and brought to trial at

Ipswich. What made the case famous was that at the first trial the jury voted eleven to one for guilty, and at a second trial another jury voted eleven to one for not guilty. Since unanimous verdicts were necessary in those days, the Director of Public Prosecutions dropped the charge, and the case was never proved. William Gardiner left Peasenhall and lived elsewhere under an assumed name, and the general presumption is that he was innocent, and had been framed by a false witness. How satisfactory it would be, in cases such as this, if the real murderers were to make deathbed confessions.

Sibton, adjacent to Peasenhall, lies at the junction of two Roman roads. Near where these roads met (or, rather, where they had once met, for they were long disused) the Cistercian Order built its only monastery in Suffolk, Sibton Abbey. When one considers the immense constructions of the Cistercians in the North of England, such as Fountains or Rievaulx, the ruins of Sibton may seem slight. But at least they are situated in isolation among the grasses of the water-meadows, reminding us that the disciples of St Bernard made a point of setting up their foundations in remote countryside and engaging in agriculture. The names of the adjoining North Grange and South Grange Farms preserve a tenuous memory of their activities.

Yoxford sounds like a rustic equivalent of Oxford, and the initial Y is because it means a ford for a yoke of oxen, not just for oxen. Like Peasenhall, it is a village that was boosted by local industry during the nineteenth century, but relapsed into agriculture in the twentieth. The Yoxford Mechanics Institution was the main employer, and there were four bakers, three blacksmiths, six shoemakers, three butchers, three milliners and two watchmakers. There was also a local poet, James Bird, who opened a stationers' shop. The village street retains much evidence of those prosperous days, with substantial Georgian houses, and pleasant architectural features such as Doric porches, and bow windows and balconies.

In 1430 much of Yoxford came into the hands of John Hopton. He owned the estates of Stricklands, Meriells, Middleton and Brendfen, all in the parish, together with large holdings in surrounding parishes; and, as we have seen, he himself lived at Westwood Hall near Blythburgh. Ten years later he purchased Cockfield Hall, and after his death his widow, Thomasin, came to live here. This resourceful woman had previously been married to William Sidney, an ancestor of the Elizabethan hero, Sir Philip Sidney. She managed her affairs carefully, as is evident from the terms of her marriage to John Hopton, whereby she retained her independent income and her moveable property. Her account books at Cockfield, where she lived to the age of eighty, reveal that the home farm provided her household with many of its needs, but that her tenant farmers paid her around half their rents in kind – cheese, butter, milk, eggs, chicken and geese; and the bailiff of the estate was obliged to keep her in fish, wine, cloth, malt and other necessities.

The present Cockfield Hall was originally built by Sir Arthur Hopton in the early sixteenth century, and the north wing of the present house, together with an impressive step-gabled gatehouse and some stables, also date from his time, distinguishable by their narrow Tudor bricks. It was to this house that Elizabeth I sent her unfortunate cousin, Catherine Grey, under house arrest. Catherine and her elder sister Jane were granddaughters of Princess Mary, Duchess of Suffolk, and Jane had already paid the supreme penalty for being put forward as claimant to the throne on the death of Edward VI. Catherine, now heir-presumptive to Elizabeth, was kept under careful watch at court, and all hell broke loose when the Virgin Queen, then at Ipswich during her tour of 1561, was informed that Catherine had secretly married Edward Seymour, Earl of Hertford, and was pregnant by him. The marriage was annulled and she was imprisoned in the Tower of London, whose Governor was Sir Owen Hopton. From here she was removed to house arrest at Cockfield Hall, where she simply wasted away like Ophelia, taking no interest in her food or her health, and dying within seven years. Cockfield Hall subsequently came into the hands of the Blois family, whose estate stretched from here to the sea. Earlier this century it comprised one of the best partridge shoots in Suffolk, and Sir Ralph Blois was such a fanatical sportsman that he had platoons of flanking beaters to funnel the birds towards him and just two other guns, with himself always in the central position.

The River Yox is, I assume, so traumatised by its encounter with the A12 at Yoxford that it seems to suffer from amnesia and forgets its name (or, more correctly, its nickname), emerging from under the road and rail bridges as the Minsmere River. From here it presses on into the Sandlings to suffer the ultimate indignity for a river – being prevented from entering the sea naturally, only through a sluice. It passes first between the parishes of Middleton (middle-place) and Darsham, and then those of Theberton and Westleton. Middleton is home to Michael Hamburger, one of the distinguished literary immigrants to our county, whose long poem 'In Suffolk' expresses his love for his latter-day surroundings. Theberton Hall was the home of Charles Doughty, the author of *Travels in Arabia Deserta*.

Here was yet another son of Suffolk who found the pastoral charms of the county too confined for his restless spirit. His account of his journey to Mecca, as part of a camel-caravan of pilgrims who set out from Damascus in 1876, is one of the most absorbing travel books ever written. He must have had an amazing personality to be able to obtain the confidence of the stern and suspicious characters who went with him, especially as he openly admitted his Christianity; and he portrays them brilliantly in his book, from the humblest camel-drivers to the proudest sheiks. *Arabia Deserta* is written in an eccentric style, designed to shun the flowery prose of contemporary Victorian writers, and in this it lacks the classical purity of the book which was published forty years later, and with which it must inevitably be compared – T. E. Lawrence's *Seven Pillars of Wisdom*. But this should not dim the fact that Doughty was an equally great Arabist and intrepid traveller in an alien world, who brought the mysterious east closer to English consciousness. This he did by his own adventures, in contrast to Edward Fitzgerald, who did it solely by his pen, without hardly leaving Suffolk. Charles's older brother, Henry, wrote an admirable and sensitive history of Theberton. I like the obsolete girls' names he has plucked from the sixteenth-century registers: Beteriss, Damaris, Annice, Amyce, Ancilla, Fyonet, Sythe, Finet, Apphia, Tryphena and Jeronomye.

Westleton is built around a village green, which slopes down to a duck-pond and is bordered by a good Suffolk mixture of houses, including Moor House, with Tudor gables, and the Crown Inn, with weathered red brick. At Westleton, as at the hamlet of Eastbridge a couple of miles south across the river, the immediate presence of the heathland is felt, and one only has to walk to the end of the village to find acres bright with yellow gorse in spring and purple ling in late summer. For we are now back in the exceptional stretch of scenery which lies behind the coastline between Southwold and Aldeburgh, just to the south of the Dunwich Forest and Westwood Marshes that we have already discovered. From Westleton or Eastbridge we stride onto footpaths leading on sandy tracks for miles between the bracken or the birch-trees, on the watch for all aspects of the natural world, from Red Admiral butterflies to red deer.

The scenery in this area has changed out of recognition in the course of this century. Previously the woodlands were confined to game coverts, and the heaths were grazed by sheep, and in consequence were mainly covered with grass. When it no longer became profitable to graze sheep on these Sandlings, they gradually became overgrown with the trees and plants which we now see. Even the marshes are not quite what they seem. They are not original wetlands, but have been artificially re-converted as such from being drained fields. This change happened partly during the last war, as a precaution against German invasion, and partly by the creation of large shallow lagoons with shingle islets, carefully designed to attract particular species of birds. For here, in the middle of the Minsmere Levels, is the Royal Society for the Protection of Birds' famous Nature Reserve. Hundreds of species of birds are identifiable, many of them migrants, including some from North America, such as the greater yellowlegs, the stilt sandpiper and the long-billed dowitcher. Here also is a nesting colony of avocets second only to that at Havergate Island on the Ore, a few miles south. Meanwhile, in the surrounding woodland are the sparrowhawks, woodpeckers, woodcocks and nightingales, and in the marshes are the marsh-harriers and bitterns. The whole area is a happy hunting ground for twitchers, though none will ever see the birds of prey once common in Suffolk, such as the eagle, gyrfalcon, and kestrel.

Close to the foreshore of the Minsmere, where formerly the river entered the sea at a small haven, there stands the ruin of a chapel. This was once a hermitage attached to Leiston Abbey, and one of the last of the abbots, John Green, became an anchorite here. The loneliness of this spot seemed to attract solitary men, and Julian Tennyson describes an extraordinary figure, apparently deranged like Edgar in *King Lear*, whom he used to encounter when wandering around these marshes. This man was obsessed by the sea, and was convinced that his long-lost son would one day return to shore just here, saved from a ship-wreck.

Leiston Abbey was founded for the Premonstratensian monks in the twelfth century. Together with Butley Priory nearby, it was established through a benefaction by Ralph de Glanville, a Lord Chief Justice of England who had been born at Stratford St Andrew. The original abbey was probably beside the chapel to which John Green retreated, but in 1363 it was transferred to its present site a couple of miles inland. The ruins of this monastery are the most extensive in Suffolk apart from St Edmondsbury. The grey of the thick flint rubble walls contrasts pleasantly with the red of the plentiful brick infills and octagonal Tudor gatehouse. The Lady Chapel, preserved for centuries as a granary, has been restored and reconsecrated; and the house that was later built among the ruins of the abbey is now used for musical courses.

The Minsmere Marshes cannot really be called lonely today because they are hardly more than a mile from the Sizewell Atomic Energy Power Station, whose bleak silhouette dominates the scene to the south. I once walked down the coast through a summer night, and passing from the moonlit dunes into the barricaded pathway that led through the construction site of Sizewell B, was like visiting Dante's Inferno. But now that it is completed I find that the enormous dome of the new pressurised water reactor is not without a certain awesome grandeur, proclaiming Suffolk to be the provider of so much energy to Southern England. And whatever our judgement about atomic power, the presence of this silent monster at Sizewell is not altogether incongruous, because Leiston, the little town just beside it, had itself become industrialised during the last century, due to the success of the local engineering company, Garretts of Leiston. When Richard Garrett, the nineteen-year-old son of the owner, took over its business affairs in 1826, it had already acquired a special reputation for making scythes and sickles, and had developed the first practical form of threshing machine. Under his forty years of enterprising direction, Garretts was in the forefront of the national drive towards the application of steam-power to agriculture and industry, particularly in the manufacture of mobile engines. Threshing machines and corn-drills and other specialist implements were also developed to ever-higher standards of efficiency.

Garretts of Leiston continued to expand, and peaked in the First World War, producing an arsenal of shells and aircraft parts, and employing over a thousand men. Thereafter it shrivelled, and in 1980 had to close down. Fortunately the Long Shop, built in 1847 for making the mobile engines, has been preserved as a museum. In it may be seen several venerable steam engines, as well as other fascinating exhibits. The Long Shop was lucky not to be damaged by enemy air attack during the Second World War, since it was in the front line for low-flying German aircraft which aimed bombs at it which fortunately failed to explode. The US Air Force, stationed at Leiston airfield with its Flying Fortresses, retaliated by some terrifying raids.

I turn now to the land to the north of the River Blyth, as far as the northern Hundred River. Here is a well-ordered landscape of fields and copses which, though enclosed, somehow gives a greater impression of space than does the comparable farmland to the south of the Blyth. Long lines of hundred-year-old oaks stand along roads and lanes, and well-built brick cottages and barns are much in evidence. These speak of large agricultural estates, and this corner of the county has been partly fashioned by three: Henham, Benacre and Sotterley (the parish of Sotterly lies just outside the Blyth Hundred boundary), whose parks embellish the scenery.

Henham (high-home) is the seat of the family of Rous, who have lived here since the sixteenth century, subsequently acquiring the title of Earl of Stradbroke, the village from which the family originated. The present Earl ('Call me Keith') is an extrovert who prides himself on being a self-made man who made a fortune in Australia. He drives around in a yellow Rolls-Royce, has sired thirteen children, and has flogged the family silver. Henham Park, though much hacked about, still retains its essential shape of parkland surrounded by woods. It was laid out by Humphrey Repton, and several of his original oaks remain. The park is approached from the south through a great ornamental lodge and gateway, from which a long drive once swept on for over a mile to Henham Hall. This, like the lodge, was a Neo-Classical structure of the early nineteenth century, but it was pulled down in 1953. Though this destruction may now be regretted, it is to my mind far less deplorable than the fate of the previous Henham Hall, a large Elizabethan mansion, of red-brick walls and stone quoins, built around a central courtyard, which was gutted by fire in 1773. The young owner, John Rous, was in Venice at the time, and the conflagration was attributed to his butler who, it was said, helped himself so liberally to his master's fine wines that he inadvertently knocked a candle on to the sawdust in one of the wine bins. By dawn next day nothing remained of Henham Hall except its frame: forty-five rooms had disappeared, and nothing was insured.

An earlier inventory of 1602 gives a delightful flavour of life in old Henham Hall. Even in an age of erratic spelling, it seems to have been rather casually or hurriedly written. For instance, in the kitchen were: 'Two rostirons, tenne spits, one pair of racks, ffower cobirons, one plate of iron to lye before the panne, two payre of ptt hockes, two frying pannes, one tray, thre chopping knyves, two clyvers, one myncinge knyfe, two stemors, three brasse ladles, two old tubbs, one fyer sholve, one fyre forke, one grate, two chopping bordes, and certain other implements'. And there were many other useful implements in the pantry, larder, dairy, malthouse and 'pastry'. The hall, gallery, parlour and dining-chamber were relatively sparsely furnished, and the most comfortable place in the house was clearly the bed in the best chamber, which comprised: 'One posted beadstead, wth ye testor and vallens and curtens of silke, one feather bed wth a boulster, two pillowes, two blanketts, one twilted covlett of silke'. The other rooms had simpler beds, and one wonders what household functions were performed by the occupants of 'Loveis' chamber', 'Arty's chamber', 'Gyrlyng's chamber', 'Powsyn's chamber', 'Heylocke's chamber' and 'Gray's chamber'. The chapel, no longer used for worship, had become a granary housing stores of wheat, rye and barley. Out in the yards were fifty hens, twenty-five ducks, twenty geese, ten pigs, twelve milking cows and a bull, seven steers and seven heffers, a flock of thirty-eight sheep, and about forty horses of various kinds.

The Benacre (bean-field) estate has been owned by the Gooch family since Sir Thomas Gooch, who was also the Bishop of Norwich, purchased it in 1743 for £15,800, some £810,000 in today's money. Since the estate would now be worth many million, it was an extremely good investment. Benacre Hall was destroyed by fire as recently as 1926, but rebuilt. Behind it the property stretches down to the sea, culminating in Benacre Broad, a delightfully naturalistic marsh and lake beside the beach, flanked by woods. Sotterley, the third of these three estates, belongs to the Barne family, who acquired it from that of Playters. It presents a more attractive ensemble than either Henham or Benacre. The Hall is Georgian, its red-brick frontage capped by a stone balustrade and pediment; and the park retains – or rather, has re-acquired – an almost medieval aspect. In the middle of it stands St Margaret's church, which is richly furnished and contains brasses and monuments to the Playters. Sir Thomas Playters, who died in 1638, is depicted with his two successive wives and his twenty-two children – an impressive progeny which, however, failed to prevent the fall of the Playters dynasty.

Wangford (waggon-ford), whose parish contains Henham Park, has been relieved from the full force of the A12 which flowed right through it till recently. But it will never be able to recapture the deep silence of the past, eloquently described in the memoirs of James Ewing Ritchie, whose father was the Dissenting Minister at Wangford during the first half of the nineteenth century. He tells us that many of the villagers had hardly been more than six miles from the village in the whole of their lives. Only the farmers, dressed in their blue coats with yellow brass buttons, would regularly drive to Halesworth or Bungay where, after transacting their business, they repaired to the inn for a smoke and a brandy. His father's house was extremely spartan. Several windows had been blocked to save on window-tax, and in the evening the sitting room was only dimly lit by a dip candle. Tea, sugar and coffee were only occasional luxuries. Most of the village went barefoot in the summer, and in the winter the women wore clogs. Yet his family was a contented one and enjoyed intelligent conversation: and 'Of the rush and roar of modern life, with its restlessness and eagerness for something new and sensational, we had not the remotest idea.'

During the eighteenth century the Dissenting Ministers often had much larger congregations than did the incumbents of the Church of England, and at Wrentham, north of Wangford, the non-comformist tradition was particularly strong. This village had earlier been one of the leading centres of Puritanism, encouraged by the enthusiasm of the Brewsters, who lived in Wrentham Hall. The large Congregational Chapel was built in 1778, and the Reverend James Hingeston of Frostenden Hall (between Wangford and Wrentham) must have felt very much on the defensive as he laboured away at that time on his manuscript on the Thirty-Nine Articles of the Church of England. Frostenden (frog-valley), though nearly three miles from the sea, is listed in Domesday Book as a seaport, indicative of the free flow of so many of the little streams which have since become diverted, blocked or sluiced.

This account of the Blything Hundred began with its architectural flagship, Holy Trinity Blythburgh. I conclude with what is to me a more wonderful church, St Andrew's Westhall, which is in many ways its antithesis. Blythburgh is famous for its prominent site and its obvious purity of style. Westhall is hard to find and even harder to understand, merits which I hope will prevent it from ever being over-run with visitors as Blythburgh is. It is tucked away at the end of a lane in a declivity and hidden between ilexes, with only a couple of houses for company, and the village of Westhall itself has vanished. It is the organic product of four hundred years of changing style, from Norman to Perpendicular, always expanding outward and upward until eventually economic decline and religious indifference left it to a slow deterioration over another four hundred. It contains a richly ornamented Norman doorway hidden inside the subsequent tower; a spacious chancel with beautiful geometric windows; wall paintings, fragments of stained glass, painted panels; and one of Suffolk's finest octagonal fonts. Such are the attributes of St Andrew's Westhall.

IX
Waveney

From its source between the villages of Redgrave and Lopham, the Waveney provides a natural border between East Norfolk and East Suffolk; that is, until it nearly reaches the sea some four miles from Lowestoft. Here it rejects the obvious route and lurches north to join the Yare at Breydon Water, and from there to flow into the sea at Yarmouth, a total distance of twenty miles instead of the four. By this deviant course the Waveney carves out for Suffolk a corner of land known as Lothingland, which would otherwise have been in Norfolk. At its northern tip Lothingland has been subsumed by the urban spread of Great Yarmouth; and although the 1974 boundary changes of English counties included some ruthless butchery, I do not think that Suffolk really suffered from the arbitrary division which was then made, whereby Norfolk gained the northern half, even though this includes the Roman fort of Gariannonum, or Burgh Castle.

Lothingland means 'the land of Hluda's people' and has nothing to do with loathing. But Michael Drayton, in his famous *Poly-Olbion*, a verse description of the whole of England, written in Jacobean times, made play with the word and referred to it as Lovingland. Here, he suggested, was where Father Neptune came to sport with those playful goddesses, the Suffolk rivers:

> When Waveney in her way, on this septentriall side,
> That these two eastern shires doth equally divide,
> From Laphamford leads on, her streame into the east,
> By Bungay, then along by Beckles, when possest
> Of Loving-land, 'bout which her limber armes she throwes,
> With Neptune taking hands, betwixt them who inclose.

More than anywhere else in Suffolk, the Hundred of

Mutford and Lothingland, almost an island, was an area of Danish settlement in the ninth and tenth centuries. This is evident from the Norse origins of many of the place names. Lound derives from *lundr*, a grove in a plain; and Fritton from Fridetuna, named after Freya, the Scandinavian goddess. Ashby, Barnby, Blundeston, Gunton and Oulton, record the settlements of Aski, Biarni, Loond, Gunna and Ali; Herringfleet, that of the sons of Herla; and Somerleyton, that of Sumerlithi – a 'summer-warrior', which is what the Danes were before they settled here. (Blundeston, incidentally, was corrupted to Blunderstone by Dickens in *David Copperfield*: he found it a convenient name for David's natal village, but his description of it is purely imaginary.)

Somerleyton is the jewel of Suffolk's Lothingland. It is an enclave of greenery which includes a large garden with a maze, a park, tracts of marshland beside the Waveney, and extensive woods bordering a lake, the Fritton Decoy. This stretch of water, over two miles long, was originally formed by the flooding of peat cuttings, in the manner of the Norfolk Broads. On its bank several large duck decoys were erected during the last century, by which flocks of tame ducks were trained to enter the decoys to feed, enticing in with them the wild duck, which were then trapped and killed for the market. (Those were the days when animals destined for the table led entirely natural lives until the final moment of slaughter.)

Somerleyton Hall is the creation of Sir Morton Peto, who purchased the estate in 1844. Peto exemplified the energy of the age in which he lived. He made a fortune from his construction company, contracting for several leading London monuments and buildings, such as Nelson's Column and the Reform Club. He became a Member of Parliament. He was also a railway entrepreneur, and founded the Eastern Counties Railway. At the same time he was a philanthropist, a builder of 'ragged schools', mental asylums and orphanages, and a Baptist. This flood of energy was now unleashed on his new property in Suffolk. Lowestoft was to be thoroughly developed, with a railway line to Norwich (with a station at Somerleyton, of course), a new harbour and a new town. The seventeenth-century Somerleyton Hall was rehashed and expanded, Peto employing as his architect a successful sculptor, John Thomas. The result was an extravaganza, part Jacobean, part Italianate, but eminently Victorian. An enormous conservatory adjoined the house. A model village was also built, a crescent of ornamental cottages beside a green. P. G. Wodehouse once wrote: 'Whatever may be said in favour of the Victorians it is pretty generally admitted that few of them were to be trusted within reach of a trowel and a pile of bricks'. But since his day we are less censorious, and the Peto-Thomas creation at Somerleyton certainly passes muster as a fine example of its period. Sir Morton's business empire crashed not long afterwards, in 1866, and the Somerleyton estate was sold to his friend Sir Francis Crossley, a carpet manufacturer from Yorkshire.

Peto's railway ran to Lowestoft past Oulton Broad, where it went right by the cottage inhabited by George Borrow. Here was another larger-than-life character, but one who was the very opposite to Sir Morton Peto. Borrow was an outsider – an awkward, tempestuous, self-opinionated man – whose driving force was expressed through curious personal encounters and through the brilliance of his writing. At the age of thirty-seven he had married a wealthy widow, but nonetheless detested bourgeois pretentiousness, and loved having rows with his neighbours. The grandeurs of Somerleyton Hall were nothing to him. The railway was anathema, and not merely for 'not in my back yard' reasons. He loathed all manifestations of industry, for he himself was by nature a wanderer, and felt affinity for gypsies and travellers. He found no convenience in the railway, for he would far rather have travelled on horseback or on foot; indeed, at the age of fifty he was to embark on a series of amazing walking tours. So he decided to leave Oulton (though he returned in old age), and must have derived a sardonic satisfaction at the news of Peto's subsequent bankruptcy.

Beccles and Bungay are both ancient towns built on buffs on the Suffolk bank of the lower Waveney. Their old market-places are only six miles apart, and their appearance bears superficial similarity, as does much of their history. Both were centres of religious protest, beginning with support for the Lollards in the fifteenth century. Both were largely rebuilt in brick during the early-eighteenth century after a series of fires had destroyed much of the wooden housing. Both derived a measure of prosperity, during the years of agricultural depression, from the establishment of enterprising printing firms: William Clowes of Beccles; John Childs, and Clay and Son, of Bungay. And both have been comparably expanded and developed during recent decades, Beccles on a somewhat larger scale. Yet it is the peculiarities of each which provide their greatest interest.

Beccles (river-pasture) belonged to the Abbey of St Edmund from before the Norman Conquest, and in consequence never became a centre of baronial power, unlike Bungay. But it was fortified, as we are reminded by the names of streets – Saltgate, Northgate, Smallgate, Ballygate, Hungate and Blyburgate – streets which shape the intricate pattern of the old upper town. In contrast to Bungay also, Beccles, further downstream on the Waveney, was in those early days involved in the fishing trade: it was assessed in Domesday Book for 60,000 herrings.

St Michael's church stands just on the edge of the high ground. Its large tower provides a particularly impressive focus for the town because it is detached from the church and stands alone. Indeed, it is the only one in Suffolk to do so, except for the small round tower at Bramfield. This separation gives the impression that the tower belongs as much to the Old Market in front of it as to the church beside it, as much to Mammon as to God, a guardian of civic as well as ecclesiastical pride, like an Italian campanile – though sadly Beccles, like other Suffolk towns, has no piazza to complement it. The tower looks especially sturdy, being made of Yorkshire stone and having angular buttresses and an unrelieved top. The south porch of the church is also of stone, and displays a lofty facade of empty niches.

Punctuating the streets and lanes of Old Beccles are many Georgian houses, ranging from the mansions of the local gentry who moved into the town during the winter, to the less pretentious houses of the traders and professional classes. These, together with their latter-day inhabitants, have been acutely observed by Adrian Bell in *A Street in Suffolk*, the last of his delightful books about the county; and I think of them in the passages where he describes Beccles on a mad March day, with bustling figures battling against the wind. But just below the town, on the river and the marshes, I think of the scene in August, with all the pleasure-craft cramming the landing-stages at this southern extremity of their cruising around the Norfolk Broads. Much of the riverine scenery around Beccles has been preserved, even though the A146 cuts through the marshes. Just outside the town is Roos Hall, a lofty Elizabethan fragment once owned by the Carolingian poet, John Suckling. Catherine Suckling, Nelson's mother, came from the rectory of the adjacent parish of Barsham to marry Edmund Nelson, curate of St Michael's. A mile east of Beccles is Worlingham Hall, a late-eighteenth-century mansion whose rich interior by Francis Sandys has recently been restored to its former glory by an energetic owner who has repainted some of the intricate plaster-moulded ceilings with his own hand.

Bungay became the castle-town of the Bigod Earls of Norfolk in the twelfth century. That is to say, it was the cluster of houses and hovels around the massive walls of the strongest castle in East Anglia: built in 1165, dismantled in 1174, rebuilt in 1294, and in ruins by 1382. Today, Bungay is a reconstructed and well-preserved town surrounding the pathetic remnants of the castle, whose curtain walls are traceable only from the curvated lines of the circumambient streets, and whose keep has undergone a melt-down into piles of rubble beside a grass lawn. Bungay, accordingly, has a hollow centre, and the Market Place with its loggia (the Butter Cross), and the great tower of St Mary's church, both lack centrality. All the same, St Mary's tower is extremely unusual and imposing, and provides Bungay with as fine a Perpendicular edifice as that at Beccles, even though most of it was built as late as 1700. The church to which it is attached comprises the former west end of the Priory Church of a Benedictine nunnery. Immediately beyond St Mary's is Holy Trinity, whose round tower is not only the oldest building in Bungay but actually antedates the castle, its coursed flints, herringbone masonry and round-headed windows indicating an Anglo-Saxon construction. And, as a later addition to this ecclesiastical sanctuary, the Roman Catholic church of St Edmund, an ornate building of red-brick and stone dressing, stands beside St Mary's to the south.

As at Beccles, there are several eighteenth-century houses in the sinuous streets of Bungay. At the time of the French Revolution one of these, Bridge House in Bridge Street, was occupied by the Vicar of St Mary, Ilketshall, whose name was Ives. A young and penniless political refugee, François René de Chateaubriand, who had in desperation accepted a position as French teacher at a school at Beccles, was befriended by Ives and came to stay in his house. Chateaubriand, a Breton aristocrat already recognised as one of the most intelligent and charming of the emigrés, was enchanted by the Ives and their teenage daughter Charlotte. When the time came for him to leave, Mrs Ives drew him aside to suggest that he might marry Charlotte, their only child. But this was a tactical error on her part, for not only did it elicit his dramatic response, 'Stop! I am a married man', but it also provided yet another romantic episode for his brilliant autobiography: 'I took the mail-coach for London, after writing a letter to Mrs Ives of which I regret that I did not keep a copy'. In his memoirs he permits himself to speculate on what would have been his life if he had settled in Bungay, but the thought of such a tempestuous and imaginative character fitting in to such a restricted and provincial society defies the imagination.

The prow of Bungay, which overlooks a great sweep of the Waveney, has been industrialised. And Outney Common, the large stretch of pasturage enclosed by the river, is separated from the town by the roaring A143. Bungay has thus had its nose cut off, and the special attraction of this natural feature has been much diminished, part of it being given over to a golf course. Outney Common was once the scene of the Bungay races, and the fair that went with them; and Alfred Munnings has given us a vivid description of them at the beginning of this century, when he was still a student. He was overwhelmed at all the music and noise, the roundabouts and coconut shies, the gypsy lads and ponies. And when he saw the thoroughbred horses with their jockeys in bright silk colours, and the thrill of the steeple-chases, he knew at once that above all he wanted to be an artist who painted horses.

In the eighteenth century a bath-house was constructed over a curative spring on the north bank overlooking Outney Common, on the site of the medieval vineyard of Bungay Castle. John King, the promoter of this venture, described the scene in very sugary phraseology: 'Those lovely hills which incircle the flowery plain, are variegated with all that can ravish the astonished sight. They arise from the winding mazes of the river Waveney, enriched with the utmost variety the watery element is capable of producing'; and he goes on to say that Bungay 'is situated on a pleasing ascent to view the pride of nature on the other side, which the goddesses have chosen for their earthly paradise'. Despite – or perhaps because of – these literary efforts, the bath-house failed to flourish.

But the best description of Outney Common comes from Sir Henry Rider Haggard, who farmed the far bank (on the Norfolk side) a century ago. He noted perceptively that the particular beauty of the Common depended not on the gold of the gorse or the green of the meadows or the wildflowers bordering the river, nor on the distant prospect of the towers and gabled roofs of Bungay, but in the constant changes of light that passed across this delectable bowl of land. He writes that in all his travels he never found anywhere more quietly and constantly beautiful than the bend of the Waveney around Bungay. Coming from such a master of descriptive style, and one who had revelled in the grandeur of the deserts and mountains of Africa, this is indeed a complement to the Suffolk scene. It is comparable to the fascination expressed in our own day by Sir Laurens van der Post, another exponent of the wilds of Africa, for the scenery around Aldeburgh.

Rider Haggard's book, *A Farmer's Year*, gives an account of its subject which is both extremely informative and delightful to read. It describes a whole community, from labourers to neighbouring squires, engaged in time-honoured farming practices which were gradually changing as a result of early mechanisation. And it demonstrates the frightening vagaries of farming without any government subsidies and without any protection from American grain. For instance, he notes that the selling price of a quarter of grain at the Bungay market in 1800 was £6 4s for wheat, £3 10s for barely, and £2 8s for oats. In his own day, in 1895, it was £1 3s 1d for wheat, £1 1s 11d for barley, and 14s 6d for oats. And this despite the creeping inflation of a century! Then again, the rent of one of his farms was £250 a year in 1868, but only £50 thirty years later. Yet somehow, through force of habit, the farms of Norfolk and Suffolk continued to be worked by farmers who could hardly pay their rent, and by labourers who earned thirty shillings a week. The author entertained his tenants to an annual New Year dinner in Bungay. This gargantuan feast helped them forget the painful reviews of their rental payments, and it concluded in a sing-song and a chorus of 'For old Bungay is a wonderful town'. Henry Rider Haggard was a widely-respected Chairman of the Bungay Bench, and deeply concerned in nature conservation. His tours of inspection on his farm were mostly by bicycle, and he also cycled regularly to Kessingland, where he had a house by the sea. On the way there, this strong man (clad, no doubt, in breeches, Norfolk jacket and broad-brimmed cap) was once blown off for several yards into a ploughed field by the force of an even stronger wind.

Beccles and Bungay are both in the Hundred of Wangford (though the parish of Wangford, curiously, is not), and this ancient administrative unit, dating from the tenth century, itself seems to have been marked out from even earlier territorial divisions. For a start, the landscape along the line of the Roman Road, which approaches Bungay from the south, contains field boundaries which suggest that they were first formed in Romano-British times. With a bit of imagination, we may feel we can detect traces of their rectangular layout (known as 'centuriation', because comprising 100 units each of about a quarter hectare). Then, the western half of

Wangford hundred comprises two groups of parishes, known at the Seven Parishes and the Nine Parishes, both of which contain clues about early Saxon times.

The Seven Parishes comprise the two in Bungay itself (St Mary and Holy Trinity) together with All Saints Mettingham, and the four Ilketshalls – St Andrew, St John, St Lawrence and St Margaret. On the evidence of the disposition of common pastures in Domesday Book, it appears that this group derives from a single unit based on Bungay. It is thought that Ilketshall is named after the Ulfcytel, who fought the Danish Sweyn in 1004 in a bloody battle near Thetford. So this might have been his domain, and Bungay his strong-point. Ilketshall St Margaret has a round tower which is possibly contemporaneous with Ulfcytel. Mettingham became the site of a castle (or, more accurately, a fortified manor-house), built for Sir John de Norwich in 1344, after the Earls of Norfolk had ceased to live at Bungay; its gatehouse still stands. Fifty years later, it was converted into an ecclesiastical college for the training of priests, well-endowed with land in this and nearby parishes. Subsequently it became a farmhouse. Among the records of All Saints, Mettingham, is a spoof Register of 1653, in the days of the Commonwealth. It is signed by 'Simon Suckbottle, Nasty Nan, John Gingerbread, Halfbrickt Man, Jumping Jones, Bounty Bridg and Dick Devill, Inhabitants of Utopia' – a testimony to the disordered state of the Church at the time, and to the contemporary sense of humour.

The Nine Parishes consist of St Mary, Flixton, together with seven all called South Elmham (one alternatively called Homersfield), whose eight small Norman churches are variously dedicated to the following: St Mary, St Peter, St Michael, St Nicholas, St James, St Margaret, St Cross (a corruption of Sancroft St George) and All Saints. Together, these are known simply as 'The Saints'. This group, which forms a Rural Deanery, was more properly called the Ferding of Elmham (elm-home), a Ferding being the fourth part of a Hundred. At the time of the Norman Conquest, the Ferding of Elmham was in the possession of the Bishop of East Anglia. It seems probable that it had been held by the bishopric from early Saxon times, and it may be that it was an estate granted to St Felix himself by the Wuffinga dynasty in the seventh century, which might account for the origin of the name of Flixton. South Elmham Hall, in the parish of St Cross, is a sixteenth-century farmhouse which contains several stone arches of a former medieval Bishop's Palace. This was a place to which the bishops would have come from time to time, and at which their steward, who managed the estate at South Elmham, would have permanently resided. Its large moat is still the host to ducks and geese, and in the fields around are British White Cattle, the ancient native breed.

'The Saints' is one of the most intimate corners of Suffolk. It has been protected from contemporary pressures by its relative remoteness from Ipswich, and it is tucked away from the main roads. Even the power lines avoid it. To enter it is like penetrating a maze, because each signpost is to another saint. Taking away the road-signs during the Second World War must have been quite superfluous, as any Panzer Group would have become hopelessly bogged down here. The lanes connecting the South Elmhams are unusually narrow, and change direction at frequent right-angle bends as they negotiate ancient land demarcations or pass by still-unenclosed village greens. The centre of the maze is the Minster at South Elmham St Cross, and to reach this the frustrated motorist has to get out of his car at South Elmham Hall and walk half a mile through fields along a most admirable trail, which itself takes a right-angle bend half way along, and leads through some narrow grass fields along the line of a winter stream.

The Minster is a place of profound mystery. Standing in a copse are the rubble ruins of the walls of a church whose design is unusual. It had an apse at one end, and the body of the church was divided by an internal wall thus forming a nave and a narthex, indicative of monastic usage. Today its site is calculated to induce an almost mystical sense of awe and wonder, not perhaps so much religious as animist. The rough copse of hornbeam, thorn and elder, is the haunt of rooks. The ground is thick with leaves and rotting timber. No fences, prepared pathways, steps or explanatory signs, are (so far) there to spoil the magic. The earthwork which we clamber across to reach the ruin may date from Roman times. One feels that here the old pagan gods have come into their own again, the ones we acknowledge every day of the week without thinking – Tue, Woden, Thor and Freia; and certainly nature herself has reclaimed what was once a site cleared of vegetation. Here in the deepest spot of the Suffolk countryside we can echo the words of the psalmist: 'a thousand years in thy sight are but as yesterday'.

The Waveney was made navigable up as far as Bungay in the eighteenth century. Above Bungay it had weirs for mills, but no locks for boats. Today, though its flow is artificially controlled and many of its water-meadows drained, it still winds its way, lethargically and unobtrusively, along its valley, breaking at sluices and passing under brick bridges and by old mill houses, its otters protected and no longer cruelly hunted by hounds, its coarse fish in plentiful stock and variety. I like this tribute to the Waveney by the nineteenth-century Suffolk poet, Jean Ingelow:

> Listen to me –
> There is a little river, fed by rills
> That winds among the hills,
> And turns and suns itself unceasingly,
> And wanders through the cornfields wooingly,
> For it has nothing else to do, but play
> Along its cheery way:
> Not like great rivers that in locks are bound,
> On whom hard man doth heavy burdens lay,
> And fret their waters into foam and spray.
> This river's life is one long holiday
>   All the year round.

During the seventeenth and eighteenth centuries the Waveney valley was the scene of the extensive weaving of linen. It began as a cottage-based activity, but gradually became concentrated in the towns, especially Beccles and Bungay; and it was associated also with the manufacture of sailcloth. The development of this industry was assisted by a large population in an area of small farms, where the cultivation of hemp fitted in well with the predominant dairy farming. It is curious to reflect that at that time the Suffolk countryside consisted mainly of grass fields; not till the Napoleonic Wars did arable begin to dominate the scene. The milk from these dairy herds was converted into excellent butter, but the thrice-skimmed residue was used for producing rocklike cheeses, dangerous alike to teeth and knives, though good for sea voyages to Australia.

Proceeding upstream, we come to the only two Suffolk villages which actually abut the Waveney, Homersfield and Mendham. At the northern end of the parish of Mendham, near where the Beck joins the Waveney, is Middleton Hall, a beautiful red-brick house with a Georgian frontage, fifteenth-century timber-framing at the back, and a fine Jacobean plaster ceiling within. I came upon it first on a misty winter day, walking across the valley from the lonely mill on the Waveney at Wortwell. The miller's house was occupied by an intensely musical family, which included a professional cellist and clarinetist, which seemed to me to exemplify the absolute transformation of the Suffolk social scene. Across the marshes to the south of Mendham is the Priory, site of a Benedictine cell founded in 1140 as a subordinate house to the monastery at Castle Acre in Norfolk; it was exceptionally well endowed, with eight parishes in Suffolk and six in Norfolk.

Mendham was the birthplace of Sir Alfred Munnings, whose father farmed there. The future artist grew up to appreciate the village characters, such as Richmer, a lame old soldier with piercing eyes and grey side-whiskers, who wore a black wideawake hat and a sleeve waistcoat; and Fairhead the carpenter, whose shop was a place of fascination, with its chisels and planes, foot-rules and nails, shavings and sawdust. Munnings was brought up to be useful and responsible from an early age. When only ten years old his father told him to ride off on his pony to overtake a waggoner who had forgotten his delivery bills. Somewhere near Metfield (meadow-field) he was thrown into a ditch, and only recovered the pony thanks to help from a farm labourer. He completed his errand caked in mud. It was from physical experiences such as this that his depictions of the Suffolk countryside derive much of their immediacy, and his lifelong absorption with horses originated. It is amazing to learn that at an early age he lost the sight of one eye when scrambling through a bush.

Fressingfield (furze-field) and Stradbroke (road-brook) are large villages, formerly market towns, whose parishes adjoin on the plateau south of the Waveney. Both have impressive churches with great west towers, and ancient buildings set around their nuclear centres. Fressingfield is the more interesting architecturally, but Stradbroke is remarkable for being surrounded by five hidden greens, whose names survive despite their enclosures: Battlesea Green, Pixey Green, Barley Green, Wootten Green and Reading Green. At Worlingworth, some three miles south of Stradbroke, detailed local records reveal something of the way in which such greens developed during the Middle Ages: much of the local population lived in tenements around the greens, away from the manor farm and glebe and village centre.

Adjoining the churchyard at Fressingfield is the former guild-house, a brick and timber building, with a corner-post carving of St Margaret of Antioch, patroness of the guild. It subsequently became the Fox and Goose Inn, and thirty years ago was the first of the old inns in this area to convert to a restaurant of haute cuisine. As I recall, Pierre Jouin, the original French owner, was so high-minded that he refused to produce a second bottle of wine because it had not been properly brought to room temperature.

The church of St Peter and St Paul is memorable for its magnificent set of fifteenth-century benches, nine on each side of the nave. The tall bench ends are all richly traceried, each to a different and imaginative design, but capped by identical poppy-heads, bursting with fecundity. The bench ends incorporate buttressed arm-rests, identical in design, but supporting carved figures of great variety. The benches evidently escaped the attentions of the iconoclasts because of their generally non-religious symbolism, but they incorporate carvings of Christ's Passion, and the delicate figure of Saint Dorothy. She is holding a basket because, on her way to martyrdom, she was jeered at by a young lawyer who asked her to send him some fruit from the garden of Paradise: an angel duly delivered to him a basket containing three apples and three roses. Contemporaneous with the benches, and further exemplifying the artistry of the fifteenth-century wood-workers, is the hammer-beam roof of the nave. Unfortunately, angels were deemed by the Puritans to be religiously incorrect, and so the roof has lost its main decoration. The roof and benches at Fressingfield are all the more impressive for never having been varnished.

Both Fressingfield and Stradbroke are birth-places of famous figures of church history. William Sancroft was born at Fressingfield in 1617, where his family owned Ufford's Hall, an isolated manor-house at the edge of the parish, which remains largely unaltered since his day. In 1662 he became Master of Emmanuel College, Cambridge, and two years later Dean of St Pauls, where he commissioned the building of Christopher Wren's masterpiece after the old cathedral was destroyed by fire. In 1678 he was appointed Archbishop of Canterbury, in which position he contested James II's attempts to impose Roman Catholicism by indirect means. He was the leader of the seven bishops who refused to sign the royal declaration of liberty of conscience. But after the fall of the king he conscientiously refused to take the oath of allegiance to William and Mary, and so was obliged to resign his high office, though, admittedly, he was seventy-two years old at the time. Twenty-three Suffolk incumbents followed his lead and were extruded from their parishes. Sancroft retired to Ufford's Hall for five years until his death, and made benefactions to the church at Fressingfield.

Robert Grosseteste, supposedly born at Stradbroke in 1175, was appointed Bishop of Lincoln in 1235, then an enormous diocese which stretched down to the Thames. He was a commanding personality and a formidable scholar, who wrote commentaries on Aristotle and Boethius, and on subjects ranging from French poems to husbandry. He entered with gusto into all sorts of contentious issues with those who contested his authority, whether the chapter of monks at Lincoln, King Henry II, or the Pope himself.

On a less exalted level, the experiences of two local vicars are instructive. James Buck, vicar of Stradbroke, was ousted by the Puritans in 1642 as being a 'scandalous minister', which meant not being a Puritan. Confined to prison at Ipswich, he was soon reduced to a diet of bread and water. He had been a martyr to gout, but this regime effected a complete cure, and he lived on to recover his incumbency, and die at the then exceptional age of eighty. John Raven, vicar of Fressingfield a century ago, and a notable Suffolk historian, tells of the first occasion when he celebrated Holy Communion here at the church of St Peter and St Paul. After receiving the bread and wine, an old woman remained standing at the altar for the remainder of the service. Only then did the sacristan say, 'Oh sir, I forgot to tell 'ee. T'owd vicar allus gave her sixpence for coming'.

In the scattered village of Wingfield are to be found the castle and the monuments of the medieval dynasty of de la Pole, Earls and Dukes of Suffolk. These are, perhaps appropriately, on a smaller scale than their equivalents at Framlingham, which comprise the relics of several dynasties of the senior earldom of Norfolk. But there is something particularly appealing in the thought that Wingfield today has relapsed into the quietude and insignificance that it held before it came into the hands of the de la Poles, and was merely the manor of the family of Wingfield.

Catherine, daughter of Sir John Wingfield, married Michael de la Pole, son of a merchant from Hull who had risen to a high position at the court of Edward III. From her father, Catherine inherited the manors of Wingfield and Lowestoft, and the Hundred of Lothingland. Michael himself became Chancellor to the boy-king Richard II and, in 1385, the Earldom of Suffolk was re-created for him. But four years later Michael fell from favour, was impeached, and, wearing peasant's clothes, managed to flee to France, where he died in 1389. His son and grandson, both called Michael, met their deaths within a month of each other in 1415 when with the army of Henry V. The father died of a fever at Honfleur, and the son was killed at the Battle of Agincourt.

The earldom devolved on the younger grandson, William, who proved to be an exceptionally forceful man, eventually dominating the government of another boy-king, Henry VI. He had commanded the English forces at the siege of Orleans, but came to support a policy of reconciliation with France, negotiating Henry's marriage to Margaret of Anjou. For three years the French royal hostage, Charles Duke of Orleans, was held under lenient house arrest here at Wingfield castle. The opposition to this policy was led by Humphrey, Duke of Gloucester, the king's uncle. But Gloucester's death at the Parliament summoned at Bury in 1447 eased the way for William, now elevated to Duke of Suffolk. Three years later he was ousted from power and, like his grandfather, fled towards France, riding from Wingfield through Fressingfield to Dunwich. Unluckily for him his boat was intercepted in the Channel off Dover, and he was summarily beheaded, with his head laid across the gunwale. Shakespeare devotes a scene to the event, including the vituperative lines:

> Pole! Sir Pole! lord!
> Ay, kennel, puddle, sink; whose filth and dirt
> Troubles the silver spring where England drinks.
> Now will I dam up this thy yawning mouth
> For swallowing up the treasure of the realm:
> Thy lips, that kiss'd the queen, shall sweep the ground;
> And thou that smild'st at good Duke Humphrey's death,
> Against the senseless winds shall grin in vain.

After this it was not surprising that the de la Poles should have adhered to the Yorkist usurpers of Henry VI. In this they were at one with the other ducal family in the county, the Howards. The Duke of Norfolk at Framlingham and the Duke of Suffolk at Wingfield lived like princes and wielded almost absolute power during a period of national turbulence. What is more, John, William's son and 2nd Duke of Suffolk, married Elizabeth, daughter of the Duke of York and sister of Edward IV and Richard III. After the accession of Henry VII, John managed to ingratiate himself with the new regime, but his sons were not so lucky. They represented a great threat as successors to the throne if the Tudor line should fail. One died leading a rebellion; another was executed; and the third, recognised as King of England by France, and known as Blanche Rose (the Yorkist White Rose), died at the side of Francis I at the Battle of Pavia in 1525.

Wingfield Castle is best seen from the far end of the open village green which verges it, and on which a few horses are still grazed. From the green it appears to be a manor house, a brick and timber Tudor building with fine chimneys. But along the south front there is a battlement wall of the 1380s which formerly surrounded the castle on all four sides. The grey of its flint-cobble walls and stone dressings further differentiates it from the bricks of the adjoining building. It makes an emphatic statement of baronial power, with everything correctly in place – the central gatehouse, flanked by tall polygonal towers, the battlements, the corner turrets, and even the original oak door. The fortification of Wingfield Castle was undertaken by the 1st Earl for very practical reasons after the Peasants' Revolt, and was no mere status symbol. But its defensive strength was of no avail to the 1st Duke when he retreated here in 1450 before his flight. Its survival for over four centuries is quite exceptional, and is largely attributable to subsequent owners of the castle having insufficient funds to modernise. Its present state of good repair is due to its occupant for nearly forty years till his death in 1980, Baron Ash (actually he was Mr Baron Ash, but Baron is certainly a suitable name for a castellan).

Out of sight of the castle, on a lane leading down to a stream, stands the church of St Andrew. It differs in design from a normal parish church because it was built to house the tomb of Sir John de Wingfield and perpetuate his memory by means of chanted offices. In order that this should be properly done, a college of priests was established. Their domestic quarters, including a hall, have been discovered and restored in the eighteenth-century structure of the adjoining College, now the centre of a well-established annual arts festival. The church was begun soon after Sir John's death in 1361, but the whole edifice was greatly expanded some seventy years later when the tomb of Michael, the 2nd Earl, was accommodated.

Although chantry priests no longer mumble Latin masses over them day and night, the recumbent effigies of the de la Poles still rest here. First in time is Sir John Wingfield, himself an important magnate, who had married a great heiress, Alianore de Glanville, and become Chief of the Council of the Black Prince. His effigy is of stone, and was originally painted red, with gold knees and elbow-pieces, and silver surcoat and helmet. Next is Michael de la Pole, 2nd Earl of Suffolk, together with his wife Katherine, daughter of the Earl of Stafford. They are carved in wood, and around the base of their monument are thirteen niches for their children. Finally, we see John, 2nd and last Duke of Suffolk of the first creation, also with his wife, who was the grandest of them all: Elizabeth Plantagenet. They lie in alabaster, and his armour is shown in exquisite detail; his head rests on a helmet surmounted by a Saracen's head, and his feet on a lion with a forked tail. Around the tombs are heraldic devices, such as the wings of the Wingfields, the leopard heads of the de la Poles, and the knots of the Staffords.

Hoxne (a spur of land) rhymes with 'oxen', but should, I feel, in justice be pronounced like 'hoaxn'. It has traded on the legend that St Edmund met his martyrdom here, as a plaque at the end of the village still asserts. This was first put about by Herbert, Bishop of East Anglia, in 1101, in order to benefit from the tremendous cult of the saint which had been fostered by the monastery at Bury. Though he couldn't claim the relics, he could at least claim the site, and a Benedictine cell was established around a chapel dedicated to St Edmund. There can be no etymological link between Haegelisdun, the as yet unidentified place of martyrdom, and Hoxne. The reason why the bishop selected Hoxne was probably because, during the previous century, it had been the southern seat of the bishopric. It also may have something to do with the fact that the church had previously been dedicated to St Ethelbert, the East Anglian prince murdered by the pagan Offa of Mercia.

Folklore at Hoxne developed its own version about how St Edmund met his death. Fleeing from the Danes, he hid beneath the wooden bridge over the stream at the end of the village green. Unfortunately for him, a courting couple came loitering by. Gazing down into the stream to look at the fish, they noticed instead the glint of Edmund's golden spurs, and went straight off to betray him to the Danes. The young oak to which he was then bound and used as an archery target grew to an incredible age, and when it finally collapsed in 1848, an old arrow-head was found deep in the wood. The stream is now called the Goldbrook, and it is considered most unlucky for a bride to cross it on her wedding day.

Such is the superstition. However, Hoxne is the site of real discoveries of far greater importance than any illusory pair of spurs. In 1797, John Frere, a Suffolk antiquary, discovered flint tools in the river gravels at Hoxne. At a time when most people believed that the world had been created in 4004 BC, Frere recognised that they came from a 'very remote period indeed, even beyond that of the present world'. These Palaeolithic artifacts are now known to date from an inter-glacial period of around 300,000 years ago. Nearly two centuries later, in 1992, a local farmer, Peter Whatling, found that he had lost a hammer when out ploughing on his tractor. He asked a retired gardener, Eric Lawes, to search for it with his metal detector. Instead of the hammer, Eric discovered Britain's largest hoard of Roman coins, together with several pieces of gold jewellery and silver objects. This was probably the accumulated wealth of a very affluent family, buried in desperation during the anarchy of the early fifth century; the head of the family might have been one Aurelius Ursicinus, and he was probably a Christian. Although it was declared treasure trove, the British Museum felt obliged to offer the full value in reward, to discourage less honest men from disposing such finds illegally.

In Anglo-Saxon times Hoxne became the meeting-place of the Hundred which bears its name; just upstream, we enter the Hundred of Hartismere. Here we come to Eye, so called because its little hill once seemed like an isle on the marshy ground around the river Dove, which flows down to join the Waveney just upstream of Hoxne. The site was selected by William Malet as his stronghold after the Norman Conquest, and his castle is the only one in Suffolk to be mentioned in Domesday Book. At that time Eye was a substantial agricultural settlement with a growing urban element, boosted by Malet's transference of the Saturday market from Hoxne to Eye. It became the centre of an Honour, associated with the Earls and Dukes of Suffolk, which held jurisdiction over estates in East Suffolk. It returned two members to Parliament between 1571 and 1832, and survived till 1885 with its own constituency of only ten parishes, its name perpetuated in larger constituencies till 1983. A Benedictine Priory was established at Eye till the Reformation, on a site half a mile east of the town, of which only some masonry remains. This monastery possessed the priceless Red Book of Eye, St Felix's own copy of the Gospels, but it disappeared at the time of the Dissolution. I like to imagine it mouldering away in the corner of some dusty old attic in Eye.

The shape of Eye Castle is reflected in the line of the surrounding streets, and the central mound thrusts the ruins of the keep high into the sky. Immediately in front of the mound stands the great tower of the church of St Peter and St Paul, and the flushwork which decorates its west front is unsurpassed in Suffolk. It is so elaborate that there is actually more stone than flint, and one feels that the admixture of the two was not so much for the traditional reasons of economy in the purchase of stone, as for the sheer joy of contrasting the two materials, and simulating narrow lancet windows by means of flint infilling. The effect is enhanced by the infilling of the equally elaborate south porch. This is of brick, and must at some time have replaced flintwork that had decayed. Such substitution would never be permitted nowadays, but the fortuitous inclusion of this third material adds to the exceptional beauty of the exterior of this church. The interior is also most remarkable, particularly for the graceful rood which divides chancel and nave. Its base and screen are medieval, but the loft and crucifix are part of the sensitive twentieth-century renovations undertaken here by Sir Ninian Comper.

Eye church stands right on the edge of the town, and the most satisfactory way to approach it would normally be along the road from the bridge over the Dove. But perhaps the approach along Castle Street is better, because it concludes at the timber-framed Guildhall beside the church, and starts by one of the most downright ugly buildings in Suffolk, the Victorian Town Hall. This disproportionate horror provides an object lesson in how not to use brick and flint together, and enhances the pleasure of walking away from it towards the beautiful church. Behind the serpentine wall of Chandos Lodge, in Lambeth Street, the great choreographer, Sir Frederick Ashton, lived a very private life. Finally, I cannot leave Eye without mentioning the revolutionary power station that has been built on a former airfield just north of the town. It is fed with poultry litter, thus providing an alternative source of energy that cheekily challenges the nuclear giant at Sizewell.

A Roman Road, subsequently known as Pye Street, traverses the Suffolk clay west of Eye and is still in use as the A140. Around the village of Yaxley (cuckoo-clearing), just west of Eye, it passes between an ancient countryside whose field systems bear evidence of what is known as a co-axial form. That is to say, the boundaries bear an element of parallelism, as can be more clearly seen from nineteenth-century maps. The road cuts across these boundaries in such a way that it is clear that they ignore it, and so they may well predate it, and have been laid out as early as Bronze Age times. Such evidence, here as elsewhere, indicates that the Anglo-Saxon settlers often established their settlements on land that had been cultivated for several centuries.

Since so much of High Suffolk consists of fields, enclosed and ploughed, it is a particular joy to come across other types of landscape, such as we do at Thornham and Mellis. Thornham (thorn-home) lies in the tract of land between the main road and main-line railway, and consists of two parishes, Thornham Magna and Thornham Parva (Latin differentiations now only in use elsewhere in Suffolk at Linstead and Stonham). Thornham Hall has been demolished, but the park in front of it is unmolested, graced with venerable oaks and natural turf. Behind it are extensive woods, laid out for pheasant shooting. The owner, Lord Henniker, has opened several miles of permitted paths through these woods and along the hedge-lines of the fields and the meadows bordering the Dove, and he believes that such permission poses no threat to the pheasant shoot, a most enlightened attitude which other large landowners should note. To walk through this large domain is rather like visiting a stately home, but with nature substituted for art and architecture. And indeed, like some old house, it is haunted; for along the Old Drive, now a grassy ride (which led towards the Hennikers' special railway halt), it is just possible that we may encounter the Lady in Pink as she canters by, and 'hear the beat of a horse's feet, and the swish of a skirt in the dew'. Incidentally, the first Henniker here had inherited from his father-in-law, Sir John Major, a Member of Parliament like his more famous namesake.

Pedestrians benefiting from a walk at Thornham should also sample the pleasures of Mellis (mills). For here is the most extensive of the unenclosed greens of Suffolk, and the walk from one end to the other is well over a mile. Unlike many other greens, it is not entirely spoilt by the road that passes through it, which skirts around the end of it and leads to hardly anywhere. Around it, behind the surrounding ditch with its hedges or fences, are the individual homesteads so typical of old Suffolk, set apart in privacy and yet communally linked by the green. Fowls still peck and horses still munch at the grass here, and it all looks so peaceful that the occasional roar of the InterCity trains can be ignored. But it had its warlike moment in April 1644, when it was used for a muster of men enrolling for the army of the Eastern Association. Archery was one of the required skills, but the training methods were rough and ready, as the following record indicates: 'Edward Gibes of Thrandeston was slayne at a muster, being shot through the bowells, and another of Wortham was shot into the thighe and three others were shot through theyre clothes'.

In the adjoining parish of Burgate (fort-gate) is another green, entirely secluded and almost secret, with thatched cottages approached by muddy tracks. And then, immediately north of Burgate, comes the scattered village of Wortham (enclosed-home), which itself is spread out between two greens nearly two miles from each other: Long Green, up by the road from Diss to Ixworth, and the Ling, down beside the Waveney. Somewhere in between is the isolated church, out of sight of both. On the unenclosed expanses of the greens one might easily imagine oneself transported into the past, except that the grass is deteriorating due to lack of grazing. The illusion is heightened for anyone who has read *The Biography of a Victorian Village*, which contains the notes and drawings of Richard Cobbold, the Rector of Wortham for fifty-five years during the last century.

Richard Cobbold, born in 1797, was the twentieth child of John Cobbold, the Ipswich brewer, who had fourteen children by his first wife and seven by his second. Richard's mother, Elizabeth, made her house the intellectual centre of the town. She herself wrote and painted and Richard, who was educated at Bury School and Gonville and Caius College, Cambridge, inherited her tastes and talents and relished the pleasures of Ipswich society, with its literary and musical soirées. He was destined for the Church, and his father acquired for him the living of Wortham. For five years Richard was able to continue to live in Ipswich and pay a curate to officiate. But the bishop then issued an ultimatum, and he was obliged to leave Ipswich for Wortham, where he had a new rectory built for himself and his young wife. The tenor of his life now changed completely. No more could he meet intelligent friends and enjoy stimulating talk. His domestic life was dull. Fortunately, he managed to triumph over his new circumstances. He wrote several novels, of which the most famous is *Margaret Catchpole*. And he established close relationships with his parishioners, and has left for us a record of them which provides an exceptional insight into village life.

Richard Cobbold's perceptive character sketches are all the more appealing because of his sympathy for his humble friends. He is shocked at the harshness of their lives, and angry at individual acts of cruelty by those in authority, such as when the Constable of the Parish took away the bedding from four very old people who entered the Poor House. He described the village poor as 'the living stones of the Church of our Land'. At the same time he was by no means sentimental about them, and was quite clear which were the saints and which the sinners. He also had little time for the elders of the chapel, with its rival services to his own.

It is always amazing to read of all the tradespeople in even quite small villages in the past. In Richard Cobbold's time, Wortham still had millers, carpenters, bricklayers, tailors, shoemakers, innkeepers, shopkeepers and school-teachers – and the emphasis is on the plural. Even the individual tradesfolk were referred to in the plural, such as Salters the Blacksmith, Youngmans the Miller, or Listers the Carpenter, as in a game of Happy Families. Besides the village shop and post office run by Mr Browne, there was also Mr Thurlow's shop, which was no more than a closet into which two people could hardly fit, selling simple necessities from tea to tobacco to buttons. At the bottom end of the social chain were the rat-catchers, turf-cutters and goose-tenders. James Taylor, who controlled the geese on Long Green, was the village 'half-wit', and clearly enjoyed the therapeutic task which had been allotted to him.

Mortality was high and life-expectancy was low, but those that did make it into old age were often remarkably fit. Martha Woods was 'Mother of 18 children, and – positively – she looks scarcely fifty'; Martha Buck at seventy-three was 'still able to trip over the fields and get over the styles with alacrity'. And old Widow Firmin looked like a forty-year-old when actually seventy-seven. Widow Crack lived to ninety-one; Dinah Garrod to eighty-five. Even Judy Fuller, who from the age of twenty-five was wont to say 'Oh! my dears, I shall not live another twelvemonth!' lived to be eighty-six, spending the last sixteen years in her four-poster bed, looked after by her husband James, who himself lived to eighty-nine. But death in time came to them all, including a well-named Mr Dye who died in Norwich, but whose widow brought his body back to Wortham for burial. A village slanderer spread the rumour that she had sold the body for anatomical study and loaded the coffin with stones. The widow insisted on an opening of the grave, presided over by Richard Cobbold. In what must have been a moment of high drama, 'there lay the silent dead in all the grandeur of truth, telling at once the slanderer that he lied'.

All by itself among the fields, with even the rectory a little way off, St Mary's Wortham presents a most curious impression, because at the west end of it is the ruin of an enormous round tower, the largest such tower in England. If anything were to convince us that the round church towers of the eleventh century were built for defence, it would be this massive circumference of flint, 7.6 metres in diameter and originally 18.9 metres high, so incongruously set against the subsequent church, and so defiant in character. It calls to mind the defensive round towers (or 'brochs') of the Hebrides, built by the Picts against the Norse raiders, into which entire communities retreated in times of crisis. But, this being Suffolk, maybe Wortham tower never had to endure a siege or even face an enemy, especially since it is quite a way from the sea.

Wortham Manor, down by the river, was for long the seat of a family called Betts, who for centuries kept all their documents in a secret chamber behind the panelling of the library, to the great benefit of historians. In 1933 it was the scene of a major incident in the 'tithe war', when farmers baulked at the heavy tax by which they were obliged to support the stipends of the local parsons. Richard Rash, incited by his literary wife, Doreen Wallace, not only refused to pay but marched his forty-five farm workers to the rectory in protest, and then most rashly obtained a guard of eighteen Fascist blackshirts to protect him from the bailiffs. The police moved in in strength, and his pigs and furniture were sequestered.

The sources of many rivers are disappointing to visit, especially with the lower water levels of today. But the source of the Waveney is a most magnificent sight, thanks to the National Nature Reserve at Redgrave and Lopham Fens, managed by the Suffolk Wildlife Trust. Here is a great wet valley fen, retaining its water by means of sluices, surrounded by natural woodland of alder, oak and poplar. The surface of the fen is mostly covered with reeds and sedges, which are cultivated and controlled. In among them are pools and water-channels, with many aquatic animals, including the Great Raft Spider, found hardly anywhere else in Britain. Kingfishers, little grebes, warblers and moorhens flit in and out of the rushes. Nowhere else in inland Suffolk can one catch such a convincing impression of what the land looked like before the advent of man, especially if one walks through it at a time when no one else is about (as I did, encountering only a bearded scientist crouching in the reeds in observation of the famous spider).

On the map, the Waveney seems to be a much more formidable county barrier than it really is today, when people cross it all the time in cars without thinking, and rivalry between Norfolk and Suffolk is reduced to sport. Even those subtle differences in local accent, once the subject of good-humoured banter, have faded away. Still, there can be no doubt about the superiority of the Suffolk bank of the Waveney in one important respect. By some lucky chance the A143 runs along the Norfolk side, consigning it to endless noise and dividing the river from its natural hinterland. The Suffolk side enjoys all the charms of narrow twisting lanes and obscure approaches to that delightful stream, the Waveney.

X
Little Ouse

North-west Suffolk drains into the Wash through Norfolk by means of the Little Ouse, which provides the boundary between the two East Anglian counties from its common source with the Waveney at Redgrave. The maritime rivers of Suffolk have always invited exploration upstream, and were once the channels by which the ships could penetrate inland. But the Little Ouse and the Lark, falling into the morasses of the fens, never exercised such military or commercial functions in their passage across the chalky plateau: the raiders and traders had already taken to their feet, treading where the very earliest human communities had trod.

Over a period of hundreds of thousands of years before the last Ice Age, isolated groups of men and women wandered about the land, engaged in uncertain combat with large mammals which at various times included woolly-coated mammoths, rhinoceroses, lions and bison in the grasslands, and bears and wolves in the forests. No human bones of these Early Stone Age people have been found in Suffolk, but at several places, notably Mildenhall and Hoxne, and also beside the Little Ouse at Barnham, Santon Downham and Brandon, their primitive hand-axes have been uncovered – pointed or oviate flint tools which would have been used to butcher animals. They managed to survive in cold climates, so must have worn some form of clothing, probably fur skins.

After the last Ice Age, during a period of ameliorating climate, the hunters of the Middle Stone Age, still able to move to and from the continent till Britain became an island, developed their skills against the animal kingdom. With bows and arrows, spears and microliths, they hunted the large animals which abounded in the extensive forests – aurochs, elk, red deer and boar; also badgers, otters, hares and foxes. They shot down duck and geese, and harpooned pike. But still there are no human bones that have been discovered of the people of these times.

The seams of flint in the chalk soil were first exploited here in Middle Stone Age times, notably at the site known as Grime's Graves, a mile across the Norfolk border. Since flint was then the best available tool, this site became a sort of Stone Age industry. With nothing better than the antlers of a red deer for a pick (the brow tine served as the pick and the beam as the handle) the primitive miners dug their shafts and tunnels and, by the light of tallow candles, cut into the seam and extracted the precious flint. Besides the all-important axes, flint was used for arrow-heads, daggers, scythes, scrapers and chisels. This stone which can produce so sharp a cutting edge remained the basic tool of ordinary people long after the introduction of bronze and later iron. At Brandon (broom-hill) beside the Little Ouse the art of flint knapping developed, that is to say, splitting the flint in two so that the smooth black surfaces of each can be used for the facing of a wall; and the material for the flushwork of many Suffolk churches probably came from here. Another use for flint, and one which continued to be important until the introduction of self-igniting ammunition, was the production of gun flints.

As early as the fifth millenium before our era, some primitive form of agriculture was first practised in Suffolk, in addition to the age-old hunting and gathering. The communities of this slow-developing Late Stone Age culture needed light land for their ploughing and for the grazing of their herds of cattle and flocks of sheep. So they tended to settle mainly at the extremities of Suffolk, on either side of the dense forests, on the chalky soils of the north-west and the sandy soils of the south-east. Though paths and tracks led through the unin-habited forests, it seems that the tribes in these two areas of settlement were distinctive from each other. For instance, in addition to the flints which they had learnt to mine systemati-cally, they also acquired implements of igneous stone. But those samples found in the west usually came from the Lake

District; those in the east, from Cornwall. Shadowy traces of large causewayed enclosures have also been discovered in both areas of Suffolk. These were great areas of tribal assembly whose precise purpose is unknown. That in the east is at Freston, and that in the west is at Fornham All Saints, together with a smaller one at Kedington. Several Late Stone Age cultures have been identified in East Anglia, largely from their earthenware artifacts: the Bell Beaker People, the Necked Beaker people, and the Corded Ware people. There must have been periodic conflicts between these different tribes of varied ancestry, particularly when fresh groups migrated into the area from across the sea or along the Icknield Way. But in between such conflicts one must suppose that their pastoral existence was untroubled by organised warfare.

The introduction of bronze tools during the second millenium quickened the pace of change. East Anglia had no copper or tin of its own, but wandering smiths would have sold new implements or refashioned old ones, as this metal gradually came into more general use, in the form of swords, daggers, axe-heads, sickles and other tools, as well as the cauldrons which revolutionised cooking. With it came a more hierarchical society, manifested by the burial mounds of tribal leaders and their families. Over a hundred of these round barrows are still visible in Suffolk, and over seven hundred are known to have existed. Though bronze tools facilitated the clearance of land, the central woodlands still remained as a barrier between east and west; and it seems that in the late Bronze Age the eastern settlements enjoyed a more advanced economy, from the evidence of the rash of ring-ditch graves in which a wider spectrum of people were cremated.

At least five hundred years before our era, settlers from the Continent had brought iron to Suffolk, though for centuries bronze was still generally used. But during the third century BC waves of iron-wielding equestrian warriors and their retainers came from the Continent and subjected the indigenous people to their rule. They are known as the 'Marnians', and were part of the conglomerate peoples of North Europe who formed the Celtic culture. Their prosperous and well-ordered societies anticipated Roman rule, and their artistic achievements are revealed in elaborate jewellery as displayed in brooches, necklets and ear-rings, in sword-hilts and horse-harnesses. They were dominated by a warrior class that lorded over slaves, and gloried in epic tales sung to them by bards in melodic incantations. But they also brought with them farmers who used broad-bladed iron ploughshares, and craftsmen who produced wheel-made pottery. Their most remarkable weapon was the battle-chariot, fitted with scythed wheels. In southern Britain they constructed enormous fortresses with vast earth embankments and wooden pallisades, although not apparently in East Anglia. This may be because of the lack of obvious defensive sites, or that for some reason the need for them was less acute. A group of Marnians came to dominate the East Anglian plains, and to form the tribe of the Iceni.

The Marnians were followed across the channel by further Celtic conquistadors, Belgic tribes even more formidable and bellicose. These eventually formed themselves into vast confederations of tribes, of whom the Catuvellauni came to dominate the south-east of Britain. During the first century BC, the Catuvellauni pressed into East Anglia and conquered the Trinovantes, whose territory was along the coastal regions of Suffolk and Essex. The conflict of these tribal groups disturbed the Roman settlement in Gaul and disrupted the delivery of wheat, livestock, hunting-dogs and slaves, on which the Romans had come to depend. Julius Caesar accordingly crossed the Channel on a punitive expedition in 55 BC and defeated the Catuvellauni. But during the ensuing decades they re-established themselves, especially under Conubelinus. After his death, the Romans came again in AD 43 under the Emperor Claudius, and this time they stayed, setting up their capital at Camulodunum (Colchester), the chief place of the Trinovantes.

Suffolk and Norfolk share the memory of the heroic figure of Boadicea, Queen of the Iceni, who led the revolt against Roman rule in AD 62. (I know she was really Boudicca, and her tribe the Ickenni, but I stick to the names I was brought up with. I also rather like the medieval transliteration of

Conubelinus into Cymbeline.) Boadicea is the first British woman known to history, but her acceptance as a tribal chief must have followed that of previous widows or heiresses who had assumed the mantle of authority among the Celtic tribes. She became a cult figure in England during the nineteenth century, which is rather surprising in view of the obvious similarities between the British Empire and the ancient Roman. And, more recently, admirers of the Iron Lady have likened her to the Icenian Lady – also surprising in view of the swift and total defeat that befell Boadicea and everything she stood for. Nevertheless Boadicea does represent the outrage felt by primitive societies which have suddenly and rudely been subjected to external power.

The Roman military government had been uncompromisingly harsh. The Trinovantes had been placed under direct rule, and their best lands awarded to colonists, army veterans who enslaved the natives. Other tribes, such as the Iceni, were indirectly ruled, but forced to pay tribute. It was in the hope of mitigating the Roman demands that Prasutagus, ruler of the Iceni, had appointed the Emperor to be his joint heir, together with his own two daughters. But this concession merely encouraged the Romans to subject the Iceni to the status of the Trinovantes. The army moved in, the Icenian landowners were dispossessed, the population was enslaved, and Prasutagus' daughters were raped and his widow, Boadicea, flogged.

The revolt of AD 62 was carefully timed to take advantage of the absence of the Roman Governor, Suetonius Paulinus, on a summer campaign against the North Welsh tribes. A vast horde of a hundred thousand warriors from several tribes assembled under Boadicea somewhere here on the East Anglian plain. It made for Camulodunum and sacked it. The colonists made a last-ditch stand in the Temple of Claudius, probably still in the course of construction; but after two days they surrendered and were slaughtered. The tribal host then moved south and sacked London. Some weeks later it was defeated by the disciplined legions of Suetonius Paulinus, who had marched back from Wales. The legionaries took a terrible revenge on the Iceni, laying waste their lands and killing and enslaving the population. We shall return to the ensuing period of Roman rule when we come to the Lark.

From medieval times the overgrazed wastelands of this corner of Suffolk were used for the cultivation of rabbits, retained for fattening and breeding within enormous enclosed warrens. Arthur Young, the leading English agricultural theorist of the late-eighteenth century, reported that one such warren near Brandon produced more than 40,000 rabbits, for fur and meat, in a year. Today, the land between Elveden and Brandon is part of the largest concentration of softwood forestry plantations in England, and Brandon Park and Wangford Warren are covered with conifers. Brandon is a centre for this industry, and has expanded from an impoverished village to a prosperous town.

Brandon gave its name to the family of the most colourful aristocrat ever associated with the county, Charles Brandon, Duke of Suffolk. His grandfather had been in the service of the Mowbray Dukes of Norfolk, and his father must have been a fine upstanding fellow, for he was standard-bearer to Henry Tudor at Bosworth. At this battle Richard III decided to stake everything on a cavalry charge, in the hope of killing Henry; but the nearest he got was the standard-bearer, before he himself bit the dust. Charles, a landless and orphaned child, was brought up at court as a companion to the king's son, who became Henry VIII. Both were strong, strapping young men who enjoyed physical exercise, especially riding and jousting; and Charles came to dominate Henry, who appointed him Marshall of the King's Household, and Master of the Horse. In 1514 came the highest possible honour for the thirty-year-old companion – a Dukedom. Charles was appointed Duke of Suffolk for political reasons. The title had been withdrawn from the de la Poles because their semi-royal blood represented a threat to the Tudors and it was necessary to quash any aspirations they might have of getting it back. It was also desirable to have in East Anglia a grandee who could counter the enormous power of the Howards, who had themselves recently been granted the Dukedom of Norfolk.

The second part of this policy never really became effective because Charles Brandon was unable to secure control over many of the de la Pole estates. Still, he did play his part in county affairs, and collaborated with the Duke of Norfolk in dealing with discontent in East Anglia. And he often came to Suffolk, usually to his manor at Westhorpe. As to the first political aim in granting the Dukedom, that of stamping out a claimant to the throne, this backfired in a most surprising way. In the same year as he was granted the honour, Charles Brandon was sent over to the French court at Paris to discuss the future of Mary Tudor, Henry VIII's sister. This lusty young woman had been married to the miserable Louis XII, who had recently died. Charles himself was a widower. They fell in love, and he had the audacity to marry her without her brother's permission. It took a few months before they were allowed to return to England. But after receiving Henry's forgiveness they enjoyed a truly happy marriage for eighteen years. Their two sons died in infancy, but their daughter Frances married Henry Grey, Marquis of Dorset, and son of the Duke of Somerset. It was her daughter, Jane Grey, who was proclaimed Queen by the Protestants in London on the death of Edward VI in 1553, for fear of the accession of Henry VIII's Catholic daughter, Mary.

Elveden (swan-valley) became supreme in the shooting of game birds as a result of the money poured into it by two successive owners, Maharajah Duleep Singh and the Earl of Iveagh. Duleep Singh was obliged to live in England after being banished from India by the Imperial Government for his part in the Sikh Wars. But he continued to receive an immense personal income from his followers in the Punjab, and he also liked to live the life of a rich English gentleman, so his lot was not a hard one. At Elveden he had the Georgian house converted into an Indian Moghul Palace, carved in close detail by Italian craftsmen. Edward Guinness, Earl of Iveagh, was the most successful brewer of his time, making Guinness a household name and Ireland's greatest export. When he bought Elveden after the Maharajah's death in 1893, he greatly expanded this extraordinary house, giving it a frontage of three storeys and twenty-five bays, creating an enormous Indian marble hall, and filling the whole with works of art.

The Maharajah had set new records in slaughtering game. In one year 19,000 pheasants were shot. He himself once shot 789 partridges in one day. Lord Iveagh managed to keep up this extraordinary performance, and on 5 November 1912, 3,248 head of game were shot, of which nearly a thousand fell to a crack shot, Henry Stonor. In order to achieve this, some twenty thousand pheasants had been reared on the estate, in addition to all the wild birds. More than eighty beaters were on parade, together with several gamekeepers. The head keeper, Mr Turner, had never seen so many birds on the wing, and at the main drive, at King's Hazard, the shooting went on continuously for at least an hour.

The parishes we now pass through are some of those whose boundaries converge, like slices of a cake, at the Rymer Point. By this means each had access to ponds for watering their grazing animals on the arid plain between the Little Ouse and the Lark. The Rymer Point was formerly known as Ringmere, and in 1010 it was the scene of the defeat inflicted on the Anglo-Saxon leader, Ulfcytel, by the Danish army under Thorkell. Taking these parishes clockwise from the north, they are: Barnham, Euston, Fakenham Magna, Honington, Troston, Great Livermere, Little Livermere, Ingham and Culford.

Euston is at the confluence of the Little Ouse and the Black Bourn. Here an enchanting landscape, contrived at different times by John Evelyn, William Kent and Capability Brown, surrounds Euston Hall, seat of the Duke of Grafton. The Hall has been reduced to under half its former size and lost its symmetry, but it still exhibits the Palladian simplicity imposed on it during the 1740s by Matthew Brettingham. The house itself had been built in the 1670s in a more florid style, with mansard roofs and with domes on the corner towers. Euston Hall is complemented by two exquisite buildings in its grounds.

Contemporary with the original house is the church of St Genevieve, standing all alone among the 'pleasure grounds' ever since the village around it was moved out of the way. It has all the elegance of a London church, and Evelyn pronounced it 'most laudable, most of the Houses of God in this county resembling rather stables and thatched cottages than temples in which to serve the Most High'. Contemporary with the remodelled house is the Temple, an octagonal folly designed by William Kent, set on higher ground at a corner of the park, and intended as a very grand box from which the dukes could watch their horses being exercised. The Black Bourn provides an ornamental sheet of water at the bottom of the valley, and beyond the park old carriageways stretch for miles in different directions through a countryside that is nowadays mostly arable, broken by windbreaks and copses designed for pheasant shooting.

The estate had been owned by the Rookwood family, but their adherence to Roman Catholicism brought about their ruin. Edward Rookwood, who had entertained Elizabeth I lavishly at Euston during her progress through East Anglia in 1578, found himself a few years later faced with penal fines and then imprisonment at Bury, where he died. Ambrose Rookwood, of the senior branch of the family at Coldham Hall, Stanningfield, was drawn into the Gunpowder Plot of 1605, and executed. In 1666, Euston was acquired by Henry Bennet, Earl of Arlington, a tough and venal man of power who had become Secretary of State to the newly-restored Charles II. Euston was a specially good investment for him because it was so close to Newmarket, to which anyone seeking to influence the king had to come.

Charles used to visit Euston for frequent overnight stays, and Arlington laid on all that he wanted. Of one such visit in 1671 John Evelyn noted: 'It was universally reported that the faire Lady . . . was bedded one of these nights, and the stocking flung, after the manner of a married Bride'; and that she 'was for the most part in her undresse all day, and that there was fondness, and toying, with that young wanton'. Also present in the house at the time was Louise de Kéroualle, the most influential French agent ever to operate in England. Louis XIV had sent her over, as a Maid of Honour to Princess Henrietta, Duchess of Orléans, with the express purpose of seducing the gullible Charles. But it was Charles's principal mistress,

Barbara Villiers, created by him the Duchess of Cleveland, who had a special interest in Euston. She wanted her second son by Charles, Henry Fitzroy, to be married to Arlington's daughter and heiress, Isabella. In this she succeeded in the following year. Henry was loaded with titles, Baron Sudbury, Viscount Ipswich, Earl of Euston and Duke of Grafton. He was the most popular of the natural sons of Charles II – headstrong, reckless and unthinking – and he met an early end at the age of twenty-seven when leading an attack on the Jacobites in Cork.

The most influential of the Dukes of Grafton was the 3rd Duke, Augustus Henry Fitzroy. He had greatness thrust upon him when for three years he headed a ministry for George III, though he was hardly up to it, and was apt to cancel meetings of the council to attend a race meeting or pay a visit to his mistress. His pride in his rank and birth was neatly pricked in a famous exchange in the House of Lords. He accused the new Lord Chancellor, Lord Thurlow, a man of lowly parentage whose mother came from Suffolk, of being of lesser worth because of his plebeian origins. Thurlow, a lawyer and an orator, replied that, on the contrary, his worth was the greater because he had earned his seat, whereas the Duke was merely 'the accident of an accident'. This phrase comes irresistibly to mind when surveying the swaggering portraits in Euston Hall.

East of Euston is a corner of High Suffolk which drains into the very Little Ouse from below its source at Redgrave. The first village I should mention here is Barningham, partly because there are said to be more than seventy ponds in the parish, and partly because St Andrew's church contains a very splendid set of fifteenth-century benches, with traceried bench-ends; but mainly because the cottage which adjoins the church, looking just like the witch's house in 'Hansel and Gretel', is where the key is obtainable, held by one of those public-spirited people without whose kindly participation our visits to Suffolk's churches would be severely curtailed.

Further east we come to three villages that run into each other – Rickinghall Inferior, Rickinghall Superior, and Botesdale. They benefited from the traffic that passed along the main road from Bury to Yarmouth in the days of the stage coaches, and the resultant eighteenth-century street of one and a half miles comprises several houses and shops with pedimented doorways and bow windows. Rickinghall's two St Mary's vie for which is superior or inferior, though Inferior probably has it, due to its most appealing round tower, crowned with flushwork battlements. Botesdale (meaning Botolph's dale, and at one time abbreviated to Buzzle) has an early sixteenth-century chantry chapel instead of a church. This later became a grammar school; and during the early-nineteenth century the horsey tenor of the town was upheld in exemplary fashion by Joseph Haddock, the headmaster, a superb horseman who kept two hunters and spent far more time riding than teaching.

The Little Ouse rises at Redgrave (reed-ditch). But the reed beds at its official source are today badly parched, and I consider that this river's legitimate head is now the artificial lake created by Capability Brown two miles south in Redgrave Park in the 1760s. It is all that remains of a rare totality in which this master of landscaping designed the house as well. Although it was to only a dull Palladian design, and his patron forbad a healthy red-brick colouring as 'putting the whole valley in a fever', Redgrave Hall, demolished in 1946, represents the many Suffolk mansions which were destroyed during the middle of the present century, such as those at Assington, Boulge, Cavenham, Mildenhall, Rushbrooke and Sudbourne.

The total elimination of Redgrave Hall and its naturalistic park is nicely offset by the survival of St Botolph's, the large parish church of Redgrave and Botesdale, at its lonely site among the workaday fields. As with so many other of Suffolk's medieval churches, the beauty of St Botolph's is greatly enhanced by its graveyard. The gravestones, many of them over a century old, display a quiet dignity in design and inscription; it is a strange paradox that the Church of England, so lax in matters of theology, is so strict in matters of taste. The graves are mercifully devoid of artificial flowers and photographs of the deceased. The grasses and bushes are less cut back and mown than formerly, for they are now recognised as being just as important as sanctuaries for wildlife as for corpses. Within St Botolph's are two glorious marble monuments which remind us of the two important men who successively purchased the Manor of Redgrave. The first of these was Nicholas Bacon, Queen Elizabeth's Keeper of the Great Seal (in effect, her Lord Chancellor): his son, Sir Nicholas, England's premier baronet, lies here beside his wife in effigies carved by Nicholas Stone. His successors foresook Redgrave for Raveningham in Norfolk, and the estate was acquired by Sir John Holt, the Lord Chief Justice under William and Mary, a reformist who abolished the trying of prisoners in fetters and ruled that the importation of slaves into England was illegal. He is shown sitting in state, attended by the robed figures of Justice and Mercy.

Returning to Euston, and pursuing our way up the Black Bourn (whilst ignoring local aircraft noise), we come first to Honington and Sapiston, both associated with Robert Bloomfield, 'the Suffolk Poet'. He was born in 1766 in a cottage beside the church of All Saints at Honington. After the death of his father, a tailor, from smallpox, his mother taught at the village school. Robert was then put to work as a farm labourer at Sapiston before fleeing to London at the age of fifteen and becoming a shoemaker's apprentice. Here he encountered only worse conditions, enduring real penury and semi-starvation. Even after serving his seven years and marrying, he was still too poor to buy a conjugal bed. He cannot have been a very adept shoemaker, because while he was working he was also composing his poem 'The Farmer's Boy', writing it down only when polished in his mind, so as to save on precious paper. That is as far as it would have got had it not been for Capel Lofft, of Troston Hall. He undertook some editing and arranged for the publication of 'The Farmer's Boy' in 1800. Virtue was rewarded when it well and truly hit the jackpot, selling over 26,000 copies in under three years, and being translated into French, Italian and Latin. But Robert Bloomfield lost all he had gained when he later went bankrupt as a bookseller.

The poem describes the annual cycle on the farm as seen through the work of Giles, an orphan labourer. It was because Bloomfield obviously wrote with such bitter experience that the simple versification had such a powerful effect on his readers. And they were pleased to note that it contained no revolutionary sentiments, for Giles works 'in cheerful servitude' for 'a generous master'. Here is Giles at work in January, breaking up the turnips for the cattle to feed:

> On GILES, and such as GILES, the labour falls,
> To strew the frequent load where hunger calls.
> On driving gales sharp hail indignant flies,
> And sleet, more irksome still, assails his eyes;
> Snow clogs his feet; or if no snow is seen,
> The field with all its juicy store to screen,
> Deep goes the frost, till every root is found
> A rolling mass of ice upon the ground.

The parish next upstream is Bardwell. Here the large church (of St Peter and St Paul) displays a colourful interior thanks to its early-fifteenth-century painted roof and its display of hundreds of blue-bordered knitted kneelers of imaginative and varied design. Half a mile to the south is Bardwell Hall, an amazing display of gables, porches and chimneys, all in Tudor brick, built around an earlier structure whose timber-framing is revealed in the dormer windows; it is closely visible from the road. Just to the west of Bardwell is Troston, the seat of Robert Bloomfield's patron, Capel Lofft. A bizarre figure, small, boyish-looking and slovenly dressed, and with literary tastes, he had succeeded to the extensive Capel estates in Troston and Stanton. He named the large trees in his park after famous men: the Homer oak, the Demosthenes ash, the Evelyn elm, and so on. In 1800, he achieved fame among the Whigs and notoriety among the Tories by interceding for the life of a poor girl who had been condemned to death for a petty theft at the Ipswich Assizes, actually making an oration on the scaffold before she swung. For this his name was struck off the roll of magistrates and he was widely ostracised in Suffolk society.

The remains of the large Augustinian priory at Ixworth lie strewn around the grass beside the Black Bourn, some of them incorporated into the house subsequently built on the site, grandly dubbed Ixworth Abbey. Behind its Georgian frontage are the vaulted rooms of the refectory undercroft, and rooms with medieval piers and arches, reminiscent of Byron's reference to his own monastic home, Newstead Abbey, where 'strength was pillar'd in each massy aisle'. Ixworth, now liberated from through traffic by an entirely sensible main road diversion, has a most attractive High Street and a worthy hostelry in the gabled Pickerel Inn.

The northward course of a Roman road, known as the Peddars' Way, crossed the Black Bourn at Ixworth. Just before this crossing, where the stream turns at the edge of the present parish of Pakenham at Grimstone End, the Romans built a fort and established a market settlement. It says something about the state of this settlement at the time of the arrival of the early Anglo-Saxons that some of the newcomers seem to have decided that they would be better off setting up their homes in the graveyard. Inside a Bronze Age ring-ditch, which had also been used for the placement of eight Romano-British crematory urns, evidence has been found of a hut which contained a working loom.

Interesting though such clues are to vanished communities, Grimstone End at Pakenham is best known today not for them but for its two mills, a water mill and a windmill, which stand in sight of each other. The water mill is on a site of great antiquity, recorded in Domesday Book, though only as a 'winter mill', implying that there was not enough water to run it during summer months, which is not surprising as it only made use of the restricted water of Pakenham Fen. The present mill dates from the eighteenth century. When it is in operation, with the great waterwheel slowly turning, and the gear wheels converting the power to drive the millstones at two revolutions a second, with all the machinery humming, the sight of the grain trickling into the waiting sacks, ready for making health-giving wholemeal bread, is supremely satisfying. The windmill dates from the 1820s and is a large tower mill, at present in use for grinding animal feed. The sight of both these mills restored to working order is all the more fascinating in the light of our increasing interest in natural energy sources, of which the two most basic are wind and water.

At Norton, a couple of miles upstream, the secluded church of St Andrew, approached along an avenue of limes, contains exquisitely carved stalls, with representations of the martyrdoms of St Andrew and St Edmund, as well as more homely scenes such as a woman carding wool and a boy being beaten. Norton is a scattered parish with several Tudor farmhouses and Little Haugh Hall, which contains a very splendid hall, staircase and landing of the 1740s, with elaborate woodcarving and plasterwork, and paintings by Francis Hayman depicting the apotheosis of Galileo and Newton. At Woolpit, on the watershed between the Black Bourn and the Gipping, the noble church of St Mary is approached through a magnificent stone porch. St Mary's possesses an outstanding roof, on which the host of fluttering angels has remained gloriously untouched for five and a half centuries. I like to think of them invoking the presence of the deity, as in the words of the psalm: 'He rode upon the cherubim and did fly; He came flying upon the wings of the wind'.

Woolpit means 'wolf-pit', but the pits that do exist around it are the remains of the former brick-making industry on which the town thrived since the late-sixteenth century. Woolpit Brick was so much in demand that the brickworks eventually had their own railway branch line to Elmswell Station nearby. The brick was a light grey-brown, being made with chalky clay, as opposed to bricks made from earth with iron oxide, which emerge from the kiln red in colour. Chalk clay is more usual in west than in east Suffolk, and hence white bricks are more common in the west. The brickworks of Suffolk began to close down towards the end of the nineteenth century, being unable to compete with superior bricks such as those from Fletton near Peterborough, which were made from a tough coal-bearing clay.

Woolpit is the site of the legend of the Green Children, as

recounted by the monk, William of Newburgh. As the story went, two children, their skins entirely green, emerged from these ancient cavities at harvest time. They spoke no known language, and refused to eat the food they were offered, until it was realised that they would eat beans. They survived on a diet of beans for many months, and were then gradually weaned on to bread. With a more normal diet, their skin began to whiten and they began to learn English. The boy soon died, but the girl lived on and married at Lynn. On being asked about her curious origin, she used to say, 'We are inhabitants of the land of St Martin'. So I have no doubt that this was an early sighting of Martians.

The Black Bourn rises in the parish of Bradfield St George, whose sister parishes, Bradfield St Clare and Bradfield Combust, lie just to the south. The dedication to St Clare, the companion of St Francis, is unique in medieval English parishes, though it seems to have been transferred to her from a Norman saint with a similar name, St Clair. The appellation of Combust refers to the burning of the hall there during the early fourteenth century. A later hall on the site was home to Arthur Young. The voluminous works of this admirable agronomist were immensely influential in his time, and, quite apart from their analytical accuracy, they were written with a clarity of style that made them easy reading for the squarest of squires, who also were usually very ready to discuss their farming with such a sympathetic man. His hall has likewise been destroyed, though his father's lime avenue remains. Bearing in mind his absorption with the quality of the soil here and elsewhere in Suffolk, I cannot help thinking that the parish would nowadays be better named Bradfield Compost, a corruption perhaps no worse than changing Clair to Clare. The eminent novelist, Angus Wilson, lived for many years in a lonely cottage at Bradfield St George.

Bradfield itself is a significant name. It means a broad space, and the implication is that the Anglo-Saxon settlers found a broad space here, rather than creating one themselves. The probability of this increases from the fact that the line of the Peddars' Way cuts along the western side of the parishes, forming the boundary of Bradfield St George, and that Romano-British burial mounds are close beside it. To have existed at all in this woodland area, the broad space must have been cultivated or grazed quite recently, and so it is to be supposed that the settlers took over an existing British estate.

The special interest of Bradfield's landscape does not end here, for at the eastern extremity of St George and St Clare a large section of medieval woodland has been preserved, administered by the Suffolk Wildlife Trust. Felsham Hall Wood and Monks Park Wood were for centuries owned by the Abbey of Bury St Edmunds, and the careful husbandry that was accorded to them is evident from the great banks which still surround them, forming the woodland edge to the cultivated fields. Monks Park Wood was also where the monks kept their deer. For this purpose it had a specially strong boundary bank, surmounted by a deer-proof wooden fence, or park pale. There were also areas of grass within the wood. The fallow deer within the park were farmed, not hunted (there was never any royal forest hunting reserve in Suffolk), and their vension was the customary meat for feasts and special occasions.

Both woods were used for coppicing, once an essential element in agricultural economy though nowadays a peripheral one. So the coppicing that continues here, mainly for education and research, is particularly important to our understanding of woodland culture. It involves cutting sections, or panels, of the wood to ground level every ten to twenty years to produce a crop of poles and firewood. The stumps, or stools, of the trees remain to regenerate another crop, and some have been doing so for hundreds of years. The woods mainly consist of ash, alder and birch, and in the initial years after the coppicing the ground is covered with oxlips, primroses, wood anemones and bluebells, while the turf of the grass rides is carefully conserved by sensitive methods of haulage. Altogether there are few places in Suffolk where the landscape of the past is so convincingly simulated as in these woods, and in walking through them in winter one can easily imagine cowled peasants at work, as in some medieval Book of Hours illustrating the countryside in January or February.

XI
Bury St Edmunds

Edmund, King of the East Angles, was murdered by the Danes under Hingwar in 869 after he had defied their army and been defeated in battle. This much is certain, though the annalists differ on exactly how he died. According to the original version, Edmund and his followers fought bravely to the last against the Danes. But another version, which became the more popular, has it that he was taken, like Christ, as a lamb to slaughter. The chronicle describes how, when it was evident that further resistance was useless, he took refuge in a church and resorted to prayer, 'exchanging his temporal for celestial weapons'. He was seized, bound, and scourged. His tormentors, furious at his continued prayers, proceeded to shoot at him with their bows 'so that there was not a place in the martyr's body in which a fresh wound could be inflicted, but it was as completely covered with darts and arrows as is the hedgehog's skin with spines'. At length, the executioner 'severed his holy head from its trunk on the 20th day of November, as he was praying and confessing the name of Christ'. This miraculous ability of the saint to retain the powers of expression under such terrible torture was extended even beyond the point of execution, for the monks who later sought to recover his head were led towards it by its own voice.

St Edmund would have made a perfect patron saint for the English nation, rather than the mythical, if warlike, St George. But although he failed to become the national icon, the East Anglian king did at least manage to enjoy an immensely influential reign for many centuries after his death, thanks to his shrine at Bury. It was in his name, and with unceasing imprecations for his guidance, that the abbots of his monastery at Bury ruled a third of Suffolk, as well as large parts of Essex and Norfolk, guarding his rich patrimony from the jealous attentions of monarchs and bishops. Suffolk as a whole fell within the diocese of Norwich (the see had been moved from Elmham to Thetford in 1078, and then to Norwich in 1094), and so it lacked the benefits which accrued to Norfolk from having a bishop and a cathedral at its centre. But during the High Middle Ages Suffolk's own importance and distinction as a county was powerfully expressed through the influence which pervaded into national affairs from the great monastery of St Edmundsbury.

For this we have to thank the Danish King Cnut. His policy was one of reconciliation with the Christian population that had been terrorised by his father, Sweyn. The relics of St Edmund, which had rested at the monastery at Beodricsworth in Suffolk for over a century, had been transported to London in 1010 to protect them from desecration by the pagan Sweyn. In London, they became the object of popular veneration, but Cnut decided to return them to Suffolk, and to give them a more prestigious status.

The Beodricsworth monastery had been established in around 630 by the early Christian king of East Anglia, Sigeberht, as his own place of retreat when he abdicated the throne. By the tenth century it had become a community of secular priests, associated with a royal residence. What Cnut did was to establish a new Benedictine monastery there, importing twenty monks from St Benets Hulme and Ely in 1020. The rather clumsy name of Beodricsworth was changed to the inspiring one of St Edmundsbury (St Edmund's fortified town). At the consecration of the new abbey church Cnut demonstrated his devotion to the cult of St Edmund by offering up his crown at the altar and receiving it back from the abbot.

Cnut exempted the abbey from ecclesiastical control, and his successor, Edward the Confessor, provided it with further privileges such as full rights of taxation and minting money at Bury. He also endowed the abbot with the famous Franchise or Liberty of St Edmund. This comprised the whole of what later became West Suffolk — the hundreds of Lackford,

Blackbourn, Thingoe, Thedwastre, Risbridge, Babergh and Cosford, together with Bury and Sudbury. The Domesday record reveals the monastery as being the fourth richest in England in terms of income, and the owner of about 300 manors. The great wealth of the abbey thus derived from four principal sources: the taxation rights over the Liberty of St Edmund; the income from the manorial estates; the livings of many parish churches under its control; and the offerings of the ceaseless flow of pilgrims to the shrine of St Edmund.

The Norman kings were content to uphold all the privileges of the monastery, and even to grant new ones; under William the Conqueror the number of monks grew to eighty. This was viewed with great hostility by the first Norman Bishop of Norwich, the Italian-born Herfast. He was unwilling to accept the abbey's chartered exemption from his jurisdiction, and he proposed that the cathedral should be moved to Bury and be superimposed upon the monastery there. Unfortunately for him, the abbot of the time was Baldwin, a Frenchman from the abbey of St Denis at Paris. He was a man of high repute, and from his knowledge of medicine had been appointed a royal physician. Baldwin took care to secure papal protection during a visit to Rome, obtaining assurances from Pope Alexander II. Later, when Archbishop Lanfranc came to East Anglia for the express purpose of mediating between Herfast and Baldwin, he happened to fall ill at Freckenham. Baldwin was summoned to his bedside, which gave him an unexpected opportunity for bending the archiepiscopal ear. Eventually Lanfranc gave an award entirely in the abbey's favour, and the furious Herfast personally assaulted the messenger who delivered the unwelcome letter from the archbishop.

Under Norman patronage a great rebuilding took place, begun under Abbot Baldwin and completed under Abbot Samson a century later. The new abbey church was comparable in size to a cathedral, in particular to the monastic cathedral of Ely. The stone was brought from the quarries of Barnack in Northamptonshire. The long twelve-bay nave led towards the sanctuary of the choir, and a vast central tower rose high above the crossing of the nave and transepts. Three apsidal chapels projected from the main apse, and other chapels from the transepts. The choir was surrounded by a stone screen, on which were painted scenes from Genesis.

The church was consecrated in 1095, and the body of St Edmund was translated to its new shrine with much pomp and ceremony. This shrine was a glorious affair. It stood on a base of green and purple marble, and was designed to look like the model of a church. It was made of wood, but intricately carved and covered with plates of silver gilt, with gold cresting at the top. Its west end was covered with a gold relief of Christ in Glory. Offerings and jewels hung about it, and it was illuminated by tall candles at each corner.

Under the central tower was an altar which could be seen from the nave, on which stood an elaborate ivory cross. There is reason to suppose that this is the cross which is now in the Cloisters, the great collection of medieval art of the Metropolitan Museum of Art in New York, where it occupies pride of place in the jewel-glittering treasury and is acknowledged as one of the masterpieces of European Romanesque art. It would have been carved within the Bury monastery, and so could arguably be said to be the most wonderful artifact ever made in Suffolk. Carved on the cross are nearly a hundred tiny figures and inscriptions, a presentation which is said to have no parallel in Christian art. On the reverse side of the cross the central medallion depicts the Lamb of God being pierced by the Synagogue, surrounded by Old Testament figures holding prophetic texts. This has led historians to suppose that the cross was intended as an iconographic sermon to the small but influential community of Jews, whose financial control over the kingdom was shortly to be abruptly ended by their expulsion.

Around the church were all the other buildings of the monastery. Immediately to the north were the cloisters, with the great hall, refectory and chapter house ranged around them. Adjoining this inner group were scores of lesser buildings of specialised function, such as the kitchen, brewery, bakery, buttery, almonry, warming house and reredorter (latrines). Separated from all these was the abbot's palace.

Here he lived in state, just like a territorial lord; indeed, as a spiritual baron, he had his own seat in Parliament. Here he received the grander guests, defined as those who arrived with over thirteen horses; lesser guests were put up by the prior. The abbot even had his own estates, distinct from those held in the name of the abbey itself.

The abbey received several important visits from the medieval kings of England. In 1132 Henry I made a pilgrimage to Bury, in fulfilment of a vow made at sea. In 1181 Henry II came to launch a crusade; in 1194 Richard I, to give thanks for his deliverance from captivity. In 1199 John paid an expensive visit, for which he failed to provide the customary largesse, in protest at the abbey's support for his brother Richard. He confined himself to the presentation of a silk cloth (borrowed from the abbey sacristan), together with a meagre thirteen pence for the celebration of a mass. But the abbey got its revenge on him, for it was at Bury that the discontented lords assembled on St Edmund's Day in 1214 to make a first draft of Magna Carta.

Henry III visited the abbey several times, and may, indeed, have died there, in 1272. In 1383 Richard II and his Queen, Anne of Bohemia, spent ten days at Bury. In 1433, Henry VI, when still a boy, was brought here for an extended visit, arriving in time for the twelve-day Christmas festival. He then returned for the whole of the following Lent, remaining for Easter and staying till St George's Day, and developed a great respect for the abbot, William Curteys. Henry VI returned in 1447 when Parliament was summoned to Bury.

With painstaking attention we can assess the life of the abbey from ancient documents. But such records can hardly penetrate the personal lives of the monks, the thoughts and tensions that lay below those tonsured heads as they knelt in prayer or ate in silence. Fortunately for us, such secrets are revealed during the late twelfth century, for one of the monks was keeping a diary. His vivid and human account of the issues of his time speaks to us with such clarity that the seven intervening centuries are eliminated. As Thomas Carlyle writes in a famous essay, 'These old St Edmundsbury walls, I say, were not peopled with fantasms; but with men of flesh and blood, made altogether as we are'.

Jocelin de Brakelond entered the monastery as a novice in about 1173, and was put under the direction of Samson, a monk who came from Tottington in Norfolk. On the death of Abbot Hugh in 1180, the monks were unable to agree on the nomination of a successor for submission to the king, and had to send a deputation to the court, of whom Samson was one. Under royal pressure, this deputation was required to put forward a name, and the one chosen was Samson. This was unexpected, for there were other more senior contenders, and Samson was not a scholar, nor a political figure of influence. He had merely made his name within the monastery as a forceful and practical man, and it was felt that the crying need at the time was to put the abbey's affairs in good order after the inadequate control exercised by the other-wordly Hugh. Jocelin was appointed to be Samson's chaplain, and so was able to observe him closely, and to write what is, in effect, his biography.

Samson excelled at making symbolic gestures, and Henry II's visit provided him with a fine opportunity during his first year as abbot. The king wanted men and money for the Crusade. Samson 'secretly made for himself a cross of linen cloth. Then, holding in one hand the cross and a needle and thread, he sought leave from the king that he might take the cross'. This request was refused, but Samson would certainly have made a doughty Crusader.

Some years later a great trial of strength arose between Samson and Baldwin, Archbishop of Canterbury, in respect of the manor of Eleigh, which was owned by the Archbishop. Eleigh lay within the Liberty of St Edmund, and when some men were accused of murder there, Samson dispatched a posse who apprehended the suspects and brought them to Bury. Both parties appealed to the king, and Samson sought the support of William Longchamps, Bishop of Ely, at that time the Chancellor of England. But Longchamps was reluctant to favour the abbey because he had personal ambitions towards the Primacy of Canterbury. This gave Samson good reason for snubbing the bishop when he later passed through St Edmundsbury. He was received with minimal attention, and when he entered the abbey next morning, by a splendid act of theatre, the priests who were celebrating Mass 'stood with unmoved lips, until a messenger came and said that he had left the church'.

An even more defiant act by Samson on behalf of the Liberty occurred in 1202. He ordered the bailiffs to lead six hundred armed men of Bury to Lakenheath to disperse the market that had been set up there by the monastery of Ely, to the detriment of the neighbouring markets. The abbot of Ely complained in person to the justiciar of England about this 'unheard-of act of daring', but in vain. Samson was less successful in a dispute with the London merchants, who claimed to be exempt from tolls throughout the kingdom. His initial stance was that 'King Henry had given the Londoners quittance from toll throughout his own demesnes, where he had the right to give it; but in the city of St Edmund he could not give it, for it was not his to give'. As a result, the Londoners boycotted the Bury fair for two years, after which the abbey yielded to them.

Much of Jocelin's account is taken up with the power struggle between the abbot and the monks. Samson was an autocrat, and took the line that he was solely responsible for all the affairs of the abbey. The custom was for the monks to elect from among themselves the heads of the various departments of the monastery. Samson felt that some of these officials were hopelessly incompetent, and the quarrel came to a head when he appointed one of his clerks to supervise the transactions of the cellerar, and then put the clerk in charge. The monks saw this as a grave threat to their status. When he also took issue with the monks about the malpractices of the chief porter of the abbey, the disturbance among them was so great that Samson went in fear of his life. His attitude towards his holy brothers was made brutally plain during the discussions about the appointment of a new prior, when he made no secret of his disdain for the over-educated monks, with their 'rhetorical colouring and elaborate verbiage, and neatly turned sentences in a sermon'.

Jocelin gives a graphic account of a fire that severely damaged the shrine of St Edmund in 1198. It was caused by a candle falling onto a heap of rags in the middle of the night. As soon as the fire was extinguished, a goldsmith was summoned to patch it up so that worshippers might venerate it in the usual way that same morning. In consequence of this fire, Samson ordered the construction of a new and more glorious shrine. After the body of the saint was transferred to it with all due ceremony, he went secretly at midnight, together with a few trusted monks, to inspect the holy relics. In a rare and solemn act of devotion, he touched the bones of St Edmund. Venerated for so many centuries, they were eventually incinerated in another fire which completely gutted the church in 1465.

Smouldering at the gates was something even more dangerous than these physical conflagrations: the pent up animosity of the townsfolk of Bury. The rule of the monks had prevented them from obtaining the liberties gained by other towns against their feudal overlords. In 1327, at a time of national anarchy with the deposition of Edward II, these simmering resentments boiled over in what was long known as the Great Riot. A mob of three thousand townsmen broke down the gates of the monastery. They flogged the monks, imprisoned the prior, and stole all the valuables they could find. The abbot was forced to agree to a charter of liberties for the town, and an uneasy truce prevailed until October when some monks staged an armed attack on the townsmen when they were at worship in their parish church. This provoked a reign of terror in which terrible damage was inflicted on the monastery and on many of its surrounding manors. It was put down by the sheriff of Norfolk who took away thirty cartloads of prisoners and imposed an enormous fine, though this was commuted a few years later in return for the revocation of the extorted charter.

When the peasants rebelled in 1381 their three most prominent victims in Suffolk were Sir John Cavendish, the Chief Justice of England, John de Cambridge, the prior of St Edmunds, and John de Lakenheath, the collector of taxes within the Liberty. The heads of Cavendish and Cambridge were exposed in the market place at Bury, and for fifteen days the prior's body lay unburied in the fields. The attitude of the townsfolk of Bury was ambivalent, and this enabled the mob to enter the abbey precincts and force the monks to surrender their charters and jewels as a pledge of good behaviour. This connivance was so explicit that at the end of the year Bury was the only town in England excluded from the royal amnesty. It took a year before the burghers were readmitted to the king's peace in return for another heavy fine.

The monastery went on to experience a revival during the fifteenth century. Immediately before the Dissolution, St Edmunds gave nearly a quarter of its net income to poor relief, quite apart from the daily distribution of food and other occasional gifts at Christmas and other feasts. All comers were received in the guest houses, and not only the great magnates of the land, but also the humblest pilgrims. During this time it had a poet in residence, John Lydgate, who came from the Suffolk village of Lidgate. He was immensely popular for his early English versifications of the Classics. They make tedious reading today, for although he wrote clearly, he completely lacked poetic imagination. But nemesis came to the monastery in 1538, when it was dissolved, and the monks were pensioned off. The Keeper of the King's Jewels came and took away the valuables, and the men of Bury were not slow to dismantle the monastic buildings. That powerful Catholic prelate, Stephen Gardiner, who became Chancellor to Mary I, was reputedly the son of a Bury clothmaker, but came to power too late to save the monastery.

The loss of such a vast edifice, comparable to the cathedrals of Norwich or Ely, has not merely left a gap in Bury, but has deprived Suffolk of its grandest monument. But at least the site of the monastery has not been built over. Instead it has become a public garden where, among the lawns and flower beds, the lines of buildings are marked out, and great mounds and pillars still indicate the awesome dimensions of the abbey church. Most amazing of all is its ruinous west frontage, seventy-five metres long. Nestling in among its stonework are various houses, just as one often sees in Italy among the buildings of antiquity. The two monuments of the monastery which do survive are the great gates which give on to the town. The Norman Gate provided the ceremonial entrance, and it takes the form of a stone tower, with large windows in its upper stories. The Abbey Gate led into the abbot's precinct, and its tower is decorated with a big ogee gable above the archway and tall blank niches at the upper level.

The ruins of the abbey church reveal the material with which the walls of virtually all Suffolk churches were built – rubble. The chief ingredient of this rubble was flint, together with various glacial boulder clays and gravels, such as septaria or coralline rag from coastal pits. The rubble was set with great quantities of mortar made of lime and sand, a slow setting cement which took a long time to dry out. For this reason, quite apart from restrictions in labour or money, work had to proceed slowly over several years, and was usually suspended entirely for the winter months from Michaelmas to Lady Day. The greatest test in construction was in the building of the tower (or steeple, as it was called). Because of its weight, the tower tended to settle further into the ground than did the body of the church, so it was often built first, before work even began on the nave.

Although flint cladding was normal for the walls of churches, dressed stone was necessary for quoins, windows and arches. It had to be imported by means of boats and barges, and the most usual stone was acquired from the quarries of the Midlands, especially those near the rivers which flow into the Wash – the Nene, Welland and Witham. St Edmund's was clad entirely with stone, and was also exceptional for the proportions of its vast central tower. Most of Suffolk's church towers were originally surmounted by spires. These were nearly all made of wood and were not usually replaced after the Reformation. As a result, the ordinary church towers of Suffolk give an impression of sturdy strength rather than elegance, of feet firmly on the ground rather than arms reaching for the sky.

One reason why the St Edmundsbury abbey church was not

preserved was that two large churches stood close by. Just beside the Norman Gate is St James's, built in honour of St James of Compostela, but still uncompleted at the time of the Dissolution. Since 1914, this has become the cathedral church of the new diocese of St Edmundsbury, and it has been given a bright new Gothic chancel for its ceremonials. To the south, on the other side of the cemetery, but still within the former abbey precinct, stands St Mary's, the principal parish church of the town. Its magnificent nave is ten bays long and supports an elegant late fifteenth-century roof, complete with large recumbent angels on the hammer beams and biblical figures on the wall posts. St Mary's contains the tomb of Princess Mary, Duchess of Suffolk, who was buried with great ceremony in the abbey in 1533 but reinterred here. Human mortality is thrust before us by the skeletal figure of John Baret on his tomb-chest, under a painted roof inscribed with his motto 'Grace me Governe'. And the civic functions of this church are emphasised by the flag-bedecked chapel of the Suffolk Regiment.

The Suffolk Regiment, whose Museum is also at Bury, descends from the Old Twelfth of Foot, raised by the 7th Duke of Norfolk in 1685. Its first major engagement was in Ireland at the Battle of the Boyne in 1690, where the Anglo-Dutch victory over the Franco-Irish forces secured the Protestant and Parliamentary dispensation that Suffolk, as much as any other county, wanted. The Regiment next distinguished itself in the hard-fought battles against the French in the Low Countries and Germany. At Dettingen (1743) it held the centre of the line under the command of George II himself. At Fontenoy (1745) it lost its highly professional Colonel, Scipio Duroure, whose motto *Stabilis* (Steady) had been adopted by the Regiment. At Minden (1759) nearly two thirds of the strength were killed or wounded. It endured near starvation during the Great Seige of Gibraltar (1779-82), following which it was regrouped and styled the East Suffolk Regiment. In India it fought at Seringapatam in 1795, when Sir Arthur Wellesley (Wellington) defeated the Sultan of Mysore.

At the outbreak of the Boer War in 1900, the Suffolk

Regiment (as it had now become) was hastily dispatched to South Africa, and the First Battalion was decimated in an attack on a hill at Colesburg. During the First World War the Regiment was made up to a strength of twenty-seven battalions, and suffered several thousand fatalities, as may be appreciated from many village war memorials. It began its engagements in this titanic struggle with an heroic defensive action at Le Cateau during the retreat from Mons in August 1914, where two thirds of the Second Battalion were lost. During the Second World War it fought with distinction in North Africa and in France, and the First Battalion captured a major German redoubt within hours after landing on Sword Beach on D-Day. In 1964 it became part of the Royal Anglia Regiment. Apart from the places mentioned above, the Regiment has served in Spain, Italy, Greece, Turkey, Cyprus, Palestine, Afghanistan, Burma, Malaya, Australia, New Zealand, Mauritius and the West Indies. The Pax Britannica was indeed a global commitment, and there are few regions of the world to which the British Army has not been.

The ancient centre of Bury was built in the time of Abbot Baldwin in the eleventh century. It was laid out in a planned grid system, the first example in East Anglia since Roman times, and the first ever in Suffolk. Churchgate Street and Abbeygate Street lead away from the two great gates of the Abbey, the latter concluding at the Great Market. At the far end of the Market is a complete twelfth-century structure, the Moyses Hall, a stone building with a large vaulted undercroft and a hall and solar on the upper floor. From its name it has been suggested that it was the house of a Jewish merchant, or even a synagogue. But more likely it belonged to the abbey, and it has at various times been used as an inn, a workhouse, a prison, a shop, and now a museum. The Great Market was a place of chronic conflict between the merchants and the abbey's bailiffs, and it became progressively encroached with buildings in place of stalls. The space immediately in front of the abbey, Angel Hill, was the scene of the Bury Fair. This took place over a period of three weeks from St Matthew's Day, 21 September, and there were also smaller fairs in Easter Week and early December. Angel Hill was also the scene of executions, and the gallows were busy here in 1643 in the hanging of witches.

The persecution of old women as witches is about the most distasteful episode in the history of Suffolk, where it was exceptionally rife. It is particularly shameful because its victims were old, lonely and defenceless, and posed no threat to society. It raged most fiercely during the Commonwealth, and so is an indictment to the inability of the Presbyterians and other sects to control the perverted and evil fantasies that had at least been curbed by the enforced doctrines of the Catholic church. The chief witch-baiter was a horrible man called Matthew Hopkins, from Manningtree, on the Essex bank of the Stour. Invigilated by the authorities in 1647, he brazenly described the methods he and his minders employed in 'discovering' the witches: seizing them, and having them stripped to find 'teats' on their bodies; obtaining the authority of the magistrates to question them; keeping them without sleep for two or three days and nights, and, by continual suggestiveness, to get them to 'confess' to their 'familiars'. These included phantasms such as Holt, a white kitten; Jarmara, a fat spaniel without legs; Vinegar Tom, a greyhound with the head of an ox; Sack and Sugar, a black rabbit; and Newes, a polecat. By these means, he proudly reported, twenty-nine local witches were condemned and hanged.

Bury's medieval foundations are not very apparent from a stroll around its narrow streets, though a few buildings, such as the fifteenth-century Guildhall, testify to the earlier period. What we see instead is a most charming town studded with buildings of the eighteenth and early-nineteenth centuries, several of them disguising earlier constructions. For instance, the Angel Hotel of 1779 is on the site of a fifteenth-century inn and stands on Norman cellars; and several of the shops in Abbeygate Street have medieval timber framing. The most elegant of the Georgian buildings is the former Town Hall, designed by Robert Adam, and decorated on all four sides with giant columns supporting capitals and pediments, framing Venetian windows. Of rather earlier date is Cupola House, built for the grocer, Thomas Macro, in 1693: Celia Fiennes, on a visit a few years later, climbed the sixty steps to the top to admire the view. Of rather later date is the Corn Exchange of 1861, a yellow-brick building with a giant portico.

By the time of the dissolution of the abbey, Bury was already a great centre for the cloth trade. When this declined it developed other industries such as leather-working and malting. But it never became swamped with large-scale industry, partly because it lay off the route of the main railway lines. It remained a small county town, and the centre of society for the local landed gentry. These families built several fine houses in the town, but were very careful not to consort socially with the tradespeople around them. For the amusement of the gentry a real-tennis court and a bowling alley were set up as early as 1591. And by the time that Daniel Defoe visited Bury in 1722, it was 'thronged with Gentry, People of the best Fashion, and the most polite Conversation'; though he also had some harsh words to say about the 'scandalous Behaviour of some People' and the blatancy of the marriage market.

Another witness to the social life of Bury during the eighteenth century was a young Frenchman, François de La Rochefoucauld. He and his brother had been sent by their father to learn about England, and François, under the guidance of his intelligent tutor, sent extremely perceptive reports back home. On their arrival early in 1784 they put up in lodgings adjoining the Angel Hotel. From here they were able to meet the English and learn to speak the language. They were very much thrust among older people, and had to endure solemn dinners with dull conversation. The girls were closely chaperoned, of course, but François was not very complimentary about them anyway. He says that they danced badly and lounged around and were poorly educated. But he enjoyed the public balls he attended because, with his excellent manners, he could easily outshine the gauche and clumsy youth of Bury. He and his brother also had a lot of fun playing billiards. After four months they moved into the house of John Symonds, the Cambridge Professor of Modern History. His Bury house was a mile out of town, and here they were held as social prisoners. They were obliged to sit for hours at his table listening to his boring monologues, and they had to attend his weekly 'at homes', when old ladies came to take tea and play cards. They could not go out after supper because the door was locked. It is pleasant to record that, faced with so many hours of boredom, these enterprising Frenchmen decided to construct a path, half a mile in length, around the Professor's garden. This involved them both in fifteen days of hard labour, which is rather touching in view of the impending revolution, which castigated all aristocrats as lazy drones.

These French visitors were able to attend the private celebration of the Mass on Sundays, the anti-Roman Catholic laws having recently been ameliorated. But Bury had remained a centre of Catholicism ever since the Reformation. Some of the gentry families kept the faith right through the reign of Elizabeth I, despite the ferocious Penal Laws against them. Jesuit priests were landed at lonely points on the coast, and then passed from house to house in the disguise of servants. The obstinacy and courage of the Catholics were rewarded when, under Stuart rule, the authorities turned a blind eye towards their recusancy, or refusal to attend Anglican services. In 1633 a Catholic College of priests was openly set up for the servicing of the faithful in East Anglia. It met usually in Bury, and a school was opened in the monastic ruins. After the Puritan ascendancy during the Commonwealth, the Catholics of Bury became so emboldened, especially after the accession of the crypto-Catholic James II, that they began to control the town Corporation, until they were forced out by riots which presaged the fall of the king.

Though the Old Catholics of Bury were never more than a small minority of the population, their story epitomises the conservative nature of the town, and emphasises the social and commercial dissimilarity between it and Ipswich. The expansion and industrialisation of Ipswich far outstripped that of Bury. Ipswich had always been the county capital, though Bury had retained a certain autonomy. When local government in England was reorganised in 1888, the county was divided as between East and West, so that Bury became a capital itself. This was done so as to protect the ratepayers of West Suffolk from the higher rates of the relatively more prosperous East. What is more, West Suffolk was virtually the same as the ancient Liberty of St Edmund, so Bury was fortuitously reassuming its medieval mantle of administrative importance. But this revival in status lasted for under a century, because in 1974 Suffolk became united under a single County Council, based in Ipswich; and the very satisfactory new Shire Hall at Bury, built beside the abbey precincts, lost its intended purpose. The story has not yet ended, however, and regionalists of West Suffolk have great hopes of regaining their autonomy in the current review of local government.

During the nineteenth century, receptions and balls were held in the Assembly Rooms, today known as the Athenaeum, built in 1804 with interiors by Robert Adam. And entertainment was provided at the Theatre Royal, built by William Wilkins in 1819. Though the ballroom of the Athenaeum has been redecorated, the whole place hardly seems conducive to elegance nowadays. But the Theatre Royal, the third oldest playhouse in England, has been acquired by the National Trust and restored to its orginal use after a spell as a brewer's warehouse; and its exquisite, intimate interior, with rows of boxes around the horseshoe pit, is once again attracting a discerning public. In 1892 it witnessed the first performance of that runaway success, *Charley's Aunt*, before a very small audience whose uproarious laughter launched it on its triumphant way.

South of the abbey is Honey Hill, with more Georgian and neo-Georgian architecture, including the town house of the Earls of Bristol, which has recently been opened as a museum of art. St Mary's Square is on the site of the Saxon market. North of the Great Market the town extends towards the railway station, a fanciful affair with gabled offices and platform end-turrets, which itself sets the tone for the early Victorian architecture around it. Outside the ring road the suburbs of Bury now stretch away for over a mile to west and north, while to the east the ancient core is dwarfed by the A14 and the enormous British Sugar storage silos, which have replaced the abbey church as the eye-catcher for arriving visitors. Glanced at from the road, the 'historic' centre of Bury looks like toy-town, shrunken by the relativity of speed.

XII
Lark

The Lark flows out of Suffolk beside the large parish of Mildenhall and joins the Little Ouse a few miles from the Suffolk border. Mildenhall (middle-hollow) is famous for its treasure, now in the British Museum. This Roman hoard is said to have been thrown up by the plough in 1942, in a field at West Row, three miles west of Mildenhall itself. The showpiece is a magnificent dish, decorated with the sea god, Oceanus, at the centre, encircled with rings of marine and bacchanalian figures. There are flanged bowls with centre medallions; ladles with Dolphin handles; and spoons with inscriptions, five of them Christian. In all, there are thirty-four pieces. It is evidently a rich man's treasure and, together with the Hoxne hoard, it demonstrates that the administrators and landowners of late Roman times enjoyed considerable prosperity. The British Museum, despite its normal scholarly caution, is prepared to postulate its origin. Two of the smaller platters have the name of Eutherius on them. A powerful eunuch of that name is known to have served in Gaul in 355–61. So the suggestion is that the Emperor Julian, or Eutherius on his behalf, presented them to a certain Lupicinus who, as is also known, was sent to Britain in 360 to quell the Picts and Scots. Lupicinus, a Christian, returned to Gaul the following year and was arrested. So his family or retainers may well have buried his treasure here, near to a villa whose hypocaust has also been uncovered at West Row.

These Romano-British residences, with their mosaic floors, painted plaster walls and Italian marble, are correctly called villas, in contradistinction to the debased use of the word for semi-detached suburban homes. Of the dozen or so whose traces have been found in Suffolk, several are in the catchment of the Lark, indicating that this was a prime area for large-scale farming. They represent the highest levels of comfortable living brought by Roman civilisation to Suffolk during three centuries of peaceful rule, since no major towns were established in what later became our county. The provincial capital to the south was Camulodunum (Colchester), and that to the north was Venta Icenorum (just south of Norwich). In Suffolk there were several large settlements, or market towns, with merchants and artisans, but none seems to have been laid out in a grid pattern, or furnished with great public buildings. The major centre on the Lark was at Icklingham. It is thought to have been called Camboricum, a name which may be faintly echoed in Cavenham, the parish immediately to the south. From its site have been uncovered large quantities of brooches, pins and bracelets, as well as coins and an Egyptian statuette. There were also two lead water-tanks decorated with Christian symbols, and a set of bronzes.

In effect, Suffolk in Roman times was merely a rural area in which agriculture was practised mainly on the lighter soils, both on large estates worked by serfs, and on subsistence holdings of peasant farmers. In the estuaries, fisheries, oyster beds and salt-pans were extensively exploited; and in the forests, grimy charcoal-burners fed the furnaces of the iron-works, and potters worked their kilns on sites near good strong clay. Under this dispensation the population grew to levels not seen again until the early medieval period. Latin was the official language, but ordinary people spoke Celtic. Emperor-worship was the official religion, but most people placated their household gods in time-honoured ways, whilst some were converted to new cults, including Christianity.

The etching of the geography of Roman Suffolk is still discernible in the lines of roads. The most important was that which led between the two provincial capitals, crossing the county from the south through Capel St Mary, and thence to Coddenham and up to Scole (in Norfolk) along the line of the present A140, with settlement towns at all these three places. Together with a parallel road on the line of Long Melford-Pakenham (two other settlements), it was probably constructed for strategic reasons during the first century, in the aftermath of the rebellion of the Iceni. From these trunk roads, with their gravel surfaces, their sections of cambered causeways and their timber bridges, other local roads penetrated into the surrounding countryside. Roads also led towards the coast, but we cannot tell exactly where because no trace of them remains on the sandy coastal belt.

Mildenhall and Lakenheath are by far the largest parishes in Suffolk, having 11,400 hectares between them, which is greater than several of the county hundreds of twenty parishes or so. Both have exceptional churches, testifying to the prosperity of these wild and lonely pastures in the days when flocks of sheep could command great wealth. The church of St Mary and St Andrew at Mildenhall is the glorious result of building programmes during the thirteenth and fifteenth centuries. The east window of the chancel is in the Decorated Style. It is so flamboyant that even a knowledgeable stranger, looking at it from the street outside, where it is flanked by octagonal pinnacles, might well suppose it was a Victorian pastiche. The great west tower and the nave of this immense church are Perpendicular, and the grand scale of things is proclaimed by having a Lady Chapel situated above the north porch. But the greatest glory of Mildenhall are the roofs of the nave and aisles, carved with intricate tracery. Those in the north aisle include delicate scenes (such as the Annunciation, St George slaying the dragon, and imps blowing at an organ) which could never actually have been seen from the ground. Around the tie-beams of the nave are several large angels with outstretched wings. These are the survivors of the time when the Puritans let loose their loutish troops to pepper them with buck shot or, if that failed, to try arrows. Even today this church has to be kept closed against the vandals who smash the glass windows and defile the porches with graffiti.

The wood-carver who made the sturdy angels at Mildenhall probably also made the sixty or so which still survive at St Mary's Lakenheath. This church presents an extraordinary admixture of style and material. For instance, the south arcade comprises fifteenth-century piers, which stand on thirteenth-

century bases, which in turn stand on Norman shafts. And the
tower is limestone at its base, but from there up incorporates
chalk, ironstone, brick and flint. Besides wall paintings, and
benches carved with grotesques and bestiaries (the favourite is
the tigress who is so absorbed by her reflection in a mirror that
she doesn't notice her cubs being snatched away), there is the
finest thirteenth-century font in Suffolk, supported by shafts
and arches.

During the Middle Ages Lakenheath and Mildenhall were
both market towns with annual fairs, Mildenhall having six
guilds. They were the subject of chronic conflict between the
Abbeys of St Edmund and Ely, being equidistant between the
two. They were on the line of the ancient droving route that
bordered the peaty fens and, until the drainages, they had
hythes, or ports, from which people took to boats. In June
1381 a most dramatic event took place at one of these hythes.
Sir John Cavendish, the Chief Justice of England, was fleeing
from the vengeance of the peasants who had suddenly risen in
anger against the restrictions under which they lived, and in
particular the imposition of the notorious poll tax, which he
had strictly enforced. Intercepted by a group of rebels near
Lakenheath, he galloped to one of these hythes, hoping to get
across to Ely. But unfortunately for him, one Katherine
Gamen, seeing the pursuit and realising he was on the run,
pushed the boat into mid-stream. Sir John was seized and
summarily decapitated. At the same time, the Prior of Bury
was captured at Mildenhall, where the same fate befell him.
When the forces of authority assembled and advanced
towards Norfolk under the Bishop of Norwich, Henry le
Despencer, they were met at Icklingham by representatives of
John Litester, the rebel leader. These, in their turn, were
unceremoniously beheaded. But it is good to learn that during
the brief revolt and its aftermath, neither side indulged in a
general blood bath.

Sir Thomas Hanmer was the big landowner at Mildenhall in
the early eighteenth century. He was an influential Tory
politician, but is also remembered for having married first the
much older widowed Duchess of Grafton, and, after her death,

a much younger girl who eloped with a son of the Earl of Bristol. Neither produced an heir for him, so the estate went to his nephew, Sir William Bunbury. At the beginning of this century the Bunburys still owned 3,300 hectares within the parish. At that time the social activities in Mildenhall, as in other Suffolk villages, were intense. There was a Literary Institute, an Amateur Dramatic Society, a Music Society, a Chess Club, a Cycle Touring Society, an Angling Association, a Cricket Club and a Football Club. These must surely have pulled in people from Barton Mills close by. This village changed its name from Little Barton because of its large corn-mill, built here in conjunction with the navigation of the Lark up to Bury, and familiar to all who travel on the A11, together with its pub, The Bull.

At Mildenhall and Lakenheath the vast bases of the United States Air Force dominate the area – environmentally, socially and audibly. Despite the hundreds of acres of concrete poured into their construction, they have at least served to preserve some sections of the ancient heathland from desecration by plough or planting. These bases are the last remaining links with the time when, fifty years ago, Suffolk was dotted with smaller military airfields; they are the twin stars into which a whole constellation has imploded. By the end of the war there were no less than thirty-three operational airfields in Suffolk, of which fifteen were leased to the United States Army Air Force. Many had concrete runways, hangars, storehouses, control towers and complexes of buildings, mainly Nissen huts. On their stands were the formidable bombers – Lancasters, Flying Fortresses and Liberators – and around them were the protective anti-aircraft batteries. No point in the county was more than ten miles from one of them, and Suffolk became, in effect, an enormous armed camp. It is probably true to say that more of the rural landscape of Suffolk was disrupted by the airfields than by all the housing development during the subsequent half century. The only difference is that most of the acreage given over to them soon reverted to farmland, and their outlines are by now hard to discern, even on foot. Those who deplore the superfluity of roads can take comfort in the thought that fifty years of disuse would bury a section of road without trace!

Four miles upstream from Mildenhall is Icklingham, whose name, together with those of Ickworth, Ixworth, Exning, and the Icknield Way, quite probably denotes the territory of the Iceni, whose history we have noted along the Little Ouse. The village of Icklingham became so prosperous during the Middle Ages that it had two churches. During the last century the original church, All Saints, became abandoned, and in 1973 was declared redundant. But the Redundant Churches Fund stepped in, and All Saints is now recognised as one of the finest examples in Suffolk of an unrestored church. Not only did the Victorian restorers pass it by, but no eighteenth-century improvements took place either; and no landed family ever erected grandiose monuments to themselves in it. Indeed, it looks very much as it would have done immediately after the Reformation, when the altar and the rood had been extracted; and the only post-Reformation furniture is the Jacobean pulpit and the Laudian communion rails, installed by order of the Bishop of Norwich 'so thick with pillars that doggs may not get in'.

To enter All Saints is to step back into the sixteenth century and forcibly experience the silent protest of Catholic worshippers against the iconoclasm of the Protestants. The south aisle is completely bare, and the nave also, except for a few rows of simple pews, some straw-filled hassocks, and a chest. Beneath the arcade stands the octagonal font, with different tracery on each side. The aisle windows contain fragments of stained glass, said to have been found by the sexton buried in the churchyard, and the chancel windows display unbroken saints, including Saint James of Compostela with his cockleshell. In the chancel also, beyond the dado of the rood screen, the entire floor consists of its original tiles, different in shape and colour and forming mosaic patterns. To cap it all, All Saints is thatched, and in its large tower are two medieval bells, respectively inscribed (in Latin) 'I am called the bell of the glorious Virgin Mary' and 'We pray thee, Andrew, receive the vows of thy servants'.

We are now in the middle of the Suffolk breckland, which comprises the entire catchments of the Lark below Bury and the Little Ouse below Ixworth, and adjoins the even larger Norfolk breckland. This is about the driest and most arid region of England. Before the tree plantings of the last century and the ploughings of the present, it had deteriorated into a desert. This is attested by the account of William Gilpin, who travelled across it in 1809. He landed from the fens at Soham and made for Mildenhall by carriage. Gilpin was an inquisitive but fastidious traveller, always on the outlook for the 'picturesque', so he can hardly have been expected to appreciate breckland. But he was not the only one to be astonished by its aridity. After a few miles of patchy grass on which grazed some thin sheep and cattle, and with not a tree in sight, he came to where 'Nothing was to be seen on either side, but sand, and scattered gravel, without the least vegetation; a mere African desert'. The sand was even driven into ridges, and they needed four horses to drag them through it. Gilpin's account adds force to the story of the breckland farmer who, when asked where his farm was, replied: 'Times thass in Norfolk, boy, times thass in Suffolk: that dew dipend which way the wind's a blowin'.

The breckland was known as the fieldings until W. G. Clarke, a Thetford naturalist, coined the name 'breckland' (a breck being a temporary arable or out-field) a hundred years ago. It stuck, thanks to his lyrical portrayal of the landscape that had so appalled William Gilpin: 'New beauties are perceptible with each succeeding dawn, – a tinge of green here, a richer purple there, sun and cloud weaving the warp and woof of the panorama of colour in the landscape, flashing on the silver trunk of a birch or the ruddy richness of a Scots pine or plunging the distant woodland into a haze of blue'. He describes the distant views of the heath in all its seasonal variety, and the trivial details near at hand, 'the tender green of a curled frond, the soft ooziness of a marshy hollow, the hawthorns and elderbushes, the startled hare or bolting rabbit'. The rabbits had been responsible for much of the devastation, and one could still sink waist high in their disused colonies of burrows.

In 1910 the poet and naturalist, Edward Thomas, decided to walk the Icknield Way, the primordial droving route along the line of the Chilterns from the Thames Valley into Norfolk. He did it for literary copy rather than for the pleasure of walking, and, as he stomped along 'on a shoeful of blisters', 'essays on walking and walking tours began to wear very thin'. Still, he has given us a perceptive account of the Suffolk breckland between Thetford and Newmarket. From Elveden to Lackford (on the Lark) the chalk track went between hedges through the heathland. After Lackford and its patches of common land, he walked between fields of corn and sainfoin, with intermittent hedges, and just before Cavenham he passed a chalk pit, with wild roses and elder on its floor. From here the track was lined by successive sequences of trees. In the oaks and elms of Cavenham Park, the doves were cooing. The trunks and branches of the elms and beeches along the side of Lark Farm provided him with mere glimpses of the sunlit barley beyond. After Tuddenham Corner the track narrowed as it went between beeches of at least fifty years old, and birdsfoot trefoil grew on the grass verges. The flavour of such scenery is hard to catch nowadays, when so much of the breckland is afforested or ploughed. But it may still be seen by anyone who walks around the small preserved section in the nature reserve at Cavenham Heath, with its birch trees, heathers and brackens, and its exposed sandy soil.

Lackford (leek-ford) is also the name of the ancient hundred which sweeps up the north-west corner of Suffolk, and which we now leave on entering the hundred of Thingoe, which means a meeting-place on a mound. Just on the border, where a track of the Icknield Way crosses the Lark at West Stow, was such a mound, and one which was a major habitation site for Mesolithic, Iron-Age, Romano-British and Anglo-Saxon communities. It is thought that the Anglo-Saxons occupied it from the fifth century, which predicates the interesting possibility that they overlapped with the Romano-British at Camboricum. If so, they probably came as mercenaries; but it cannot have been long before they would have dominated the countryside and presided over the eventual ruination of Camboricum.

After the Anglo-Saxons abandoned this site during the early seventh century, the entire mound became covered by a sand dune. This, together with the acidity of the soil, protected it from disturbance. Excavations have revealed more about an Anglo-Saxon village than anywhere else in England, and, so as to popularise the fruits of their labour, the county archeologists have reconstructed several buildings. Volunteers, dressed in supposedly Saxon garments, demonstrate some of the skills by which the villagers survived: 'Do you speak English?' was my irreverent question to them.

What the West Stow site shows is that there were basically two types of building. The larger ones, ten to twelve metres long and with a door on the south side and a central hearth, were the family houses. The smaller ones, huts of four metres long, were used for a variety of purposes, some as dwellings, others for storage or weaving, or for the family pig. There were seven houses and sixty-eight huts, and from the way they were placed it is evident that each house had its satellite group of huts. Archaeologists refer to these houses as halls, and to the huts as houses; but I wonder what the villagers called them? Altogether, the tiny community was largely self-supporting, with its weaving looms and its fields of wheat, barley, oats and rye; its hens, geese and goats, and its herds of sheep. It would also have had its parasites, of course; and if the social study of the thirteenth-century Pyrenean village of Montaillou is anything to go by, a favourite spare-time occupation would have been picking the lice off each others' bodies.

In its passage below Bury, the Lark flows past a clutch of parishes whose parks and houses have failed to retain their former splendour. Fornham (trout-home) St Genevieve is the site of the battle where the Flemish force of the Earl of Leicester was defeated and butchered in 1173, but it seems to have been badly defeated itself in the battle for conservation. Its church was burnt down in 1782 and not rebuilt; its hall was demolished in 1950; and its park, after being used for infantry training during the war, has since become the site of sewage works. A similar deterioration has taken place at Livermere, just north of the Fornhams. An artificial serpentine lake, called

Ampton Water, was created to beautify the parks of the mansions at Great Livermere and Ampton. But the former was pulled down in 1923 and the park has all been ploughed up, and the sense of desolation in this featureless stretch of landscape is broken only by the tall tower of the ruined church of Little Livermere, and the pyramidical wooden tower of St Peter's, Great Livermere. M. R. James, a brilliant scholar who became Provost of King's College, Cambridge, and wrote antiquarian works on East Anglia, was the son of a rector here. Then there is Culford Hall, now a school, but once the seat of the Marquess Cornwallis, the great English general and proconsul of the late-eighteenth century, born at Brome Hall, near Eye. Charles Cornwallis fulfilled the roles of Viceroy of Ireland and Governor-General of India with distinction, and the portrait of him by Gainsborough reveals at a glance his imperative personality. He had earlier waged a successful campaign in North America until finally cornered (not through his own fault, but that of his Commander-in-Chief, Sir Henry Clinton) at Yorktown by General Washington.

But scenic imperfections such as these are more than offset by the charms of Hengrave Hall, just downstream on the Lark. Hengrave Hall was built for Sir Thomas Kyston, a rich London cloth merchant. He had purchased the estate from the last Duke of Buckingham of the first creation, and it seems that he was anxious to emulate the grandeur of this aristocrat. His chief mason, John Eastawe, was instructed to build a house similar to the Duke's new mansion, Thornbury Castle in Gloucestershire. Indeed, because Hengrave is built in white brick up to first floor level, with dressed stone from there upwards, it has the appearance of being in a stone-bearing county. Construction started in 1525 and it was completed in 1538. Though considerably altered since, Hengrave Hall is one of the finest houses of its period in England. At the centre of its battlemented frontage stands the gatehouse, flanked by mitre-headed turrets. Between them is a flamboyant triple-bay window, whose curvacious stonework looks rather like an elaborate organ-loft, with tall mullions for the organ pipes. It is Gothic in design and decoration, except for the sculpture at the base, where painted cherubs and armorial shields proclaim the early influence of the Renaissance (the two outsize cherubs, who support the three fishes of the Kytsons, are dressed in Roman armour and look like hearty soccer players). In the stone-faced courtyard is another great bay window, which lights the hall; and in the domestic chapel the windows still have their original stained glass.

This rare survival of medieval glass is particularly apposite at Hengrave because of a most exceptional continuity of Catholic faith within this magnificent mansion. Sir Thomas' widow supported Mary Tudor, who came to Hengrave on her way to Framlingham to rally support for her claim to the throne in 1553. His son, also Sir Thomas, despite his attempts to placate Queen Elizabeth by entertaining her in style in 1578, and presenting her with a costly jewel, remained a recusant. He and his widow also preserved a musical tradition by housing John Wilbye, one of the leading madrigalists. Their daughter, Penelope, married Sir John Gage, and for nine generations Hengrave remained in the possession of this Catholic family. During the French Revolution, Hengrave was lent by them to the Canonesses of St Augustine, who had fled from Bruges. In 1952 the house became the property of the nuns of the Assumption. After running a girls' private school here for twenty years, they have converted Hengrave into an Ecumenical Retreat and Conference Centre. Thus a great private house has become a religious house, in pleasing contrast to the monastic buildings which were converted into private houses after the Reformation, such as the Priories at Ixworth and Butley.

Not only in the house, but in the little church within its grounds, has Catholic tradition been long preserved. In 1589 this was converted into a private mausoleum, and has been used for Catholic services since the eighteenth century. At the west end is a massive Anglo-Saxon round tower, with a font within it. At the east end are the splendid tombs of the Kytsons, lying in apparent promiscuity with consecutive spouses. The first Sir Thomas lies below his wife, who is between her two subsequent husbands; and the second Sir Thomas is between his two successive wives. One wonders what they would all have to say to each other if they awoke! The church was originally dedicated to St John the Baptist but now it is called the Church of Reconciliation. When I opened the door of this pewless place of prayer, a silent group was seated. I sat and joined them, and the first thing I noticed was a memorial plaque concluding with the words of St John's Gospel: 'In my father's house are many mansions'. This seemed a most appropriate motto for Hengrave today.

One and a half miles away is the free-standing gatehouse of West Stow Hall, contemporary with Hengrave Hall. Seen from the road, its soft red-brick colouring contrasts pleasingly with the harsh flintwork of the nearby walls and buildings; and behind the gatehouse is a sixteenth-century colonnade which connected it to the former Hall. Set high on the gatehouse frontage, between two pinnacled turrets, are the arms of Mary Tudor, Duchess of Suffolk. Inside the first-floor room are depicted four ages of man. The youth out hunting says, 'Thus do I all the day'; the young man embracing a woman says, 'Thus do I while I may'; the middle-aged man watching says, 'Thus did I when I might'; and the old man with a stick says, irascibly and unmetrically, 'Good Lord, will this world last for ever?'.

Passing upstream through Bury, we come to where the Lark is joined by the Linnet, a stream which drains the large Ickworth estate. This came into the hands of the Drurys in the fifteenth century, and from them, by marriage, to the Herveys. During the eighteenth, the Herveys grew immensely rich through advantageous marriages and, as Earls and later Marquesses of Bristol, became second only to the Graftons at Euston as the leading grandees of west Suffolk. In recent years the estate has largely been sold and the house is now the property of the National Trust. The present Marquess and his late father have revived the family reputation for wild living – both having served prison sentences – but neither could emulate the style and panache of the 4th Earl, Frederick Augustus Hervey, the builder of Ickworth House.

As a younger son his expectations were modest, especially

when, at the age of twenty-two, he married, for love and not for money, Elizabeth Davers from the neighbouring Rushbrooke Hall. They lived on the Ickworth estate, at Horringer (winding-stream), and though he took holy orders he never sought an incumbency. Fourteen years and six children later, Frederick's lucky break came when his elder brother, Lord Bristol, was appointed Lord Lieutenant of Ireland and was able to get him appointed Bishop of Cloyne. In the following year he became Bishop of Derry, the richest bishopric in Ireland. Frederick, quick, clever, enthusiastic and very amusing, at first poured his abundant energy into improving the finances of the diocese, and engaged in public works and in support for reform. But he also indulged in tremendous expenditure on his own account, his attitude being exactly that of Pope Leo X who said 'God has given us the Papacy; let us enjoy it'. He cultivated the company of intelligent men (when in Suffolk he regularly saw Arthur Young and John Symonds), but neglected his wife and family; any form of consideration for others was uncongenial to such a solipsist.

He built a house for himself on the extreme north coast of Ireland, so exposed to the Atlantic that it had front entrances on both sides, against the wind. Then another Irish house, carefully sited in a scenic landscape, its central building in the shape of an oval drum. Both were designed to house the great collection of works of art which he now set about acquiring in Italy. His income, already enormous at about £20,000 from Derry, was almost doubled when he succeeded his second brother as Earl of Bristol in 1779. He was now both Earl and Bishop, but his outrageous hedonism put God very much in second place to Mammon. Rushing around Italy and buying up paintings and sculpture, he became the prototype of the English milord, the eponym for all those Hotels Bristol.

In 1796 he decided to go ahead with a 'villa' at Ickworth, on a site near the disused manor house. Though he commissioned Francis Sandys to build it, he was himself its true architect, writing endless instructions from Rome and Naples, but never visiting the site. He rejected the idea that the house should be built of strong white brick, as opposed to red brick covered with stucco: 'White brick always looks as if the bricklayers had not burnt it sufficiently, had been too niggardly of the fuel; it looks all dough and no crust'. His house should 'unite magnificence with convenience and simplicity with dignity'. This meant principal rooms thirty feet high, to avoid stuffiness, and flues which extended to the topmost crown of the domed roof, thus eliminating the need for chimney-stacks.

Externally, what we see is his design: that is to say, a colossal oval rotunda, covered with a dome, banded with columns and decorated with terracotta friezes. From it a pedimented portico protrudes, and two curving wings extend on either side to pavilions, which themselves are large houses. The Earl's intention was that the rotunda should provide his private quarters, while the wings and pavilions should house his collection. Things didn't work out that way, however. A great part of his collection was seized by the French army in Italy in 1798; and he died in 1803 when travelling towards Rome, his end made pathetic by a pious peasant who refused to let the heretic die in his house and had him taken to a barn. His son and heir, saddled with the terrible burden of Ickworth, never completed the interior and reduced the planned size of the pavilions; the stone staircase was only put in earlier in the present century, and to a less spectacular design.

Among the pictures that hang in the awkwardly-shaped rooms at Ickworth are many Hervey portraits, including Gainsboroughs of the Earl-Bishop's brother, nephew and son, and a Romney of his daughter. But perhaps the painting which best evokes the rather wicked high spirits of the family is Hogarth's *Holland House Group*. Here we see the Earl-Bishop's father, Lord Hervey, the witty fop beloved of Queen Caroline, gossiping on the terrace with the Fox brothers, Lord Ilchester and Lord Holland. With his back to them is a clergyman standing on a chair and surveying the countryside in search of a fat living: Hervey is about to topple him into the moat below.

The Earl-Bishop selected a site which was at the edge of the landscaped park, and his great house is secluded behind ilexes and cedars. This is perhaps fortunate, because such a grandiose structure would surely look rather out of place among the clumps of oaks and naturalistic contrivances that grace this eighteenth-century simulation of a medieval deer park. Together with the outlying woodlands that surround it, Ickworth Park provides some of the most beautiful landscaping in West Suffolk, all the more beneficial for lying right at the edge of Bury St Edmunds.

The Lark rises in the parish of Hawstead. Hawstead is celebrated to all concerned with local history because of Sir John Cullum's *History and Antiquities of Hawstead*, first published in 1784. The author, both squire and rector, delved deep into ancient records and produced a fascinating picture of Hawstead during the late Middle Ages. For instance, he gives examples of the method of tenure and service in the fourteenth century. Thomas Frame, we read, has to pay the Lord of the Manor an annual rent of twenty shillings, together with a Christmas offering of four pence and a cock and two hens. He also has to work in the Lord's meadow for four days at mowing the grass and eight days at reaping the harvest. During this work he receives set rations of bread and cheese and herrings and beer. When a tenant managed to arrange a commutation of his service to the Lord, he often had to provide a symbolic tribute, as when Thomas Smyth was granted a piece of land called Dockmeadow for the annual payment of a rose.

Cullum's description of the medieval harvest is most appealing: 'What a scene of bustling industry was this! for, exclusive of the baker, cook, and brewer, who, we may presume, were fully engaged in their own offices, here were 553 persons employed in the first year; in the second, 520; and in a third, of which I have not given the particulars, 538: yet the annual number of acres of all sorts of corn did not much exceed 200.' All the inhabitants of the village, male and female, young and old, were mustered for the harvest, whose success depended on getting it in as quickly as possible, in a matter of two or three days. The operation was supervised by the Lord of the Harvest, chosen by the harvestmen, and usually one of the tenants of the lord of the manor. During the year that he held this office he was exempted from his rents and services.

Cullum contrasts this with the harvest of his own day, which was more spread out in time because of the different cereals grown. During this period the harvester could expect to earn about £3. Another difference between the two periods was in the rotation of crops. The old system was for land to lie fallow every second or third year. By Cullum's time many farmers had moved to a four-crop rotation, typically turnips, barley, clover and wheat.

In Suffolk the old custom of calling for largesse from visitors to the harvest field was normal in Cullum's day. The visitor could hardly refuse to make his donation, and it would be greeted by the whole line of reapers who would cry out 'Holla! Largesse! Holla! Largesse!', followed by two short screams and then a shout continued as long as their breath could hold. The other custom was the consumption of tremendous quantities of beer. But in between these necessary interruptions the really impressive thing about those pre-mechanical harvests was the rhythm with which the men went about their work hour after hour, with the scythes swishing through the corn in unison, each man spaced regularly behind and to the side of the one ahead. This stately motion was rather like that of a rowing eight, but because it was done for work, not sport, it was not without a certain solemn dignity, an almost reverential exhibition of manual labour at this culminating moment in the agricultural year.

After the harvestmen had finished their work, the gleaners were admitted by bell on to the field. Dozens of women and children scrabbled and seized the ears of the stalks that remained on the ground and put them into their sacks. The family's bread ration in the winter could be crucially dependent on how much they had gleaned after the harvest, but the pathetic nature of their work could not altogether extinguish the dry humour of the gleaners, as seen in a poem in John Lushington's *New Suffolk Garland*, published in 1866, of which the last verse reads:

Dear me! there goo the bell agin — 'tis seven, I declare;
An' we don't 'pear to have got none: — the gleanin' now don't fare
To be worth nothin'; but I think — as far as I can tell —
We'll try a comb, some how, to scratch, if we be 'live an' well.

The old Suffolk vernacular has today become very diluted, as is inevitable in a television age. It is only heard in pungent accents on the lips of a few old people, and even then probably not with the authenticity of Lushington's time, before education had taught the village children to 'talk proper'. The dialect, full of punchy words, many of them corrupted or misinterpreted from standard English, was not peculiar to Suffolk, but belonged to the whole of East Anglia, and had much in common with rustic speech all over southern England. But it was the precise pronunciation that could distinguish a Suffolk man from one from Norfolk or Essex. For instance, the consonants were clearly articulated, not swallowed as in Norfolk. The East Anglian accent was characterised by a curious sing-song intonation, with a higher note at the end of the sentence, and strange vowel sounds. Robert Forby, whose *Vocabulary of East Anglia* was published in 1830, was an early etymologist who disparaged such sounds. Of the 'au-w' as in low or mow, he writes that 'it is not to be conceived that any natural organs can give easy and habitual utterance, if any utterance at all, but those of a native East-Angle, or of an old he-cat'.

Forby is delightfully instructive on two very common words of address. 'Bor', often pronounced 'baw' he correctly identifies as an abbreviation of neighbour, and nothing to do with 'boy'. Thus, he writes, 'one old woman may, without absurdity, say to another, "Co' bor, let's go a sticking in the squire's plantations". And the other may answer, "Aye, bor, so we will" '. Similarly confusing is 'mawther', which has nothing to do with mother, but is an awkward girl. In Edward Moor's *Suffolk Words and Phrases* (1823) the following example of Suffolk speech is quoted: 'How stammin cowd tis nowadays — we heent no feed nowhere, an the stock run blorein about for wittles jest as if twa winter — yeow mah pend ont twool be a mortal bad season for green geese, an we shan't ha no spring wahts afore Soom fair. I clipt my ship last Tuesday (list a' me – I mean Wensday) an tha scringe up their backs so nashunly I'm afreard they're wholly strayed – but 'strus God tis a strange cowd time.' (Stammin means surprisingly, and nashunly means greatly.)

Before the Cullums the manor of Hawstead was owned by the Drurys. The leading Drury was Sir William, who was Lord Deputy of Ireland under Elizabeth I, and who gets a charming mention in Thomas Fuller's *Worthies of England*: 'His name in Saxon soundeth a pearl, to which he answered in the preciousness of his disposition, clear and hard, innocent and valiant, and therefore valued deservedly by his queen and country'. (Fuller is a bit off course here, for Drury is from an Old French word meaning 'sweetheart'.) Nothing remains of the Drury's house at Hawstead (cattle-shed), nor at neighbouring Hardwick (sheep-farm), nor, indeed, of their London house except for the street it stood in, Drury Lane. But in the Christchurch Mansion at Ipswich there is a set of painted panels from a parlour at Hawstead, which depict scenes on the theme of mortality and the inescapable human condition. Best of all are the Drury monuments at All Saints, Hawstead. These include a masterpiece by Nicholas Stone in black and white marble, which comprises a plain sarcophagus for Sir Robert, watched over paternally by the bust of Sir William in a niche above; and an alabaster effigy for Sir Robert's daughter, Elizabeth, who died aged fifteen, with an elaborate Latin inscription.

The little river Kennett flows close to the western edge of Suffolk to where the Lark takes up the task of providing the boundary. It rises near Lidgate (swing-gate), where the church (St Mary's) is built high up on the site of a Norman castle, whose size is etched by formidable earthworks. And just before it joins the Lark it flows past the chalk mound of another Norman strongpoint at Freckenham. The parish of Freckenham had, until 1837, the distinction of being an ecclesiastical 'peculiar', responsible to the Bishop of Rochester, not to the Bishop of Norwich. And Moulton, also on the Kennett, was one of the three 'peculiars' in Suffolk which were under the jurisdiction of the Archbishop of Canterbury. The medieval road between Bury and Newmarket passed through Moulton, and the narrow three-arched pack-horse bridge has been most satisfactorily preserved, a mass of rough flints standing beside the ford, now usually high and dry above the bed of the depleted Kennett.

The Suffolk boundary would, in all logic, follow the line of the Kennett throughout its course. But by one of those administrative anomalies rather like the Church of England's old peculiars, it extends west to embrace Newmarket. Newmarket lies in a pocket of land that was within Cambridgeshire at the time of Domesday Book. But during the twelfth century it was drawn into Suffolk and became a detached part of the hundred of Lackford. Happily, this arrangement has survived the rationalisations of 1974, when several quirky county boundaries were tidied up. So, from the ancient ford over the Kennett at Kentford, we proceed five miles west along the line of the Icknield Way at the edge of the parish of Moulton, to enter that of Newmarket, attached to the rest of Suffolk by a narrow gap of only one hundred metres wide.

Newmarket is quite distinctive from anywhere else in Suffolk, and not just because of this umbilical chord. It has for nearly three and a half centuries been hitched to one single source of prosperity – horseracing. It is the heart of English racing, and the whole of the racing world known as 'the turf' actually originated here on the chalk plains of Newmarket. This association with sport goes back to even earlier times in the history of the town. It was founded, as its name implies, as a new market, in around the year 1200. In 1227 it was granted an annual fair, and began to outstrip the ancient village of Exning, in whose parish it then was. It also enjoyed the great advantage of lying right on the main route between London and Norfolk. Within a century it had become a place where tournaments were held, and Edward II twice issued proclamations warning his barons and knights not to tilt and joust here without his express permission, a precaution dictated by his apprehension that the tournament might turn into an insurrection. Horse thieves were already at work, including a dare-devil who, on being arrested by the bailiff, stole that officer's purse and belt, and bolted.

It was James I who really put Newmarket on the map. He came ostensibly for hare-coursing and hawking, and he was certainly an intrepid if clumsy horseman, always giving the animal its head. But the real attraction for him was to escape from the stifling formalities and tedious state affairs of London and the Court. Here he could be among his favourite courtiers, and avoid uncongenial advisers and awkward decisions. If he wanted intellectual stimulus, he could always summon up dons from Cambridge, fifteen miles away. The House of Commons grumbled at his chronic absence at Newmarket, and when they sent a deputation to him in 1621, his curt reception and response led towards a rupture between him and Parliament.

His son, Charles I, continued to patronise Newmarket. As Prince of Wales he had participated in the festivities that characterised life in the 'royal village', appearing on stage in a masque by Ben Jonson, and entering the lists as a tilter. During his reign regular spring and autumn meetings began to be held, at which the main sport was hunting the deer, as well as shooting pheasants and partidges and playing tennis and pall-mall. His last visit to Newmarket was under different circum-stances, as a prisoner of Parliament in 1646. At first he was permitted to lead a normal life, to ride on the Heath and receive calls from the neighbouring gentry. But after the army revolted he was kept under close arrest, before being taken away to Hampton Court.

After the austerities of the decade of the Commonwealth, it was at Newmarket, more than anywhere else, that the hedonism of Charles II and his court was most vividly exhibited. He himself was ensconced in the 'palace', really a hunting lodge. Squeezed into uncomfortable lodgings in and around the town were his confidential ministers, his mistresses, his natural sons, and lots of gilded youths and lusty girls. Horseplay as well as horseracing was the order of the day. John Wilmot, Earl of Rochester, was the court jester, and

James Howard, Earl of Suffolk, the leading dispenser of hospitality. Gambling was the great thrill which kept them all up late into the night. The king was immensely active physically, both on horseback and whoresback, but indolent to a degree when it came to political affairs. It was said that the only time to catch him was when he awoke from his afternoon nap. The French and Spanish ambassadors left Newmarket disgruntled by his lack of attention. The aldermen of Oxford, unable to gain an audience, were obliged to petition him on his way to the race course, where they were the target of abuse from the race-course roughs.

But the really significant thing about Charles II's visits to Newmarket was the development of horse racing. The earliest races were very rough and ready events, secondary to all the hunting, coursing and hawking that still provided the main excitement. A course was laid out on the chalk turf of the Heath, marked by tall white posts, along which noblemen and gentlemen matched each other, with the king himself sometimes entering a race. The Town Plate was established by him in 1664. The royal stud farm acquired mares with eastern strains, and the serious business of breeding began to preoccupy the stables of Newmarket. Under the later Stuarts the sport developed, with more specialised courses and stricter rules; though well into the mid-eighteenth century, the custom was for mounted spectators to gallop along behind the contestants for the last half-mile towards the finishing line in a shambolic cavalry charge. The Beacon Course of 4 miles, 1 furlong and 168 yards became the main field of combat, and was the scene of such remarkable events as the match between Sir Harry Tempest Vane's horse, Hambletonian, and Mr Cookson's Diamond in 1799. The stake was 3000 guineas, and the whole of the sporting world had bet heavily on this crucial race, won by Hambletonian by half a neck.

Before the accentuation on shorter and faster racing (the Classic 1000 Guineas for three-year-old fillies was first run at Newmarket in 1814), extraordinary contests of endurance were held on Newmarket Heath. In 1754 a mare completed 300 miles in sixty-four hours, twenty minutes. In 1761 John

Woodcock, a professional jockey, rode 100 miles a day successively for twenty-nine days, using fourteen different horses. In 1831 Mr Osbaldeston did 200 miles in eight hours, thirty-nine minutes, changing horses every four miles. And in 1809 the famous pedestrian, Robert Barclay, walked 1000 miles in one thousand hours, covering one mile in each and every hour. Several of these crossed the massive earthwork, the Devil's Ditch, constructed to defend the ancient Kingdom of East Anglia at its most vulnerable point, the eight miles of level plain between the woodland and the fenland.

Grooms and stable-boys began to form that permanent community that is still the basis of Newmarket. Their life was hard, but they were well housed and fed and, as Thomas Holcroft, who joined as a stable-boy at the age of thirteen in 1758, wrote, 'I was mounted on the noblest animal that the earth contains, had him under my care, and was borne by him over hill and dale, far outstripping the wings of the wind'. When Surtees took his Mr Jorrocks to Newmarket in the 1860s, that amiable foxhunter found the conversation entirely confined to 'Heath', 'Ditch in', 'Abingdon Mile', 'TYC Stakes', 'Sweepstakes', 'Handicaps', 'Bet', 'Lay', 'Take', 'Evens', morning, noon, and night. 'Really', said Mr Jorrocks, 'I'm not a betting man'. 'Then, wot the 'ell business have you in Newmarket?' was all the answer he got.

Today Newmarket is surrounded by stud farms, from which are produced the yearlings for the all-important sales held here, and where strings of horses are exercised along grass rides fringed with belts of beeches. The sheer professionalism of all aspects of modern racing gives it a very different flavour from the early and more carefree days of the sport. The town has changed, too, and the High Street, from the Jubilee Clock Tower at the Bury end to the Cooper Memorial Fountain at the Cambridge end, contains hardly any relics of the old days, except in the Museum of Horseracing in the Jockey Club, and the Rutland Arms, a fine example of a late-Georgian coaching inn. Charles II's 'palace' was pulled down by order of Queen Victoria, and the present non-conformist chapel is on its site. The last monarch to use it had been George IV when Prince of

Wales; but he never returned after leaving Newmarket in a tiff in 1792, following the Jockey Club's insinuation that his jockey, Sam Chiffney, had pulled back the favourite, Escape, to fourth place.

If the wind is from the north, the sound of the A14 drones relentlessly over Newmarket Heath. Some people assert that from a distance the monotonous roar of our motorways and trunk roads is no different from the sound of breakers on the sea-shore, but I cannot agree. The audible tone may perhaps be similar, but the sensation is entirely antipathetic: the sea is elemental and soul-soothing, the traffic is mechanical and maddening. Here, at the western edge of Suffolk, the muffled roar reminds us how closely our county is soldered to the rest of England, and it jerks us out of our perusal of the past and forces us into the present, as we ourselves thunder on towards the twenty-first century. The sensitive admirer of Suffolk may well take fright at the thought of what is to come, and fly from such feverish contact. His thoughts will turn again to the coast and the sea, and on the way he will linger over the manifold facets of our county, human and natural, which we have encountered on our way up the rivers, unseen and unfelt by all those who make it from Newmarket to Felixstowe in under the hour.

Short Bibliography

Addison, William: *Suffolk*; Robert Hale, 1950

Blythe, Ronald: *Akenfield*; Penguin, 1994

Brakelond, Jocelin de: *Chronicle* (translation, L.C. Lane); Chatto & Windus, 1907

Cautley, H. Munro: *Suffolk Churches and their Treasures*; Batsford, 1937

Dewes, Simon: *A Suffolk Childhood*; Hutchinson, 1959

Dymond, David, and Martin, Edward: *An Historical Atlas of Suffolk*; Suffolk County Council Planning Department, Ipswich, 1988

Fletcher, Ronald (editor): *The Biography of a Victorian Village*; Batsford, 1977

Haggard, H. Rider: *A Farmer's Year*: London, 1899

Heard, Nigel: *Wool, East Anglia's Golden Fleece*; Lavenham, 1970

Holmes, Clive: *The Eastern Association in the English Civil War*; Cambridge U.P. 1974

James, M.R.: *Suffolk and Norfolk*; Dent, 1930

Jebb, Miles: *East Anglia: An Anthology*; Barrie & Jenkins, 1990

Jennings, Celia: *The Identity of Suffolk*; Suffolk Preservation Society, 1980

Parker, Rowland: *Men of Dunwich*; Collins, 1978

Scarfe, Norman: *Suffolk in the Middle Ages*; Boydell Press, 1986

Scarfe, Norman: *The Suffolk Landscape*; Boydell Press, 1987

Tennyson, Julian: *Suffolk Scene*; Alastor Press, 1987

Victoria History of Suffolk, London 1907

Wilson, Derek: *A Short History of Suffolk*; Batsford, 1977

Young, Arthur: *General View of the Agriculture of the County of Suffolk*; 1804

Index